Charlie Dancey's

COMPENDIUM
of
Club Juggling

'The Galaxy's Greatest Guide to Gravity'

Charlie Dancey's COMPENDIUM OF CLUB JUGGLING
Copyright © 2001 Charlie Dancey.
All rights reserved.

Published by Butterfingers, Devon.
+44 (0)1647 441188
mailbox@butterfingers.co.uk

First published in 1995. Reprinted 1997. Revised and
reprinted 2001.

Cover design, illustrations and typesetting
by Charlie Dancey.

http://www.dancey.net
charlie@dancey.net

Body text and headings set in Garamond,
other text in **Gill Sans**.

A C.I.P. catalogue record for this title is available from
the British Library.

ISBN: 1 898591 14 8

Introduction

Welcome to the COMPENDIUM OF CLUB JUGGLING. This book, like its companion volume, THE ENCYCLOPÆDIA OF BALL JUGGLING, contains a large, but *incomplete* collection of juggling tricks arranged in alphabetical order. The idea is that since there is no *sensible* order in which to catalogue juggling tricks, I might as well make it easy for you to find your way around!

The whole book is cross-referenced to the point of absurdity. This is to encourage you to dip in and follow the links so that you end up reading it in the order that suits *you*. The last thing I expect any reader to do is to read it from cover to cover!

I have written this book for anybody who wants to learn more about club juggling than they could possibly make up for themselves. It's aimed at both beginners (who will, I hope appreciate the chatty explanations and tips) and experts (who will, no doubt, read the book like the instructions on a packet of frozen pizza). If each reader was to learn just two new tricks from the book I would consider it a job well done!

Club juggling is seen to be inherently more difficult than ball juggling and, insofar as one never seems to meet anybody who learned to juggle clubs without learning to juggle balls *first,* I suppose this must be true. Because of this I once believed that I would never be able to do as much with clubs as I could with balls but I hadn't reckoned on **Passing Patterns**, which, according to many, is what juggling clubs are *made* for. This is therefore a bigger book than the ENCYCLOPÆDIA and at a rough count, there are somewhere between seven and eight hundred tricks, or 'things you can do' in these pages. So where do you start?

Beginners should go straight to the section on the **Three Club Cascade**, stopping off briefly at **How Many Clubs Should I Buy?** on the way. Experts can try **Mike's Mess**, an amazing solo pattern for three clubs. Club passing fanatics will certainly enjoy the very sociable **Boston Circle**.

Ambitious jugglers who are reaching for the sky will want to learn the incredible **Five Club Cascade** and if they get stuck they'll find that the story in the back of this book, **Zenith and the Art of Pattern Maintenance** has been written with them in mind.

Neither the COMPENDIUM OF CLUB JUGGLING nor the ENCYCLOPÆDIA OF BALL JUGGLING could have been written if it was not for the amazing openness of jugglers when it comes to sharing their tricks. This attitude has probably done more for juggling than the invention of the beanbag. The list of people who have contributed to this work would require a book in itself, so if I talked to *you* while I was working on this book — thanks a million.

Don't fall into the trap of thinking that you need to master every trick in the book to be a great juggler. The best juggling is the juggling *you* do best —not what others do. Aim for invention and dare to be different. If you discover something wonderful then be sure to let me know so that it can be included in future editions of the COMPENDIUM OF CLUB JUGGLING.

Charlie Dancey
Bath, November 1995

Acknowledgements

I could save myself quite a bit of effort here by simply saying, 'If I have ever met you — thanks'. Nevertheless there are one or two names that I'd like to mention because of special help they have given me in preparing this book:

Ray Bowler, he made the chair I'm sitting on; **Pete Douglas**, who is vital to the well-being of my Macintosh; **Haggis McLeod**, who can do *most* of this stuff; **Tarim**, the famously ambidextrous 'third person' who co-incidentally learned to juggle at *exactly* the same time as I did despite his claims to the contrary; **Martin Frost**, who is mentioned all over the COMPENDIUM because it's quite impossible to talk seriously about club-passing without borrowing a few of his ideas; THE CATCH, KASKADE and JUGGLER'S WORLD for their encouragement, support and for saying nice things about the ENCYCLOPÆDIA; **Barry Bakalor** for providing the wonderful Juggling Information Service on the Internet; **Colin Wright** for mathematical advice and interesting conversations; 'H' of BEARD JUGGLING EQUIPMENT for providing information about the design and manufacture of juggling clubs (and some samples too); **Peter Chippindale** for literary advice and constant encouragement; **Ian Wood** for giving me a cyber café to play with; **Laurie Lea** of BUTTERFINGERS for having the faith to keep publishing my stuff; **Garlic** for keeping me company; and finally, **Lorraine**.

Contents

Contents A to Z

Contents A to Z

Charlie Dancey's

COMPENDIUM
of
Club Juggling

How to use this book

The COMPENDIUM OF CLUB JUGGLING is in alphabetical order, so if you know the name of the trick you want to look up then you can either go straight to it or look it up on the contents page. You'll see many words and phrases in bold type, like **Three Club Cascade** for example. These are cross references. The best way to navigate the COMPENDIUM is to dip in and start following these links so that you end up reading the book in the order that suits *you*.

Occasionally I have cross referenced to a ball juggling trick from the ENCYCLOPEDIA OF BALL JUGGLING, these references have a little **'EBJ'** tacked onto them —for example **Behind the Back Catch**[EBJ].

If you are a beginner then look up **Three Club Cascade** where you'll find advice and tips on learning to juggle with clubs as well as suggestions for tricks you can learn once you can handle the basic pattern.

There is quite a lot of juggling notation and many technical-looking diagrams dotted around the COMPENDIUM. You don't *have* to understand these to be a great juggler but they are often the most elegant way of explaining juggling tricks on paper, especially when it comes to dealing with some of the more exotic tricks that you can throw in **Passing Patterns**. To find out about these systems, see **Notation**.

The COMPENDIUM is divided into 190 separate headings and each of these may contain a number of different 'things you can do' each of which is preceded by a '•' symbol. There are somewhere between seven and eight hundred '•'s dotted through the book.

You are not supposed to try and learn 'every trick in the book'. This book is intended as a source of ideas and inspiration that will, with luck, encourage you to go out and invent your own tricks.

After all, how do you think all this stuff was invented in the first place?

Albert

This trick is named after the great and world-record holding juggler *Albert Lucas*. The **Albert** is a reverse **Under the Leg** throw, made from front to back, without either foot leaving the floor. It's almost aggressively flashy and well suited to the traditional high speed circus style of juggling. Think tight lycra costumes, think figure skating, think Saturday Night Fever —it's *that* sort of trick.

• The throw is made from a **Three Club Cascade**. Swing the club downward and between your legs, allowing your grip to slip all the way down to the knob. You release the club at the last possible moment and it rises behind the opposite hip, hopefully to a reasonable catching position. It's good form to keep your legs as straight as possible with *both feet flat on the floor*. **Albert** experts frown on any subtle contortions as if you are 'cheating'. This is a trick with a pedigree and there is a 'right' way and a 'wrong' way to go about it.

It's not an easy throw to make because unless you have arms like an orangutan, the club is being handled at the limit of your arm's stretch which seriously reduces your control over it.

*An **Albert** throw in a **Three Club Cascade**. It's **Under the Leg** thrown backwards, neither foot leaves the floor.*

• The *reverse* of an **Albert** is called a **Trebla** (get it?) —you make an **Under the Leg** throw *without* taking either foot off the floor. Once again, the Scandinavian judges will mark you down for any leg-bending or contortion (though leaning your body forward a few degrees is acceptable).

• If you can juggle **Alberts** and **Treblas** you are ready for the *big one*. You throw continuous **Alberts** and **Treblas** in every possible combination, wrapping those clubs around your thighs every which way without *ever* putting in a single **Cascade** throw. For traditional circus jugglers this trick is a 'must-have'. Very impressive, very difficult and somehow completely ridiculous —all at the same time.

• An **Albert** can be thrown as a pass in a passing pattern, it's very similar to a **Slapover** except that the club passes between your legs.

You need to practically wrap the club around your thigh so that it ends up heading for your partner spinning in reverse —**Tomahawk** style. A right hand throw will 'wrap around' your right thigh and you'll need to bend well forward during the throw.

See also **Trebla**, **Under the Leg** and **Slapover**.

Albert

Armpit Grip

Simple, easy and effective —some of the best juggling tricks are like this. The **Armpit Grip** is easily learned and adds a certain devil-may-care adroitness to your work.

•Juggle a **Three Club Cascade** and, instead of making a normal throw from the left hand you tuck the club under your right arm. Grip it here for two **Beats**, while you keep the rest of the cascade going. Then grab the knob with your right hand's finger and thumb, flicking it back into the air with a neat **Double** spin.

You'll have trouble reaching the knob if you have tucked the club too far into the **Armpit Grip**.

•You can also use the **Armpit Grip** while passing clubs with a partner. Let's assume that you are passing **Every Others**.

Place a club, from the left hand, into a right hand **Armpit Grip** on the *two* beat (the beat *after* the pass). Now keep juggling for two beats and then flick the club out of the **Armpit Grip** straight into a pass to your partner. You can juggle this continuously and it looks like you just don't give-a-damn.

•Back to solo juggling; a smooth move is to place *two* clubs into opposite **Armpit Grips** —one directly after the other and then pull them out to resume your cascade. The key to all of these moves is to keep the rhythm of the underlying cascade running evenly throughout —that's what gives these tricks that certain special feel of polished *inevitability*.

See also **Neck Grip**, **Khyber Pass** and **Stevie Spangle Shuffle**.

Back Crosses

You rarely hear club jugglers talking about throwing 'behind the back', instead they talk about throwing **Back Crosses** —making throws that pass from one hand to the other behind the back. Most jugglers find it easier to juggle **Back Crosses** with heavier and slower-spinning clubs because they give your hands more feedback than light, snappy, fast-spinning clubs.

•You can learn to throw **Back Crosses** in a **Three Club Cascade** as **Singles**, **Doubles** or **Triples**. Each variety feels completely different to juggle. Most beginners find **Doubles** the easiest to master.

Practise with just one club to begin with, making **Double** spin **Back Crosses** in both directions until you start to get a feel for what your juggling club is doing while it is out of sight.

Your throwing hand should swing in a lazy ape-like arc and propel the club so that it rises from behind the opposite shoulder in such a way that you don't need to turn your head *too* far to see it, you should be looking more *upwards* than to the side.

•When you throw a **Back Cross** in a running **Three Club Cascade** the throw should seamlessly follow the catch. It's a single flowing movement.

As with throwing balls **Behind the Back**[EBJ] you need to develop the knack of looking in the *opposite* direction to the **Back Cross** throw. You only glance at the **Back Cross** as it peaks. If you fail to do this then you will catch the **Back Cross** but you'll drop the club that was peaking as you made the throw.

*As your right hand throws a **Back Cross** you look* away *from it. This is the 'secret' of the trick.*

It's easy to panic and try to rush the move, which causes all kinds of problems, concentrate on juggling the whole move *slowly*. It's *control* that gets you through it, not speed!

•Obviously, once your **Back Crosses** start to take shape you will want to learn to throw continuous **Back Crosses**. If you are using **Doubles** you will find that you can see everything you need to by looking straight up.

•**Single** spin **Back Crosses** are harder to learn, the tempo is faster and the clubs rise to the sides of the pattern, rather than descending from above You'll need to develop a good 'head flick'. On a right hand throw you look to the right, as you throw with your left you look to the left —always in the *opposite* direction to the throw you are making! You have to learn to snap your head from side to side without getting giddy and disoriented.

Once again it's *control* rather than speed that makes the move work.

•**Triple** spin **Back Crosses** are very high, slow and lazy, you look straight up as you throw them. They are the least frantic of all but you must have very good control of the spin to succeed.

•Megastars can juggle continuous **Back Crosses** and move up from **Singles** to **Doubles** to **Triples** and back down again without a fumble.

Continued overleaf...

Back Crosses...

•Four club jugglers can throw **Back Crosses** in the **Triple-Singles** pattern. Usually it's the **Triple** that's thrown behind the back although some keen types do it with the **Single**. I dare say somebody is working on doing both at the same time — such is juggling.

You can't throw a **Back Cross** in a **Four Club Fountain** because this pattern has no crossing throws. Instead you go into one 'round' of **Triple-Singles**, making the **Triple** a **Back Cross** and then drop back into a **Fountain**. Alternatively throw a four club **Flash** as four consecutive **Triple Back Crosses** and drop back into the **Fountain**.

•One of the more dizzy heights to which those exalted masters (and mistresses) of the **Five Club Cascade** can rise is that of throwing continuous **Triple** spin **Back Crosses** from a **Five Club Cascade** — enough said!

•On a more easily attainable level, a good exercise (and performance piece) for the three club juggler is to juggle a mixture of fancy **Double** spin throws in a **Cascade** pattern.

Start with a steady **Double** spin **Cascade** as your 'base pattern'.

Now add **Under the Arm** throws, **Dip** throws and **Back Crosses**, making *every single throw* a **Double**. The effect is of the three clubs winding around your body like snakes —a circus-style display of pure skill and control!

To make this a perfectly balanced exercise (i.e. right and left hands sharing the work evenly) you should try throwing *three* **Back Crosses** followed by *three* **Dips** followed by *three* **Under the Arm** throws and then *three* plain **Doubles**. This is very satisfying to juggle and wonderful to watch.

•Now impress your audience by throwing two *simultaneous* **Back Crosses**!

Juggle a **Three Club Cascade** and then launch a **Double** straight up (as if going into **One-Up Two-Up**). Now throw the two remaining clubs as **Back Crosses** simultaneously.

•Another move worth learning is the club juggler's equivalent of the **Behind the Back Catch**[EBJ].

Juggle a **Three Club Cascade** and throw what *looks* like a right self **Double**. While the club is in the air your *left* hand throws a **Double** spin **Back Cross** and catches the first **Double** while still wrapped around behind your back. You can make the catch from either the normal **Back Cross** position or from under the arm —it's up to you!

Back to Back Passing

•**Back Crosses** can also be thrown in 'behind the back and under the arm' style, rather like juggling the **Contortionist**[EBJ].

•When passing clubs with a partner you can use **Back Crosses** either for your self throws or for making passes. Experts at **Single** spin **Back Crosses** can make *all* of their selfs behind the back and it's very common to see jugglers making passes to their partners from behind the back.

•A really dramatic trick is to throw a **Right-Left-Triple!** combination as three **Back Crosses**.

See also **Under the Arm**, **Under the Leg**.

Up-Down-Go! is the usual way of synchronising yourself with your partner when starting a **Passing Pattern**. It does *not* work when you are juggling back-to-back with your partner because you can't see each other. Instead you 'clack' your clubs together —*Clack!-down-go!*

•Audiences are very impressed by **Back-to-Back Passing** so it's a good trick to include in a show routine.

Both jugglers are throwing **Dropbacks** to each other, usually with **Double** spins.

This messes up the usually smooth rhythm of a six-club **Passing Pattern**, but who cares?

Start with three clubs each, do a *Clack!-down-go!* followed by a **Slow Start** and then pass a **Four Count**. You will both be looking *up* to catch the passes and it's very helpful if you let each other know how good or bad the incoming passes are.

•Almost any two-person club passing rhythm or routine is suitable for **Back to Back Passing**. Try a **Three Three Ten**, and practise some double-handed work with a **Three Count** as well so that your left hand learns to throw **Dropbacks** as well.

•Seven clubs juggled as **Staggered Doubles** is a very good pattern to use for **Back-to-Back Passing**, especially so because it's *meant* to be juggled on **Double** spins.

•To save clonking your partner on the head (or getting clonked) you should call **Hup!** as soon as your end of the pattern has become a disaster area, otherwise your partner may continue to chuck clubs at you without realising that you have already given up!

See also **Dropback Line**.

Back to Back Passing

Backdrop

The **Backdrop** is not to be confused with the **Dropback** though it probably will be. A **Dropback** is the action of tossing a club nonchalantly over your shoulder and expecting somebody else to catch it. A **Backdrop**, on the other hand, is the action of placing a club on your shoulder and letting it fall to a blind catch in the other hand.

• Juggle a **Three Club Cascade** and then, instead of making a right hand throw, quickly place a club on your right shoulder so that it hovers there, just for a moment, before falling down your back.

You should continue your cascade while this is going on so that two **Beats** later your left hand is free to quickly nip around the back and catch the club as it plummets toward the floor.

Note that the **Three Club Cascade** has not been interrupted by this trick, all you are doing is altering the path that one club takes for one throw.

Blind catches like this take a some work before they are solid. A good tip is to *visualise* the path of the club —this really helps.

• If you stoop forwards while you place the club for the **Backdrop** you'll be able to freeze the pattern for a moment with the club balanced on your shoulder. To resume you just straighten up a little and the club falls. Somehow this always reminds me of Frankenstein's pal, Igor.

Place the club on your shoulder...

..let it fall and catch it blind two beats later.

Balance

Balance is a trick in which a club is balanced on end, you'll also hear jugglers using the term when talking about the feel of their juggling clubs —to read about club design see **Juggling Clubs**, to find out about **Balance** tricks read on!

• The classic **Balance** is the trick of standing one club on its knob, supported by another club held in the hand.

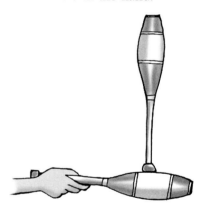

To get into this position from a **Three Club Cascade** you throw a right to left **Triple**, and then **Balance** the club held in your left hand on the one held in your right. You have about half a second to establish the **Balance** before your left hand needs to let go and catch the **Triple**.

•Alternatively, you can use a left self **Double** to achieve the same thing. In either case you'll be catching the high club more or less *blind* because you cannot take your eyes off the **Balanced** club once it's in position.

Many people believe that the secret of balancing is to keep their eyes firmly fixed on the *top* of the object in question. This isn't quite true, you should gaze fixedly at the object's *centre of gravity* instead.

•Having got your club into a **Balance** you have a number of options. The simplest is to toss it up and resume the **Cascade**.

•Experts can flip the **Balanced** club from its knob to its nose! Balancing a club this way up is a lot harder because the centre of gravity is lower.

It's a lot easier for readers of the COMPENDIUM *though, because they know that you don't stare at the knob, you stare at the club's Centre of Gravity.*

•A really elegant move is to toss up the **Balanced** club and then place the supporting club into a **Balance** on the left hand club —effectively the **Balance** has swapped sides.

You can repeat this move continuously for a great 'sleight of hand' pattern.

*The expert at the **Balance** gazes fixedly at the centre of gravity of the balanced club.*

*After holding the **Balance** for a moment or so the club is tossed up..*

*...and the supporting club is placed in a new **Balance** on the 'spare' club...*

...remember to catch the one you tossed up!

•The **Balance** is often used as a flashy trick in a **Passing Pattern**.

To buy yourself enough time to set up a right hand balance you can throw an **Early Double** from the left hand.

*OK, that's the **Balance**, but which club shall I throw as my next pass?*

This leaves you with a number of options for your next move —which will be a pass to your partner.

•The standard move is to toss the **Balanced** club to your partner and then resume the regular pattern.

Continued overleaf...

Balance...

• Rather than passing the **Balanced** club across you can throw the supporting club. First toss the **Balanced** club up a few inches, then pass the supporting club from underneath it.

• Yet another variation is to maintain the **Balance** and pass the club in your *left* hand!

• Alternatively you can smash the **Balanced** club across by hitting it with the 'spare' club, **Tennis** style.

• Experts may flip the **Balanced** club onto its nose before making the pass.

• When you have exhausted the possibilities of club-on-club balances you can always move on to club-on-body balances. Take one club and practise balancing it on your *forehead, chin, nose, hand, elbow, shoulder, knees and feet.*

• Of all these **Balances** the *forehead* **Balance** is the most popular (though my own personal favourite is the *nose* **Balance**).

The classic trick is to hold one club in a forehead, nose or chin **Balance** while juggling three more clubs in a **Three Club Cascade**. When dramatic tension has reached that 'magic moment' the juggler lets

the **Balanced** club fall and gathers it into a **Four Club Fountain**.

There is nothing easy about this, balancing the club is hard enough, but juggling at the same time is virtually impossible. Nevertheless it *can* be done and the audience will appreciate your selfless devotion *almost* enough to make the whole thing worthwhile!

The secret is to focus *completely* on the **Balance** and let the **Cascade** take care of itself! Don't make the mistake of forming the **Balance** and then waiting until it starts to feel solid before beginning to juggle. Instead you should form the **Balance** and *immediately* start to juggle. Let the **Cascade**

collapse if it must, but don't let that club fall off your face —no matter what!

• In another popular **Balance** trick the juggler 'rolls' clubs across their face from a **Three Club Cascade**.

Juggle three clubs and place a club into a *chin* **Balance** with your right hand. Without breaking the rhythm of the pattern you allow the **Balanced** club to fall smoothly to the left, where it is caught by the left hand. Done well it just looks as if a club has gone into slo-mo for one throw, the whole thing is one flowing movement —the club never actually **Balances** at all!

Practise rights, lefts, every right, every left, same club every time and...

• ...you can't go for *every* throw because you have only one chin! Instead you can use a combination of chin and forehead.

The right hand puts a club into a forehead **Balance**, the left hand goes for a chin **Balance**. As the forehead club falls off to the left it's caught by the left hand and as the *chin* club falls it is caught by the right hand, with careful control you can keep a sort of **Cascade** of three clubs going in this way. There are two secrets to this trick; firstly you must be able to place the clubs perfectly, and secondly you must learn to shift your attention from one club to the next at exactly the right moment.

•A club in a nose, chin or forehead **Balance** can be thrown back into your pattern with a **Head Flip**.

Allow the **Balanced** club to fall backwards, and as it starts to 'roll' over your head you nod forwards quickly. This will throw the club upwards, hopefully with a nice **Single** spin, to a convenient catching position.

The **Head Flip** is 'one of *those* moves', practice is the only secret!

•Masters and mistresses of the nose, chin and forehead **Balance** develop their skills by walking around for large parts of the afternoon while balancing a club and trying not to bump into things or fall downstairs. This should not be done in the immediate vicinity of heavy traffic.

•Sitting down while still balancing a club is a highly regarded skill, actually *lying* down for a moment gains you humungeous thrill points and massive rounds of applause.

•A version of **Gladiators** is sometimes played at juggling conventions in which all the participants **Balance** a club (again nose, chin or forehead) and the last one to drop is the winner —as with other versions of **Gladiators** those are the *only* rules!

•The *foot* **Balance** is also worth a mention. Stand on one foot and **Balance** a

club on the other —it's a great way of falling over!

It's a good idea to practise the move by *dropping* the club into the **Balance**.

•Once that is working you can try dropping a club from a club-on-club **Balance** into a *foot* **Balance**. Ok, it's not easy, but that's juggling for you!

•It's also possible to throw a club directly into a *foot* **Balance**, use a very lazy **Single** spin throw —this is another of *those* tricks again!

*One more **Balance** trick overleaf...*

Balance...

• A really silly **Balance** trick is to set a club up in a club-on-club balance so that it actually rests on your *thumb* rather than the lower club. This is invisible to an audience, then you let the 'supporting' club drop out from underneath it —the **Balanced** club magically stays in place, it looks surreal!

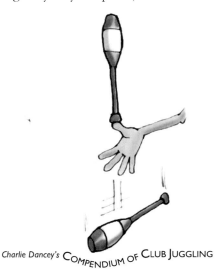

Beat

The underlying rhythm of a juggling pattern can be measured off in **Beats**. In most juggling patterns (say a **Cascade** of three or a **Fountain** of four), one throw is made on each **Beat**. In patterns where the hands throw together (like **Spreads**) the hands usually throw together on every other **Beat.**

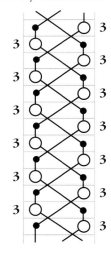

*A **Cascade** of three written in **Ladder Notation**.*

When a pattern is written down in **Ladder Notation** you can clearly see the pulsing of those beats as represented by the 'rungs' of the chart. In the chart for a **Cascade** of three objects you can see that there is a throw made on every **Beat** and that each throw spends two **Beats** in the air.

SiteSwap notation takes a simpler view, the number **3** represents a throw such that the thrown object is ready to be thrown again three **Beats** later. A **4** is thrown again after four **Beats** and so on. Because it takes a little time for the hand to 'process' a throw you'll find that a **3** actually spends just *two* **Beats** in the air, the extra **Beat** is the time spent in the hand (**SiteSwap** conveniently ignores this for the sake of mathematical simplicity but then gets into a complete twiddle about **Multiplexes** and stuff like that).

Club jugglers invariably refer to different weights of throws as **Singles**, **Doubles**, **Triples** rather than thinking in terms of how many **Beats** they spend in the air. Here's a table of how the various different ways of looking at throw weights compare:

3 = *two beats in the air* = **Single**

4 = *three beats in the air* = **Double**

5 = *four beats in the air* = **Triple**

6 = *five beats in the air* = **Quad**

—and so on.

Bear in mind that the actual amount of **Spin** on any given throw is arbitrary. *Normally* jugglers will throw a **4** as a **Double** but they don't have to. Similarly, in the **Five Club Cascade** every throw is a **5** which *ought* to be a **Triple** but jugglers almost always use **Double** spins.

When juggling **Passing Patterns** it's good to keep the rhythm of the pattern going in your head by counting off the **Beats** as you juggle. In a **Three Count** you can count:

pass - *two* - *three* - ***pass*** - *two* - *three...*

Now, if I say that you can make an **Early Triple** pass on the *two* **Beat** you'll know exactly when to throw it.

You'll find more words about the **Beat** (some of them quite long) in the ENCYCLOPÆDIA OF BALL JUGGLING.

See also **Single**, **Double**, **Triple**, **Ladder Notation**, **SiteSwap Notation** and **Causal Diagrams**.

Bounce

Juggling clubs will **Bounce** if they hit the ground just right. It can be expensive to practise this because if they are smashed hard into the ground 'just wrong' you may be needing some new props! It's not the force of the throw that makes a club bounce, it's control of the contact that the club makes with the ground.

•The easiest **Bounce** is a *'Flat Bounce'*. The club is thrown straight down at the floor as a **Flat** and you must ensure that both the knob and the body of the club hit simultaneously. If they do then the club will bounce back up with a satisfying and healthy-sounding *'boink'*.

If the knob and body *fail* to contact simultaneously then all of the force of the throw will absorbed by the structure of the club, there will be nasty sound of potential (or actual) damage and you'll look like a complete idiot who has just thrown their club at the floor.

It's therefore wise to practise the move gently at first and with your *own* clubs.

•You can use the *Flat Bounce* in solo juggling to great effect. Juggle three clubs, throw one as a high **Triple** or **Quad** and simultaneously **Bounce** the other two clubs once before catching the high one.

•A more impressive (and satisfying) **Bounce** is the **Tomahawk Bounce** which can be used either as a solo throw or as a pass. The club is thrown **Tomahawk** style, aiming for simultaneous knob and body contact as before. A well aimed **Tomahawk Bounce**, thrown as a pass, will rise as a **Flat** into your partner's hand.

Continued overleaf...

•Alternatively, you can throw a *Tomahawk* **Bounce** to yourself.

Tomahawk the club straight down to the ground and you should be able to get it to rise with normal spin, back into the throwing hand.

Boston Circle

This is an extraordinary **Passing Pattern** for *any* number of jugglers from three to a dozen or so. It's a type of **Feed** and the amazing thing about it is that *everybody* gets to pass with *everybody*. It's a very good pattern to play with at juggling conventions and workshops. This pattern has also gone by the names *'Turning Circle'* and *'Feast'*.

It also works on *any* passing rhythm so you can use **Two Count**, **Three Count**, **Four Count** or whatever you like. I'd recommend the **Three Count** because that gives about the best balance of skill and practicality.

•Arrange yourselves in a circle, facing inward, everybody has three clubs and prepares for a right handed **Fast Start**.

Each juggler passes in turn, clockwise, to each other juggler including *themselves*. This might sound crazy but let me explain (I'll assume that there are six of you juggling the **Boston Circle**).

Suppose your first pass is to the juggler on your left. Your next pass will be to the juggler two spaces to the left, then you'll pass to the juggler opposite and then you'll carry on around the circle until the next

person is you! As soon as you reach yourself you just miss a pass (this is *passing to yourself*) and then you go around the circle again.

It's that simple, everybody is doing the same thing except that they all start at different points in their 'sweep' All you need to know is how to start.

•Assume the role of *organiser* and explain to your confused companions that on *your* first pass you'll be exchanging passes with the juggler to your left. Take the line of this pass and then imagine a set of parallel lines across the formation between the other jugglers. This is the layout for everybody's first pass.

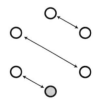

The direction of your first pass (you are the grey blob at the bottom) determines where everybody else starts.

If you were working with an odd number of jugglers then somebody would be passing to *themselves* (i.e. throwing a self) on the first pass.

• You're ready to go, everybody does an **Up-Down-Go!** and the clubs start to fly.

*Here's the full sequence of passes for a six-person **Boston Circle**. In the hexagonal pattern every second pass sees two jugglers passing to themselves.*

*Right-handed jugglers will probably prefer to use a **Two Count** but it's much better to be truly ambidextrous and use a **Three Count**.*

The pattern can be reduced all the way down to three people (a pretty minimalist version) or increased up to a practical limit of eleven or so.

Box

There is a ball juggling trick called the **Box**ᴱᴮᴶ which is a difficult three ball **Square Juggling**ᴱᴮᴶ pattern. It is virtually impossible to juggle with clubs though it has been done and we'll see how in a moment. When club jugglers talk about juggling a **Box** they are more likely to be referring to a passing pattern arrangement for four jugglers. We'll see how *that* works right after the **Square Juggling**ᴱᴮᴶ three-object pattern.

• Firstly it has to be said that *right angles*, while fairly unusual in ball juggling are almost mythical in club juggling. The props just don't lend themselves to that style.

DOUBLE

DOUBLE

VAMP

In the solo **Box** both hands throw simultaneously, the right hand throws a self **Double** while the left hand **Vamps** a club across with no spin. On the next throw the left hand throws a self **Double** while the right **Vamps** the no-spin club straight back.

Each club stays in its own part of the pattern, one on the right, one on the left and the third **Vamping** back and forth.

Before attempting this with clubs you should make sure you can juggle the ball version. That done, it's probably best to start the pattern from a running **Three Club Cascade**. Lead into it with a self **Double** on one side before starting the 'paired' throws.

You may also find it easier if you throw both the **Doubles** and **Vamps** as **Flats**. Completely removing the spin from the pattern can make it considerably easier to handle.

*The **Box** is very difficult because it involves simultaneous but different throws from each hand —one hand throws a **Double** while the other throws a **Vamp**.*

•The four person passing pattern arrangement known as the **Box** is a bundle of fun.

Take three clubs each and arrange yourselves on the four corners of an imaginary square facing inward. Each juggler passes only to the person diagonally opposite. Many different passing rhythms can be used —we'll begin with a **Four Count**.

All four of you do an **Up-Down-Go!** and start to juggle. One pair does a **Slow Start** (*One-and-two-and-Pass!*) while the other pair juggles a *very* **Slow Start** (*One-and-two-and-three-and-Pass!*). In this way, and as long as everybody keeps time, collisions in the centre of the pattern are avoided.

You'll find that you can get away with throwing **Doubles**, **Triples** and other **Syncopations** as long as everybody keeps to the rhythm. You should even be able to **Drop** and recover.

•When this starts to feel too easy you can start to pile on the pressure. It is possible, with extreme care, for both pairs to pass to each other on a **Two Count** in which case all four jugglers pass *simultaneously*. The four clubs will pass very close to each other in the middle but, if perfectly timed, they'll miss! It helps a lot if you pass wide (so that the imaginary tramlines are a long way apart).

•Done that? I'm impressed. Now try the deadly **Three Three Ten** in the **Box**. Start as you did for the **Four Count**, so that one pair are lagging one pass behind the other. Things don't get tricky until you hit the ten **Showers** at the end of the routine. Remember to juggle wide, as in the last exercise. Finish on a high **Triple** and take a bow.

The great thing about the **Three Three Ten**, as always, is that you stand a good chance of completing the exercise *without* a drop. When juggling straight **Two Counts** and **Four Counts** it's usual to juggle *until* you drop. This is bad psychology (because you always end up feeling like a failure) and *rotten* performance technique.

•Another popular **Box** routine manages to avoid collisions by juggling on a high-low principle. All four jugglers start together and everybody juggles a **Two Count** —but...

*The **Box** is all about timing and avoiding collisions.*

One pair throws four passes to each other as **Doubles** while the other pair throws six passes as ordinary **Singles** — then the roles reverse, the former high jugglers throw six **Single** passes and the former low people throw four **Double** passes.

The rhythm is wonderful, four **Doubles** take *exactly* as long to execute as six **Singles** and there's a wonderful adrenaline moment at each change.

•If all four members of your team can juggle seven clubs on **Staggered Doubles** then you simply *have* to try the *fourteen* club **Box**. The elegance and sheer wonder of this pattern is utter joy. Two intersecting seven club patterns mesh in space and time. The passes in the middle miss each other by scant inches and *half a beat* of time.

The start is everything. I'm assuming that you are all working right handed (which is a pretty safe bet).

You'll be standing in the square ready to go. Two jugglers will have four clubs each and two will have three clubs. Now call me Sherlock if you must, but I can say for a positive fact that the two jugglers with four clubs will be standing *next* to each other.

Not only that, one juggler will be standing *to the left* of the other*.

It's that juggler, the one on the left with four clubs, who is to throw the first club — triggering the first seven club pattern into life. The other juggler with four clubs is to deliver their first club *half a beat* later.

Now *half a beat* is not something that jugglers are used to and the natural tendency is to throw *one whole beat* later. Wrong! This must be the *second* club into the air, *equal* second is too damn late.

It's going to take you a couple of tries to make this happen but when it does you are going to be rewarded with a truly exceptional juggling pattern.

See also **Triangle** and **Star**.

---

*You see, I *think* about these things!

Brain Damage

No, this is not what happens to a juggler when they try to work out patterns in **SiteSwap Notation**, it's a very stupid three club trick in which you bash yourself on the head as you juggle.

•Juggle a **Cascade** of three clubs and smash yourself on the head with one of the clubs. The timing and feel of the move is rather like a **Chop**. You don't break the rhythm of the **Cascade**, you just use the time between the catch and the throw.

Some clubs are OK for this trick and others are definitely not! With a soft-bodied club you can hit yourself *very* hard without injury, but with others the trick may well live up to its name!

Brain Damage

Butterfly Pass

From the same family as the **Half Spin Pass**, this throw is designed mainly to shock and surprise your partner in a **Passing Pattern**.

•Instead of making a normal **Single** spin pass you give the club a good crack of the wrist so that it does a **Double** spin while travelling at the same height. It's a vicious spin and if you apply it carelessly it can injure your partner —be careful!

•**Butterfly Passes** look incredible when juggled with fire torches at night. However, the risk of injury means that they really shouldn't be thrown without your partner's full knowledge and consent.

Buzz Saw

A club thrown with a truly reckless and violent amount of spin is known by **VolleyClub** players as a **Buzz Saw** for obvious reasons.

Your partner is unlikely to appreciate such a throw in a **Passing Pattern**, though they are very good to throw in solo practice. You can get an audible hum from a club if you **Spin** it fast enough.

It's just alphabetical coincidence that the **Buzz Saw** and the **Butterfly Pass**, two very closely related tricks, appear right next to each other in the Compendium.

See also **Spin.**

Capacity

Working out juggling patterns on paper is something that appeals to some of the more technically and mathematically minded jugglers who may use **Ladder Notation**, **SiteSwap Notation**, **Causal Diagrams**, massive computers or curious systems of their own invention to make their calculations.

One of the important features of a juggling pattern is its **Capacity**, the number of objects that it can contain. In most cases this is pretty obvious —a **Five Club Cascade** contains five clubs, but things do get considerably more complex than that.

Imagine a **Feed**, one feeder and two other jugglers. The feeder juggles a **Two Count** passing **Triples** alternately to right and left, while the two other jugglers pass **Singles** back on a **Four Count**. Now, how many clubs fit into such a scheme? And then suppose you manage to work that out and decide to add one more club to the pattern, how do you adjust your throws to make room for it?

It's not obvious is it? What's called for here is a little *theory*.

•If you can get your pattern down on paper in the form of **Ladder Notation** (no

*A **Butterfly Pass**.*

mean feat for a **Feed**) then the number of objects is the number of lines criss-crossing down the chart.

•In **Causal Notation** it's considerably easier, the number of objects is the number of causal lines *plus* the number of hands.

•In **SiteSwap Notation** the number of objects being juggled by any individual is equal to the number of the *average* throw they make. So if the feeder is juggling **Triples** from the right (**5**'s) and **Singles** from the left (**3**'s) this averages out to *four* objects. If the two fed jugglers are working **Singles** (**3**'s) they have three each —adding this up we find that the pattern is a ten club pattern.

Sometimes, when you do this, you'll find jugglers working with fractional numbers of clubs (like *three and a half* each in the seven club **Staggered Doubles** pattern) but as long as the total number of clubs in the pattern is a whole number you haven't made any mistakes!

•Another useful rule of thumb is that objects in the air are *usually* separated from each other by *two beats of time*. In a **Three Club Cascade** it takes a club exactly six beats of time to complete one circuit of the

pattern and get back to where it started. Each club follows the previous one exactly *two beats* later.

This explains not only why it's necessary to increase the throw weights of a passing pattern to fit in more clubs but also *how much* of an increase you need to make.

In the six-club **Two Count** or **Shower** pattern you'll find that it takes a club exactly twelve beats to complete a circuit. If you want to add a seventh club you need to increase the length of this circuit by two. The standard way of doing this is to upgrade your passes from **Singles** to **Doubles** which results in the **Staggered Doubles** pattern. Other possible ways of increasing the **Capacity** of the pattern include keeping your passes as **Singles** while your partner throws you **Triples**. Alternatively you could both keep passing **Singles** and one of you could throw *self* **Triples**.

Capacity[EBJ] is also discussed in the ENCYCLOPÆDIA OF BALL JUGGLING.

See also **Beat**, **SiteSwap Notation**, **Ladder Notation** and **Causal Diagrams**.

Cascade

A **Cascade** is a figure-of-eight shaped juggling pattern for an odd number of objects. You cannot juggle an even number in a **Cascade** —you need a **Fountain** instead. However, any number of objects can be juggled in a **Shower** pattern.

Cascade, Fountain and Shower.

In a **Cascade** the hands throw alternately and each throw crosses the pattern. There's a problematical collision point in the middle.

The **Three Club Cascade** is the first pattern that a club juggler learns and quite a few go on to the **Five Club Cascade**.

Beyond that level few survive. The **Seven Club Cascade** has been achieved by a handful of jugglers through the ages, but at the time of writing, as far as I know, the *Nine Club Cascade* remains an unreached goal.

Causal Diagrams

While I was putting together the COMPENDIUM OF CLUB JUGGLING I came across a new form of juggling notation that produces charts known as **Causal Diagrams**, invented by the well-known club-passing 'guru', Martin Frost*. This system has two great advantages over other systems of notation; firstly it shows how a juggling pattern 'feels' to the juggler, and secondly it it can describe large and complicated patterns without looking like the wiring diagram of a telephone exchange.

The key to understanding **Causal Diagrams** is to realise that while **Ladder Notation** and **SiteSwap Notation** attempt to record the movement of every object in a juggling pattern, **Causal Diagrams** simply track the movement of the juggler's *problem*. Let me explain what I mean by that.

At any given moment in a **Cascade** of three objects the juggler has a *problem* — there is one more object than there are

---

The first published examples of this notation were seen in Martin Frost's regular column 'Juggler's Workshop' in JUGGLER'S WORLD (the International Juggler's Association magazine, Summer 1994 issue). Martin had developed the idea some time before then as part of his excellent work on **Passing Patterns**. I'm very grateful to Martin for the invaluable help and support he has given me.

hands. The *problem* approaches the hand and it *causes* the juggler to make a throw; so now there is a new *problem* heading for the other hand. A **Causal Diagram** tracks, not the motion of the *objects* but the motion of the *problem* that *causes* the objects to be thrown.

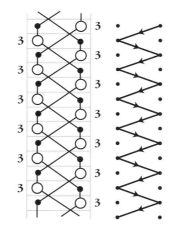

*The **Ladder Notation** for a **Cascade** of three, compared to a **Causal Diagram** of the same pattern.*

The **Ladder Notation** of a **Cascade** of three resembles a braid of three strands of hair, the **Causal Diagram** of the same pattern gives a single line that zigzags from side to side. Each line in the **Causal**

Diagram leads from one throw to the throw that is *caused* by it. The little dots are simply place markers so you can read off the succession of beats in the pattern.

To my way of thinking the **Causal Diagram** accurately models the *feel* of juggling three objects. I'm convinced that this zigzag line is far closer to the image of the pattern in the juggler's mind than the braid of three in the **Ladder** chart. How about you? Perhaps the **Causal Diagram** for the **Box**[EBJ] might further convince you.

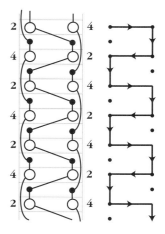

Notice how the **Box's** crossing 2's cause *simultaneous* self 4's to be thrown, hence the causal arrows representing these throws travel *horizontally* across the chart.

Here's a **Shower** of two objects. Note that the left hand **Feeds**, or places balls *directly* into the right, hence the throw symbols for the left hand are actually touching the catch symbols for the right.

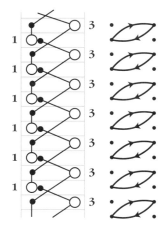

According to this **Causal Diagram** the action of throwing a **3** with the right hand *causes* the left hand to throw a **1** (a **Feed**) one beat later. This seems fair enough (you need to empty the hand in order to catch the **3**), but how about the idea that the throwing of a **1** by the left hand *causes* the right hand to throw the selfsame **3** a beat *earlier?!*

This isn't as crazy as it seems. In order to place an object directly into your right hand

you have to have emptied your right hand *first*. This does seem a little odd at first but if you think about it for a moment I'm sure you'll see how the **Causal Diagram** has captured the 'spirit' of the **Shower** perfectly.

Each arrow in a **Causal Diagram** starts from the point at which a throw is made and ends at the point at which a *caused* throw is made. Notice that the arrow for a throw of weight **3** always moves *one* beat down the chart, while a **4** moves *two* beats down the chart. This leads to a simple mathematical rule:

Each causal arrow moves down the chart two beats less than the weight of the corresponding throw.

That's why the **2**'s in the **Box** become horizontal arrows, moving *zero beats* down the chart. It's also why the **1**'s move one beat *up* the chart (two less than one equals *minus one*).

Numerically minded readers will already have guessed that **0**'s (**Gaps**) produce arrows that move two beats *up* the chart.

Spooky!

Here are three more examples of popular **SiteSwap** patterns, from left to right they are **534**, **531**, and **504**.

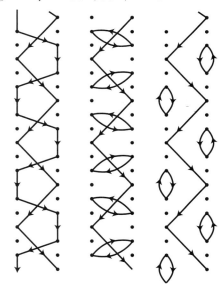

Here's the next mathematical rule for **Causal Diagrams**:

The number of paths running down the chart is equal to the number of objects in the pattern minus the number of hands.

Think of it this way —the surplus of objects over hands is the number of *problems* that a juggler has to deal with in a pattern.

Causal Diagrams...

This rule seems to fit perfectly well for the **Three Ball Cascade** diagram (one line zigzagging), the three object **Box** (one line square-waving) and the four object **534** pattern (two lines criss-crossing) but what about the two object **Shower**, **531** and **504** diagrams? All of these charts are complicated by the fact that arrows are moving *up* as well as *down* the chart.

In the two object **Shower** there should, by rights, be *no arrows at all* because the number of objects minus the number of hands is zero, hence (in theory) no *problem* to deal with and therefore *nothing to juggle!* The answer to this is that there is indeed *nothing to juggle* but the juggler decides to juggle *anyway* by throwing a **3**, creating a problem where there was none. The payoff is that the juggler then un-creates the problem by throwing a **1**, producing two causal arrows that *cancel each other out.* Arrows that move *up* the chart 'cancel out' arrows moving *down* the chart.

This 'cancelling out' idea can also be applied to the diagrams for **531** and **504** which contain closed loops. Once the loops are taken out of the picture the two patterns are revealed for what they are —three object patterns.

Causal Diagrams really come into their own when applied to **Passing Patterns** and it was in this context that I first saw them in Martin Frost's article. Martin drew his example diagrams with time running from *left to right* which is the conventional mathematician's way of doing things.

In this book I have used **Causal Diagrams** extensively to record and explain **Passing Patterns** and **Syncopations**. I've also drawn them left-to-right as Martin originally did.

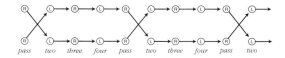

*A **Causal Diagram** of a six-club, two person, **Four Count**.*

Each juggler's throws are represented by a single row of circles, labelled 'L' and 'R'. The passes are the throws that cross from one juggler's row to the other. It's important to remember that the arrows do not show the movement of clubs around the pattern, they just indicate how one throw 'triggers' the next.

Causal Diagrams are very easy for a club juggler to read because an arrow that travels one beat along the chart happens, by a lucky chance, to be a **Single**. Similarly a two beat arrow is a **Double**, three beats for a **Triple** and so on.

Here's the trick **Right-Left-Triple!** being thrown in a **Four Count** (the juggler represented by the top row of the chart is the one throwing the trick). The dotted lines simply mark the 'normal' sequence for reference.

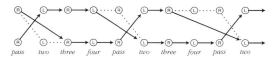

The **Causal Diagram** captures the essence of what is going on in this trick far more simply and effectively than either **Ladder Notation**, **SiteSwap Notation** or simple words of explanation. It really is a very lucky chance that the length of the arrows should fit in so neatly with the **Single, Double, Triple** style of terminology favoured by club jugglers.

The **Right-Left-Triple!** combination creates some spaces in the chart during which a juggler simply holds a club for a

Beat or two. A hold like this is denoted by a **2** in **SiteSwap** which *should* convert mathematically into an arrow that moves *zero beats* down the chart.

In other words, to be truly consistent, those isolated dots should be drawn with arrows that lead back onto their own tails!

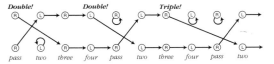

The **2**'s are shown as causal arrows that *cause themselves*. This is not quite as crazy as it sounds, the plain English translation of this mathematical oddity is that you are holding an object *because* you are holding an object.

There are two other 'weird' throws to watch out for, the **1** and the **0.** The **1** is the **Feed**, the action of passing a club directly from hand to hand, and this produces a causal arrow moving one beat to the *left*. It seems to be illogical but it actually means: *to place a club into that hand you had to empty it first!*

The **0**, or empty hand, produces a highly unlikely looking arrow that moves *two* beats to the left. The meaning of this is: *for the hand to be empty you must have made a throw from it beforehand.*

Mathematics may seem crazy but it *does* make sense —honestly!

Chops

Here's ultra-violence for the club juggler! A **Chop** is a wild and expressive slicing sweep of a club taken diagonally downward through the pattern. Good **Chops** can take years to perfect so you may as well start now.

•Begin by making an **Under the Hand** throw with the left hand and notice how your right hand instinctively 'dodges' the **Under the Hand** throw with a small curving movement. The fully fledged **Chop** is a development of this small dodge into a faithful rendition of a mad axe-wielding lunatic's death blow.

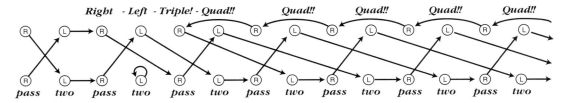

*Here's a **Causal Diagram** hard at work, this example comes from the* COMPENDIUM *entry* **Two Count**. *It includes* **Singles**, **Doubles**, **Triples**, **Quads**, *empty hands (**0**'s) as well as a hold (a **2**). What's happening here is that the top row juggler is switching from the regular six-club pattern into juggling with the left hand only —**Three in One Hand** style.*

Chops...

You make the change by shifting the focus of your concentration from the *left* hand as it throws **Under the Hand** to the *right* hand as it executes your embryonic **Chop**. Work on increasing the power and distance of your **Chop** until you are catching the 'axe' high to the right hand side of the pattern and sweeping it diagonally down and to the bottom left of the pattern.

• **Chops** work best as a continuous pattern, and this is what you should be working on. Many jugglers find it easier to use **Double** spins when doing **Chops** as this gives them more time to put expression into the move. You'll find that the pattern feels quite different depending on whether you use **Singles** or **Doubles** and the hard truth is that you really need to learn *both*.

In the fully **Chopped** pattern each throw is made *straight up*, the right hand throwing on the left of the pattern and the left hand throwing on the right. All of the sideways movement happens in the **Chop**. Your head will be flicking from side to side as you **Chop** —like juggling **Back Crosses** while you **Chop** to the *left* you are looking to the *right*.

• There is an often-missed point of finesse in the juggling of good **Chops** —it's a slight **Flourish** of each club before it slices down. This is not easy to get right so begin by practising with just one club. Hold it in your right hand in a **Normal Grip**.

Turn your hand outward (clockwise) as far as it will go. Now loosen your grip on the club and let the nose fall and rotate under its own momentum through three quarters of a turn. You end up holding the club as if you have just caught a pass.

That's the **Flourish**. Now add a **Chop**, slicing the club down to the left like a Kung Fu maniac, toss it as a **Single** or **Double** spin (your choice) and repeat the whole sequence with your left hand.

That's how really elegant **Chops** are done.

*A **Three Club Cascade** juggled with really wide **Chops**.*

• A good game to play with **Chops** is juggling them really *wide*. Stand with your legs wide apart and as you **Chop** to the left you move as far to the left as you can (never forget that you have to be looking to the right while you do this). Then on the next **Chop** you swing to the far right.

You'll probably need to be juggling **Doubles** to get away with this. The trick looks dramatic because you are always so far away from the club in the air. A good juggler can get the two sides of the pattern as much as ten feet apart.

Circus Grip

•A variation of the **Chop** is the *Outside* **Chop**. This does not lend itself to being juggled as a continuous pattern.

Instead of chopping the club down through the *middle* of the pattern you 'axe' it to the *far side* of the pattern. A right hand *Outside* **Chop** is chopped *over* the left arm and is then thrown up with **Dip** spin.

•**Chops** are also useful in **Combat Juggling** where they can be used as a menacing display to terrify a nervous opponent before you move in for the kill.

When you prepare to juggle three clubs you must hold one club in one hand and two in the other. The **Circus Grip** and the **Normal Grip** are the two alternative grips you can use for those two clubs.

It is generally agreed that the **Normal Grip** is the best choice for the beginner since you are less likely to get a club in your teeth if you fumble the start of your pattern. However, the alternative **Circus Grip** has some special uses.

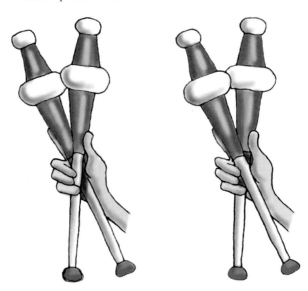

•To form a **Circus Grip** you hold one club in its natural position in your right hand and lay the second club on top so that its body lies to the right (in a **Normal Grip** the top club lies to the left).

•It's very important to realise that when starting from a **Circus Grip** you throw the *bottom* club first. If you value your lovely toothy smile, don't *ever* throw the top one first —it'll snag the other club as it leaves your hand and if it doesn't hit you in the face you've probably *swallowed* it!

Traditional circus performers (in England and Europe at least) favour the **Circus Grip** because it's easy to lead straight into a snappy up-tempo **Triple** spin pattern from a cold start. Club jugglers of the modern, cool, laid-back and recreational school of thought prefer the **Normal Grip** because they believe it to be safer and more natural.

Continued overleaf...

*The **Circus Grip** (left) and the **Normal Grip** (right). In each case it's the club pointing to the left that gets thrown first, that's the bottom club in the **Circus Grip** and the top club in the **Normal Grip**.*

Circus Grip...

• It's interesting to note that if you hold two clubs in one hand in a **Normal Grip** and then pass them as a unit across to the other hand, they will magically transmogrify into a **Circus Grip**. The two grips are mirror images of each other!

• When you stop your three club pattern you can choose whether you end up in a **Circus Grip** or a **Normal Grip** very easily. For a **Circus Grip** you make the last catch with the 'already held' club on the *inside*. To stop in a **Normal Grip** you make final catch with the held club on the *outside*. This

is easier to do than to explain and it's well worth practising because it's often useful to get two clubs into a **Circus Grip** in mid-juggle instead of stopping the whole pattern and fiddling around.

Why? Because the **Circus Grip** is the right way to hold two clubs for a two club **Multiplex** throw. Try it!

• Hold two clubs in a **Circus Grip** and throw them both together (**Double** spins look best). Notice how they split cleanly and under full control. Try the same move from a **Normal Grip** and they will tend to snag on each other and fly unpredictably.

• Putting some of these exercises together; juggle three and stop on the right in a **Circus Grip**, toss the pair up as a **Double** spin **Multiplex** and then resume the pattern before repeating the same sequence on the left. Keep that up for half an hour and you'll be an expert!

See also **Three Club Start**.

*How the last club is caught for a **Circus Grip** (shown on the left with the previous club on the inside) and for a **Normal Grip** (on the right with the 'already held' club on the outside).*

Club Swinging

Club Swinging is the art of manipulating two clubs while holding them by the knobs. It is a high art with an ancient military pedigree, a physical discipline and a form of dance. **Club Swinging** has as infinite a range of complexity as any other form of juggling.

It is a beautiful combination of the curving momentum of clubs controlled by the shape of the human body. The shapes made by **Club Swinging** moves always remind me of Leonardo da Vinci's famous drawing of the proportions of the human body matched to the circle and the square.

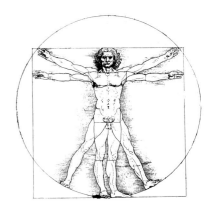

Club Swinging lies beyond the scope of the COMPENDIUM OF CLUB JUGGLING but there are a number of excellent books on the subject and the serious club juggler should make it their business to have at least a basic grounding in the art.

•CLUB SWINGING *by W. J. Schatz* originally published in 1908, now reprinted by Brian Dubé Inc. ISBN 0-917643-08-9

•THE BOOK OF CLUB SWINGING *by Ben Richter* 1994, published by Circustuff ISBN 0-9520300-4-7

•MODERN CLUB SWINGING *by Anna Jillings* 1994 published by Butterfingers ISBN 0-9513240-8-X

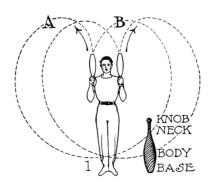

Illustration from CLUB SWINGING *by W. J. Schatz*

Combat Juggling Techniques

In the wonderful game of **Gladiators** and in other hostile juggling situations it is as well to have prepared in advance some defensive, or just plain *aggressive* techniques, if you hope to win the day.

•At the beginning of a large game of **Gladiators** there may well be a couple of hundred jugglers intent on doing each other to drop. Indeed most of them *will* drop in the first few seconds. Therefore the wise juggler takes a position near the edge of the arena, ensures that nobody is behind them and bides a little time. This is the *only* point in the game at which there is any justification for a temporary treaty between two jugglers who may stand back to back for the first half minute or so to avoid possible danger from behind.

•Next, as the first casualties leave the scene, you should start moving around and then keep moving at all times. Move unpredictably and constantly and don't ever forget that if you don't know what's happening behind you then *you'll never know what hit you!*

•At some point you will need to attack another juggler, but it's a good idea to intimidate them first with some well executed **Chops** or a **Lovegrove Loop**. These moves are both very unsettling.

•Now execute a neat **One Eighty** and *reverse* straight into their pattern. This will finish off all but the better players.

•Similarly, if you see somebody reversing into *your* pattern you can use the **One Eighty** to turn your back on *them* and then tussle it out back-to-back.

•The *Rotivator* is another cunning technique. Juggle **Two in One Hand** with your left hand while holding your third club at arms length as far away from the other two as possible. Now advance on your victim, twisting the club to and fro as you send it burrowing right into their pattern.

Continued overleaf...

•The classic attack move is to throw a club out of your pattern very high and right over the top of your victim. You are now utterly committed so you run screaming straight at them, your two remaining clubs brandished like war hammers. Smash down through their pattern and then run on to catch your high throw.

Often neither juggler survives this move.

•There is no honour in combat, despite what some would have you believe, so consider this; approach another juggler and simply steal one of their clubs. As you pinch it throw one of *your* clubs to the floor at their feet so that it looks as if *they* have dropped. It's a nasty little move and if it's noticed the crowd will probably boo you horribly and then *everybody* will be after you!

•If you end up as one of the last two surviving **Gladiators** then you can suggest to your opponent that you pass clubs with them in the spirit of fair play, good sportsmanship and all that.

Make the offer sound really genuine and they will start to consider the risks of your proposal. ("I pass a club, but what if I don't get one passed back?"). They may decide to go for it (poor fool, they shouldn't have trusted you) or they may decide that it's a ridiculous idea. Either way they'll *still be off guard for a moment* while they think about it. Smash 'em then!

•Of course if you do actually start to pass clubs then you deserve whatever you get!

•I've just been to the very wonderful *Boggle Juggling Shop* (who, incidentally, sell more copies of the ENCYCLOPÆDIA OF BALL JUGGLING than just about anyone else hence this shameless plug). I bought myself a pair of *Secret Spy Look-Behind Dark Glasses*. It's like having rear view mirrors on your head! On top of that they look amazingly cool as well. I'm not sure if it's cheating to use these in a game of **Gladiators.**

But if it is —I'm using them!

Cradle Pass

Fanatical ball jugglers collect, compare and invent *three-ball tricks* because there seems to be an endless infinity of them. The equivalent passion for the club juggler is that of collecting passing tricks that can be thrown in **Every Others** (the six-club **Four Count**). Here's a very collectible item for you.

•Immediately after throwing a pass to your partner you throw a **Flat** from your right hand and catch it in the crook of both elbows so that it lies across your chest as if you were cradling a baby. You are holding a club in each hand as you make the catch.

For your next pass you straighten both arms quickly, propelling the 'baby' as a **Flat** across to your partner.

•If you are on the receiving end of a **Cradle Pass** then you can catch it directly into **Cradle Pass** position at *your* end of the pattern and chuck it back again.

•There's a similar matching move in which you throw the 'baby' *over your head*.

The first thing to learn is the throw itself, working out how to get into the throwing position comes later!

You need to get one club in each hand and have them resting on each shoulder (like shouldered rifles). As you tip your head forward the third club, the 'baby' lies across these two clubs and rests on the back of your neck. Making a pass from this is rather like doing a **Scoop Pickup**. You tip your head down and swipe the two held clubs forward which zooms the 'baby' across to your partner as a **Flat**.

The throw is really very easy to make, but it's setting the move up that takes skill! You gather two clubs into your left hand, in a **Normal Grip** and then raise all three clubs into the throwing position in one smooth movement. You'll need to practise this solo until you can do it without thinking about it before trying to pull the move off in a running pattern.

Cradle Pass

Crown

The **Crown** is a special way of stacking three clubs —a pretty silly thing but what the heck. It takes quite a bit of fiddling about to get it to work at first but who knows, this might be just the thing you've been looking for.

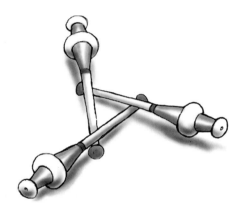

• Stack three clubs in a triangular formation so that each handle rests on the end of another club. It seems natural at first to place the knob of each club under the taped middle section of the next but a slightly smaller triangle is more stable. Different clubs behave differently so when you've perfected your **Crown** with one set of clubs, don't expect it to feel the same with another!

• Now your **Crown** is assembled you can balance the whole arrangement on your head and, um, —look pretty silly!

• By grabbing two of the **Crowned** clubs and flicking them forwards you can propel the third forwards at dramatic and possibly dangerous speed, a great way to start a **Passing Pattern**!

Dentist

Here's a trick to add to your repertoire of silly **Every Other** tricks and twiddly bits. It *looks* as if you are executing a very skillful chin **Balance** but actually your are just a shameful cheat. Your penalty for this fraud is that you could lose teeth!

• Juggle **Every Others** with your partner and throw them an **Early Double** pass. Using the brief **Gap** in your pattern you place your left hand club in your mouth so that your teeth are actually *biting* the knob. Take care not to bite the screw in the base of the knob if you value the enamel on your teeth.

On your next pass you bat the club out of your mouth with the club in your right hand, striking it level with its point of balance so that it crosses the pattern as a **Flat**. For goodness sake make sure that you release the grip of your teeth *before the impact* or there will be a couple of extra objects flying across to your partner.

•Jugglers who are masters of the **Balance** (i.e. who can balance a club on their nose, chin or forehead and juggle at the *same time*) will frown on this trick as a cheap gag and proudly demonstrate the genuine version, executing a perfect chin **Balance** *without* the use of the teeth.

Good for them, someday I too may be able to emulate their awesome skills.

See also **Oral Six**.

Devilstick Trick

This trick is almost, but not quite completely, impossible. I know this because I have been doing it for many years now. I honestly thought that it might have become a very fashionable juggling trick, but since it hasn't it must be harder than I thought.

The idea is that in mid-juggle you switch from **Cascading** three clubs into a devilstick pattern. You need to be a reasonably good devilsticker to do this trick.

The main problem is that juggling clubs make *really hopeless* devilsticks because their surface is far too slippery. They also make hopeless devilstick handles for the same reason. In fact just about all that a set of juggling clubs has going for it as a set of devilsticking equipment is that there are exactly the right number of bits —three.

•Hold two clubs (the handles) by the fat ends and stand the third (the devilstick) on its nose, on the ground, in front of you, balanced between the two handles.

Kneel down and try devilsticking from this position.

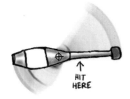

You'll find that it is best to clack the devilstick club just above the tape at the top of the handle and that it is *absolutely essential* that the devilstick club is exactly horizontal for each clack, swinging through a full 180 degrees between taps.

Many devilstickers work with smaller amounts of rotation than this but they are

Devilstick Trick...

using *grippy* props, not skiddy juggling clubs.

It's not easy is it?

As soon as you have had some degree of success (say six *clacks* without a drop) you are ready to move on to the full trick which involves going from a **Three Club Cascade** straight into a frenzied bout of devilsticking and then recovering back to the **Cascade**.

• To go into the **Devilstick Trick** you need to get two clubs flipped around to **Wrong End** catches and then throw the third club with **Dip** spin into the first *clack*.

The sequence I prefer is a right to left **One and a Half Spin**, then immediately left to right **One and a Half Spin** and then a right to left **Dip** which gets *clacked* on the right hand club. This takes you from **Cascade** to devilstick mode in just three short throws. When practising you might like to set up the two **Wrong Ended** catches a few throws before you throw the **Dip** so that you have time to think about it.

Once into devilstick mode you should try to keep it all together for just a few *clacks* and then knock the devilstick club high into the air and recover back to **Three Club Cascade**.

It's a complete nightmare but so very satisfying when you pull it off without a drop.

• Keen jugglers may like to put in a couple of **Propellers**[DD] into the **Devilstick Trick**.

The word **Propellers**[DD] is marked as if there were such a book as CHARLIE DANCEY'S DICTIONARY OF THE DEVILSTICK. I'm afraid I haven't written that one yet. So here's an extract from it that you might find useful.

Propeller

The **Propeller** is the awesome trick of keeping a devilstick in the air with *one stick only*, while it rotates continuously in one direction.

The really stupendous secret of this trick is that it is not nearly as difficult as it looks. For normal devilstick work you *clack* the stick just *above* its centre of gravity, for the **Propeller** you *clack* just *below* this point.

Normally a **Propeller** is executed clockwise when using the right hand and anti-clockwise when using the left but either direction is possible.

Difficulty

In the ENCYCLOPÆDIA OF BALL JUGGLING I dealt with the subject of **Difficulty**[EBJ] at some length and I presented a mathematical formula (not to be taken *too* seriously) by which you could calculate *Dancey's Juggling Index* for the difficulty of juggling a given number of balls in a given number of hands:

$$d = b/(h + h/b)$$

The formula is all very well as far as it goes but what the novice club juggler wants to know though is *how much harder is it to juggle clubs than balls?* That's a tough question for which there is no precise answer. When the ball juggler first moves on to clubs they may feel that they will never be able to juggle as many tricks as they could before with their new props.

It's true, they won't, but they *will* be able to learn entirely new tricks that take advantage of the **Spin** of the clubs, and when it comes to **Passing Patterns** —well, clubs are just made for that!

A rule of thumb you *could* say that juggling three clubs is about as hard as juggling four balls. Similarly, a five ball juggler is using about the same level of skill as a four club juggler. These are very rough comparisons of course and they will vary from juggler to juggler.

As far as the practical limits of skill go you'll find that, just as ball juggling enters the realms of fantasy after about nine balls, club juggling starts to become highly unlikely beyond seven. Both of these numbers have, of course, been exceeded, but only by *very* few people.

In any case, what does it matter? Juggling is *supposed* to be difficult!

*The **Seven Club Cascade,** this is about as far as club juggling goes.*

Dips

Dips are throws made with side spin, in other words *propellerwise*. A **Dip** throw from the right hand will spin clockwise (from the juggler's point of view) as opposed to an **Over the Top** throw which would spin anticlockwise.

Dips are so-named because of the 'dip' that your wrist makes when you do the throw.

• Begin with just one club in your right hand —fat end pointing forwards. Now turn the club so that its nose faces due *left*, you'll find that the most comfortable and relaxed way to hold the club in this position is with the back of your hand upmost.

Now **Dip** the nose of the club and throw it with a **Single** spin to a catch in the left hand —easy. Toss it back and forth a few times to get used to the feel of this throw, which is, after all, at ninety degrees to the usual way of thinking. Note that most of the action of **Dipping** a club is in the 'dip' itself. Your wrist feels like it is throwing the club for you by virtue of the natural springiness of the tendons in your wrist.

• Now juggle a **Three Club Cascade** and try putting in **Dip** throws; first from the right, then from the left. Now throw every right as a **Dip**, then every left, then the same club every time and finally *every single throw*.

• You can throw **Doubles**, **Triples** (and more!) as **Dips** too. Continuous **Double** spin **Dips** look wonderful. Work on developing a very relaxed action.

• **Dips**, especially when thrown as **Doubles**, are excellent throws to include in your **Fire Juggling** routine because they paint lovely swirls of light in the air.

Dips

Double

A **Double** spin, in club juggling, usually equates to a **4** in **SiteSwap Notation**. This is not a hard and fast rule since the amount of **Spin** on a club is completely independent of its airtime or the height to which it rises. Nevertheless, you will generally find that where **SiteSwap Notation** would describe a throw as a **4** a **Double** will be the most likely amount of **Spin**. It doesn't have to be that way, but the balance, rhythm and springiness of the human arm seems to naturally agree with this scheme of things.

• As your juggling skills improve you will learn to handle larger and larger amounts of **Spin** with accuracy. Learning **Doubles** is the first step on this road. Good practice patterns are the **Three Club Cascade** (juggled on **Double** spins), **Two in One Hand** and **One-Up Two-Up**.

You need to have to have perfect control of your **Doubles** before attempting the **Four Club Fountain**.

• When throwing a **Double** (or indeed any other amount of **Spin**), you should concentrate on watching the *knob* of the club as it turns —after all, it's right on the end of the handle, the bit you have to catch!

*When throwing **Doubles, Triples** and other multi-spinned throws you should concentrate on watching the knob of the spinning club.*

*A **Double** spin pass.*

• In **Passing Patterns** you'll find **Doubles** being used to make **Syncopated** throws, (like the **Early Double** and the **Late Double**). When making these throws it is the *airtime* of the throw, rather than the number of spins, that makes the difference between a well-timed and catchable throw and a club that comes flying out of nowhere and then carries on until it hits the floor. It's quite easy to catch a club at the **Wrong End** but it's very hard to catch a club that arrives at the *wrong time*.

A **Double**, to be on time, should rise to two and a quarter times the height of **Single**. It's tricky to judge height with a spinning object but a rough guide is that if your **Singles** peak at head-height, your doubles should be peaking at about the maximum height you could reach to on tippy toes with your arm stretched right up.

See also **Single**, **Triple**, **Quad** and **Spin**.

Double Return

Double Returns were discovered during a particularly productive club-passing session at the old Walcot Village Hall workshops back when I were a small wee lad. In those days you could nip down to your local juggling workshop, learn six new tricks and then juggle for seventeen hours without a break and still have enough beanbags left over to juggle a **Five Ball Cascade**[ERBJ] before turning in for the night and doing the same thing all over again the next day. We thought *nothing* of it. These young jugglers of today don't know how lucky they are —etc.

The **Double Return** is a particularly interesting and useful **Syncopation** of the **Four Count** (**Every Others**) passing pattern. It's fun to juggle because you and your partner can make a game out it, and it adds a new dimension to *Long Distance Passing*, the **Dropback Line** and other patterns.

If both you and your partner can throw well-timed **Early** and **Late Doubles** in a **Four Count** you are ready to learn **Double Returns**.

• Juggle **Every Others** and get your partner to throw one pass as a tramline **Double** instead of a **Single**. That's all they have to do, keep to the regular rhythm but throw one pass as a nice, slow and lazy **Double**.

This pass will arrive *late* in your left hand, so your pattern will 'freeze' for a beat while you wait for it. As the **Double** approaches your left hand you respond by throwing a left to right self and then immediately pass back to your partner with a second **Double** thrown from your right hand.

In other words, they throw you a **Double** and you respond with:

pause - and - **Double**.

Your **Double** arrives bang on time at their end of the pattern and the regular **Four Count** resumes.

It may take you a couple of attempts to get the timing right but it's really very simple. Your partner throws you a **Double** that arrives out of time, you *return* the favour and two wrongs magically make a right. As soon as it 'clicks' you should reverse roles, so that you both get familiar with the concept.

• The person that throws the first **Double** is said to be *'leading'* and the person that returns the **Double** is *'following'*.

Now the fun really starts. You'll find that the *leader* can throw a series of **Doubles** (say, three consecutive passes) and the *follower* simply responds each time with:

pause - and - **Double**.

—in effect the *follower* is juggling a slow and lazy **Two Count** to the *leader's* **Four Count**.

Take it in turns to play the *leader* until both of your are mesmerised by the metronomic rhythm of the **Double Return**.

• It gets better! Juggle the **Four Count** again and have your partner throw a **Double** on *every* pass. They are now 'hogging' the *lead* but you can steal it from them.

Continued overleaf...

Follow for a few passes and then, instead of responding with:

pause - and - **Double**.

You respond with:

pause - and - one - and - **Double**.

..in other words, get *three* selfs in before you return the **Double**. This transfers the lead to your end of the pattern so that now you are leading and they are following. You may find this a bit confusing at first, but if you both keep to the rhythm it will seem very smooth and natural. Now you can play **Double Returns** all day and hypnotise yourselves with the trick's wonderful tempo.

• The *follower* has a big **Gap** in their pattern to play with, which I'm sure you'll be able to find many uses for. For example you can easily **Flourish** every club before returning the **Double**. All you have to do is to catch each left hand self in a **Reverse Grip** and the **Flourish** follows naturally.

• The **Double Return** principle can also be taken up a level to **Triples**. Your partner throws you a **Triple** pass on the normal *pass* beat and you wait through the **Gap** and respond likewise, now *they* get a **Gap** and

then the pattern resumes as normal.

This isn't *quite* the same thing as the **Double Return** because you both get a **Gap**, but it's useful nevertheless.

• *Long Distance Passing* competitors would do well to practise **Double Returns** because it gives you an advantage. In *Long Distance Passing* competitions it's usually arranged that one partner 'toes the line' while the other moves steadily further away. You should agree that the line-toer *follows* while the other *leads*. Begin with a couple of rounds of regular **Four Count** to get synchronised and then shift up into **Double Returns**. When you get too far apart for comfortable **Doubles** you change up into **Triple** returns. **Quad** returns are also possible but by the time you reach this stage you are getting pretty desperate —you are going to have to rely on pure skill rather than clever technique.

See also **Dropback Line** and **Overhead Feed** for more elegant uses of the **Double Return**.

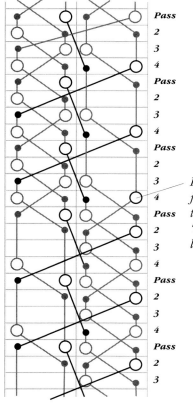

*A **Ladder Notation** chart of some fun and games with **Double Returns**, to begin with the juggler represented by the left hand ladder is 'leading' by throwing **Doubles** out of a regular **Four Count** while the other juggler follows. The **Doubles** are shown as darker lines.*

Pass
2
3
4
Pass
2
3
4
Pass
2
3
4
Pass
2
3
4
Pass
2
3
4
Pass
2
3
4
Pass
2
3

Here the juggler on the right 'steals the lead'.

Drop

A **Drop** is not so much an accident as a fact of life in juggling. Readers of the ENCYCLOPÆDIA OF BALL JUGGLING will already know my opinion of the suggestion by another well-known juggling author that a 'drop is a sign of progress'. It isn't. It means that you have *made a mistake*.

•If you want to be as sure as a juggler ever can be that you are going to get through your show or routine without a

Drop then you should apply the **Five Times in a Row** rule to the material you plan to use —if you can juggle a trick five times consecutively without a **Drop** then the chances are that you'll be able to pull it off in front of an audience.

It's especially important to avoid **Drops** in fire shows because, quite honestly, nothing looks worse or breaks the hypnotic spell of whirling fire so totally as a fire torch hitting the floor.

•The great rule about all **Drops** is not to let them rattle you, this is especially important in performance. You can't ignore a **Drop** because it's just so damn obvious, but you can win back the audience's approval by remaining in control of the situation. One way of doing this is to play on the theatrical possibilities of the problem with wise cracks and gags (known in the trade as "drop-lines"). For example, if you **Drop** in a **Passing Pattern** you can wait for your partner's next pass to replace the missing club and then carry on juggling a solo **Cascade** so that *they* are left with just two clubs — *'I've got my three!'*.

•Alternatively you can execute a 'dramatic recovery'. For this you need to master such skills as the **Kick Up** (the

classic recovery) the **Toe Kick** and the **Pickup**.

•If you don't feel like making the recovery *yourself* in a passing pattern, you can always kick the club across to your partner saying, "It's *your* problem!" which always gets a big laugh.

•Sometimes a club will drop and roll out of reach, down a hole, off stage or perhaps be stolen by a passing dog. In these situations it is very uncool to start moaning about how much the thing cost you, instead you should whip off a hat or a shoe and carry on juggling with that instead. Audiences appreciate quick thinking!

•Occasionally, when a club is dropped, it will **Bounce**. It's good to remember this because sometimes, just sometimes, you can catch the club after the bounce and make it look like a deliberate move. I wouldn't rely on it though!

•I have heard it suggested that the reason for the very 'watery' names of juggling patterns (**Cascades**, **Fountains** and **Showers** etc.) is because the very *first* thing a juggler learns is the **Drop.**

Drop Kick

Here's yet another silly pass that you might see juggled in the **Four Count** or other **Passing Patterns**. Add this to your collection along with **Bounces**, **Tennis**, **Tomahawks** and all the other whacky ways of throwing things at your friends.

•Juggle a **Four Count** and right after the pass, stop your pattern with two clubs in your right hand and hold the third club out in front of you horizontally, pointing from right to left.

Judge the timing correctly and drop the club, kicking it across to your partner on the *pass* beat. Go for control rather than force, using the top of your foot to kick it.

•You can dispense with the 'cheat' of stopping your pattern before you make the kick if you wish. The club you **Drop Kick** across is the club that you have just received from your partner (the one you would return as an **Early Double**). Just loft it across your pattern as a **Flat** and kick it over.

Although this is 'better juggling' I don't think it looks as impressive to an audience as the easy version (i.e. with the *stop*). By stopping your pattern you are giving the audience a better chance to focus on what you are doing.

Dropback

Chucking a club backwards over your shoulder is called a **Dropback**. This is how clubs are thrown when passing **Back to Back** or when juggling a **Dropback Line**. The throw is made completely blind so you need to develop a feel for where it is going —despite the name of the throw the idea is *not* to actually end up with a **Drop**.

•A **Dropback** is usually thrown as a **Double** to another juggler standing right behind you. Juggle a **Three Club Cascade** while your partner stands a few feet behind you. Now throw three consecutive **Dropbacks** (two over the right shoulder and one over the left) and your partner will have the whole pattern.

•Now it's your turn to run behind your partner and practise receiving their **Dropbacks**. You should both be outspoken in your criticism of each other's throws, yelling 'Over!', 'Under!' and other similar complaints. In no time at all you'll start to get that all-important *feel* for where those clubs are headed.

•Make sure that you both practise leading from both hands, using *left-right-left* as well as *right-left-right*.

*A **Dropback**.*

Dropback Line

Multi-person passing patterns are usually arranged in such a way that you can see everybody that you are passing with —not so the **Dropback Line**. Here jugglers are throwing clubs backwards over their shoulders, in other words —using **Dropbacks**.

•The simplest **Dropback Line** is an arrangement for three jugglers, working with nine clubs. Two jugglers, A and B, stand face to face. The third, C, stands between them facing A.

A is the only juggler who can both see and be seen by everybody and therefore orchestrates the start. It's best to start with a **Four Count** to keep life simple.

•The basic nine club **Dropback Line** has a serious problem with its timing. The **Singles** from A just don't match very well with the **Doubles** thrown by B and C and it can be a bit of a struggle keeping the whole thing together. One answer is for A to throw **Doubles** to C which at least means that everybody is making the same sort of throws.

*A passes **Singles** to C, who throws **Dropbacks** to B (**Doubles**), and B passes back to A, throwing **Doubles** over C's head.*

*Every pass is made right to left as usual but note that since C is facing the same way as B, C's **Dropbacks** need to be diagonal —from the right shoulder to the left hand. Some jugglers throw this **Dropback** over the left shoulder and some over the right, it's up to you.*

•A far better solution is possible if you use **Double Return** technology. What follows may sound complicated but it results in a very elegant timing which is far easier to juggle than the standard **Dropback Line**.

Arrange yourselves as before, only this time A gets four clubs, B gets three and C gets two. Juggler A starts first, throwing a **Single** to C's left hand. C responds, using **Double Return** timing, by making a **Dropback** over the shoulder to B who starts to juggle *one beat* after this **Dropback** throwing a **Double** all the way back up the line to A.

A continues, passing **Every Other** right to C, C juggles **Double Return** style **Dropbacks** to B and B is passing **Every Other** right, as a **Double**, back to A.

As long as you are all experienced with **Double Returns** the whole thing fits together like magic. Note that C, who usually has the hardest job with those **Dropbacks**, is now juggling the easiest part of the pattern. This is an enormous improvement on the 'standard' **Dropback Line** though it can only be juggled as a **Four Count**.

Continued overleaf...

Dropback Line...

•Another way of 'improving' the **Dropback Line** is to add an extra club. The ten-club pattern has none of the timing problems of the nine-club version because it actually *needs* those **Doubles** to make room for club number ten. The ten-club **Dropback Line** is juggled as a **Two Count**.

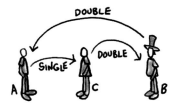

B starts with four clubs and A and C have three each. B makes the first throw, a long **Double** to A. A and C both respond simultaneously, **Seven Club Passing** style, when B's pass is halfway across. This is a little tricky for C since poor old C cannot actually see the starting pass being made. So the start has to be clearly signalled to C.

•Once you are happy with ten clubs you'll probably want to try adding more. You can make room for it by upping the value of B's passes to A from **Doubles** to **Quads**. **Numbers Jugglers** will no doubt find their own way of taking this theme to its absolute limit.

•Adding more people is great fun too. You can try just about anything you like but there's a good argument for using a bit of envelope-scribbling in preparation (check out **Capacity** for some hints on working out how many clubs you can fit into a pattern). Here's one that works well for four people and fourteen clubs.

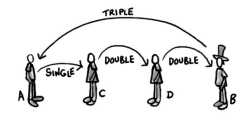

A will be passing **Singles** to C, who throws **Dropbacks** to D who throws **Dropbacks** to B who throws **Triples** back to A.

B starts with five clubs, everybody else gets three. You all juggle a **Two Count**. B leads straight off throwing **Triples** to A.

A and C start on B's *second* pass, D waits *one beat longer* before throwing their first **Dropback** to B.

If you can get past the start it runs like clockwork!

See also **Philadelphia Line**.

Early Double

The **Early Double** is often called a *'left to left double'* because if you are passing *right handed* (as just about everybody does) then that's exactly what it is —a **Double** thrown from your *left* hand to your partner's *left* hand. In the COMPENDIUM I need to be a little more careful with my terminology, because this book deals with right-handed, left-handed and ambidextrous patterns. The term **Early Double** is much more elegant and exact*.

The **Early Double** is usually the very first **Syncopation** that a juggler learns to throw in a **Passing Pattern**. You throw a pass a beat *early*, as a **Double**, from the 'wrong' hand which is timed to drop into your partner's hand just when they were expecting the normal pass. It can be used in any pattern of the 'three clubs per juggler' variety. The reason that the **Early Double** doesn't mess up the pattern is that, as long as a pass arrives on time, it doesn't matter when or how it was thrown.

•We'll start with the right-handed **Four Count** (**Every Others**) since this pattern is pretty much the favourite for beginners.

---

*I'm not sure who coined this phrase but if it *wasn't* Martin Frost (the American club-passing guru and inventor of **Causal Diagrams**) then it *should* have been. He has a very clear way of looking at this sort of thing.

The count of this pattern goes:

Pass - two - three - four- Pass - two - three - four...

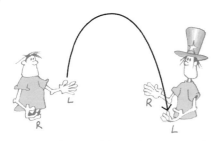

The **Early Double** is thrown on the *four* beat diagonally across the pattern from your left hand to your partner's left hand where it should arrive *bang on time!* As a reward for this skillful throw you get a short pause, or **Gap**, in the juggling at your end of the pattern.

It can be flummoxing working out exactly when the *four* beat is, especially if you aren't used to this sort of thing. Just remember that you throw an **Early Double** with the *club that you just received from your partner* —as their pass comes in, you catch it and **Double** it straight back, diagonally across the pattern.

To make the trick run like clockwork your **Double** needs to be well timed and this means getting the height of the throw right. If your partner complains that the pass is coming early (a common fault) then throw a bit higher. If the pass arrives late then you are throwing too high and you need to drop down a bit. Perfectly executed **Early Doubles** run like clockwork with no stress on the timing of the pattern at all.

You can throw each other **Early Doubles** *whenever you like* without prior arrangement or warning, provided of course that they are all thrown on the *four* beat.

•The **Early Double** can be thrown in many passing patterns of the three-clubs-per-juggler variety; the **Two Count**, **Three Count**, **Four Count**, **Five Count** and so on. In each case the **Early Double** is thrown on the beat before the *pass* beat.

You cannot throw an **Early Double** in a **One Count** though because there *is* no beat before the *pass* beat —every throw is a pass!

•Bear in mind that you don't *have* to throw an **Early Double** with a **Double** spin. They usually *are* thrown that way but it's entirely optional, you can use **Singles**, **Flats**, even reverse spin if you like. All that really counts is the airtime of the throw.

•When you have mastered this throw, learn the **Late Double** and the **Early Triple**.

See also **Syncopation**, **Causal Diagrams**, **Late Double**.

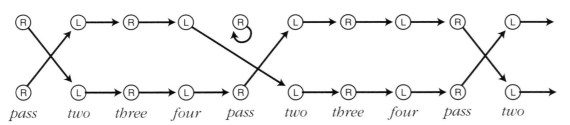

pass — two — three — four — pass — two — three — four — pass — two

*A **Causal Diagram** of the **Early Double** thrown in a six-club **Four Count**. Only your pattern (the top line) is altered by the throw.*
*Astute readers will immediately spot the potential for **Early Triples** and **Quads** which can also be arranged so as to drop into your partner's left hand when expected!*

Early Double

Early Triple

Following on in a fit of pure logic from the previous entry we come to the **Early Triple**. This is a pass made *two* beats earlier than a normal **Single** pass which nevertheless arrives in your partner's hand on time (and hopefully the right way around).

The principle of the throw is that you are going to make a **Triple** pass (four beats in the air) instead of a normal **Single** (two **Beats** in the air). In order to ensure that the pass arrives when expected in your partner's catching hand the throw has to be made *two beats early*.

•In the ever-popular **Four Count** the **Early Triple** is thrown on the *three* beat. In other words, the next right hand throw after a regular pass. Having thrown the **Triple** you get a pause at your end of the pattern (holding a club in each hand) and your regular **Four Count** rhythm resumes on receiving the

next pass from your partner. There's enough time to turn a **Pirouette** if you feel like it.

Pay attention to the height of your **Triple**, it should drop into your partner's waiting left hand *exactly* on time. Throw it too low and they'll receive it too soon, too high and it will come too late. Timing is *more important* than getting the thing to arrive the right way around.

•Throwing an **Early Triple** in a right handed **Two Count** is slightly more complicated, because it has to be thrown as a *combination*. The usual way of doing this is by setting yourself up with an **Early Double** and then immediately following that with the **Triple**:

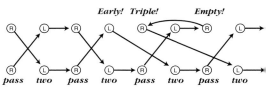

You get a **Gap** as a result of this move, leaving your right hand *completely empty* for two beats. An empty hand creates a backwards-pointing arrow in a **Causal Diagram** which is a little unsettling but makes perfect mathematical sense.

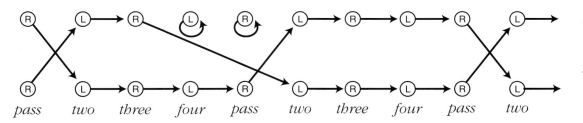

*A **Causal Diagram** of the **Early Triple** thrown in a right-handed six-club **Four Count**. This is astonishingly similar to the **Early Double.** The pass is made early, and arrives 'on time'.*

Only your pattern is affected by the throw.

• You can take advantage of the empty hand by **Feeding** a club into the empty right hand from the left and throwing another **Early Triple**. Keep going in this style and you are juggling the club-passing equivalent of a three club **Shower**. Here's the move with an **Early Double** lead.

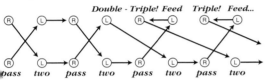

Double - Triple! Feed Triple! Feed...

pass   two   pass   two   pass   two   pass   two

Great throwing practice for you, great catching practice for your partner!

• In a **Three Count** the **Early Triple** is thrown on any *two* beat, that's immediately after the *pass* beat.

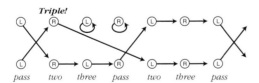

Triple!

pass   two   three   pass   two   three   pass

After the **Triple** you get a pause while holding two clubs. The two holds appear as arrows pointing back to their own tails.

Since the **Three Count** pattern is ambidextrous you need to practise both left and right handed **Early Triples**.

• In a **One Count** you can make a tramline **Triple** pass on *any* beat (every beat is the same in the **One Count**). Technically, one could argue about whether this should be called an **Early Triple** or a **Late Triple** but either way, it amounts to the same throw.

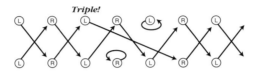

Triple!

Both you and your partner share the **Gap** this time as you wait for the **Triple** to descend.

• Finally, as with all the **Syncopations** you don't *have* to use a **Triple** spin on an **Early Triple**, it's just that you usually do. The important thing is the airtime (four beats). You can experiment with **Flats**, **Reverse Spins** or just about anything you like —just try to get that club to drop into your partner's hand at precisely the right moment —and hopefully the right way around!

See also **Late Triple**, **Right-Left-Triple!** and **Causal Diagrams**.

Eight Club Passing

Once two jugglers start passing with more than seven clubs they have entered the territory of the **Numbers Juggler**.

• The first pattern that eight-club duos learn is usually a **Two Count** in which every pass is a **Triple**. This pattern can be thought of as a passing version of the solo four club pattern **Triple Singles**. Every **Triple** is a pass to your partner, and every **Single** is a self.

Stand face to face, four clubs each, and do an **Up-Down-Go** —leading with a tramline **Triple** pass. Now just keep going, every left is a **Single** self and every right is a **Triple** pass.

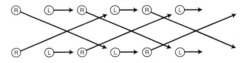

Causal Diagram *for eight clubs.*

Syncopations are difficult to add to this pattern because the passes are *already* **Triples**, any variation on the rhythm is going to involve making a higher throw somewhere —that means **Quads** at least.

Continued overleaf...

Assuming that you are passing a right-handed **Two Count** the following selection of **Syncopations** are all possible.

•A left to left diagonal **Quad** pass can be made on the *two* beat (any left hand throw). This is the equivalent of an **Early Double** in a six-club **Two Count**.

•Likewise the **Late Double** pass of the six club pattern converts to a right to right **Quad** pass on the *pass* beat.

•Which means that the familiar **Right-Left-Triple!** combination for six club juggling must be thrown as two **Quads** and a **Quin**. Impressive but unlikely!

•Many jugglers prefer to juggle the eight club **Two Count** using **Double** spins instead of **Triples**. Cutting the amount of club rotation in the pattern makes it easier to control and less prone to mistakes and fumbles caused by **Wrong End** catches. The down side is that the timing of the throws becomes uneven, instead of juggling a smooth rhythm of *lefts* and *rights* you may find yourselves juggling:

leftright - leftright - leftright ...

You will also be juggling faster than before, since you are fitting the same eight

The miracle of **Eight Club Passing** *being achieved with a* **Two Count** *on* **Triples**.

Note that there are a couple of hiccups in this picture, firstly, the Guy in the Shades has just made a **Wrong End** *catch (not unusual in this pattern) and secondly, the Guy in the Hat's face is obscured by a club —juggling photos nearly always come out like this!*

clubs into a smaller airspace. In this pattern the **Syncopations** become virtually identical to those that you can throw in the seven club pattern **Staggered Doubles**.

•Juggling the solo four club pattern, **Triple-Singles** using **Doubles** for the high throws is good practice for this pattern.

•Eight clubs can also be juggled using **Single** spin passes. In this version the throwing rhythm is completely altered so that right and left hands throw *in synch* rather than alternately. If you work out this pattern on paper you'll see that every throw is actually a **4** (usually a **Double**) but because you are juggling so low it *feels* as though every throw is a **Vamp**.

You start with four clubs each, do an **Up-Down-Go** and lead from *both hands simultaneously*. The right throws a **Single** pass and the left throws a **Single** self. Now keep going if you can.

•Expert eight club partnerships can switch up and down between the three modes (**Singles**, **Doubles** and **Triples**) *without* stopping.

See also **Five-Three-Four** for two more complex eight club patterns, using mixtures of **Singles**, **Doubles** and **Triples**.

Eight Clubs Solo

There are a few jugglers who have managed short bursts of an eight club pattern (I have a photo of Anthony Gatto at the controls) but nobody to my knowledge that has a **Solid**[EBJ] pattern. Juggling eight clubs is something that jugglers can *attempt* rather than actually *do* in any practical sense.

•The most sensible pattern is probably the **Fountain** which means that you are juggling four clubs in each hand. I had always assumed that **Quads*** would be the most suitable throws for the pattern but then I discovered that Gatto had used **Triples** (interestingly when somebody asked him what throws he used, Gatto claimed that he didn't know and had to ask his dad —*weird!*).

The combined difficulty of the four club lead from both hands and the collision problems make this pattern one that lies at the upper limits of human capability.

Good luck!

---

*This is probably one reason why I have never had any success with the Eight Club Fountain. Another is my total lack of dedication.

Elbow Throw

Here's another funky club passing throw that you can add to your **Four Count** juggling repertoire along with the **Khyber Pass** and other wonderful nonsense.

•Juggle a **Four Count** and right after a *pass* beat you place a club, from your left hand, into the crook of your right elbow where you grip it for a moment before throwing it as a pass by straightening your arm in a lunging motion.

•As you make this pass you can place the club in your right hand into the crook of

your *left* elbow and make a pass from there on the next pass beat.

•To complete the combination you can turn one hundred and eighty degrees to your left and place a club into a **Knee Catch** position and throw *that* club in a similar manner —it feels like a Kung Fu kick!

See also **Armpit Grip**.

Elbow Throw

Eleven Club Feed

There is more than one way to juggle an eleven club* **Passing Pattern** between three people, but this is probably the simplest. It's a standard three-person **Feed** in a normal vee formation. The feeder juggles a **Two Count**, making **Triple** passes alternately to right and left, while the 'fed' jugglers work **Four Counts**, tossing **Triples** back to the feeder.

•Arrange yourselves in vee formation and label yourselves A, B and C. A is the feeder and faces B on the left and C on the right. A and B start with four clubs each. C has three.

You all do an **Up-Down-Go!** and start to juggle. A and B both pass on the very first throw, but, surprisingly, A passes to the right, to C —*not* B!

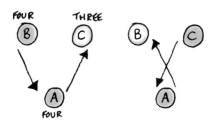

*The first and second passes of the **Eleven Club Feed**. On the first pass A is receiving from B but passing to C (who isn't passing to anyone). On the second pass B selfs while C passes to A and A passes to B.*

Now the pattern is running, on the next pass, two beats later, A is passing to the *left*, to B and receiving from C on the *right*.

The feeder keeps passing **Triples** alternately to the left and the right and the other two juggle their **Triple-Self** patterns two beats out of synch with each other.

•This is pretty hot stuff, so as far as **Syncopations** go I'm not going to say much more than 'good luck'. The feeder can throw tricks that would work in an eight club **Two Count** juggled on **Triples**.

B and C can throw tricks that would work in a two person, seven club **Triple Self** pattern.

Good luck.

See also **Eight Club Passing**, **Triple-Self (seven clubs)** and **Feed**.

*A **Causal Diagram** of the **Eleven Club Feed**. A is feeding B and C and every pass is a **Triple**.*

---

*The first time I tried this pattern my partners and I managed to miscount the number of clubs and ended up trying to juggle an **Eleven Club Feed** with just *ten* clubs. 'There's a **Gap** in this pattern, your theory is all cock-eyed.' complained HMG. 'No, it should work, honestly!' I replied, checking my scribbled notes. It was some half an hour before we realised the mistake!

MORAL: if you are having serious difficulties with a pattern it might be an idea to check you are using the right amount of equipment!

Every Others

This is a popular name for the universally popular **Four Count** passing rhythm. Every fourth throw is a pass, and since most of us are right-handed this usually means that **Every Other** right hand throw is a pass.

See **Four Count**.

Fake

Club passing is not *supposed* to be competitive but we like to have our little jokes on our partners from time to time.

• Juggle a **Four Count** and make as if you are throwing an **Albert** pass while actually throwing an **Early Double**.

You have to *try* it!

Fast Start

A **Fast Start** is the method of starting a passing pattern in which the *very first throw* is a pass.

The alternative is the more sedate **Slow Start**, in which the jugglers make a few throws to themselves in order to synchronise the pattern.

Feed

The term **Feed** has two meanings in juggling, depending on whether you are talking about solo juggling or **Passing Patterns**.

*A three club **Shower** pattern. One hand throws **Triples** while the other **Feeds** clubs back across.*

In solo juggling terms a **Feed** is the action of placing a club directly from one hand into the other. The Americans use the term **Hand Across** to describe this 'throw'. A **Feed** is a throw with an airtime of *no time at all* and in **SiteSwap Notation** it is called a '**1**'. Despite having no airtime it still takes one **Beat** to catch the thing and get rid of it again. The **Feed** is the throw on the *easy* side of a **Shower** pattern.

In **Causal Diagrams** the **Feed** produces a causal arrow that moves one **Beat** *backwards* in time. This seems rather peculiar at first glance but, when translated from diagram to plain English, it just means that in order to **Feed** an object into a hand you have to empty the hand *first*.

In **Passing Patterns** a **Feed** is an arrangement of jugglers in which one juggler (the feeder), acts as the hub of the operation and is involved in every pass while the other jugglers (the 'fed' or as some would have it, the 'feedees') pass only to the feeder, taking it in turns.

The most common **Passing Pattern** arrangement for a **Feed** involves three jugglers.

Continued overleaf...

Feed...

•Grab nine clubs and two other jugglers and call yourselves A, B and C.

A is to be the feeder and stands facing B, to the right, and C, to the left. A will be juggling a **Two Count**, passing from the right hand to B and C alternately. B and C will be juggling **Four Counts** taking it in turns to pass back to A

When all three are ready to begin they raise their clubs into the air and bring them down together in the classic jugglers' **Up-Down-Go!** synchronisation move. A and B immediately pass to each other while C selfs. Next it's A and C that pass while B selfs and so the pattern continues with A passing out alternately to left and right.

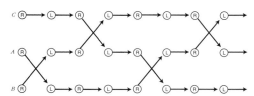

*A **Causal Diagram** of a six-person nine-club **Feed**. The feeder is represented by the middle line and is juggling a **Two Count** to the fed jugglers' **Four Count**. More ambidextrous arrangements are also possible using rhythms like the **Three Count** and **Pass-Pass-Self**.*

The fun really starts when the jugglers start to throw tricks. Everybody in the **Feed** can throw **Under the Leg**, **Tomahawks**, **Slapovers** and all that sort of stuff pretty much whenever they feel capable of it. These tricks are not specific to the **Feed** pattern itself so I won't deal with them here. Instead we'll concentrate first on the possible **Syncopations** or 'timing tricks' that can be thrown in the **Feed.**

The feeder can throw **Syncopations** that work in the ordinary six-club two-person **Two Count**. Here are a few of the possibilities.

•Substitute a **Late Double** pass for the ordinary pass.

•Return a caught club to the thrower

with an immediate **Early Double**.

•While throwing an **Early Double** use the pause in your pattern to turn a full pirouette.

•The feeder can do the **Right-Left-Triple!** combination by starting with a **Late Double** (in place of a regular pass) to B, *immediately* followed by an **Early Double** to C, *immediately* followed by a **Right to Left Triple** pass to B.

•The feeder can spice that move up even more by following the **Triple** with a left to left **Quad** to C! Then they pause through the **Gap** before resuming at the more placid normal level.

•Alternatively, don't pause at all after the **Quad** in the last trick, instead just keep catching those passes as they come in and returning then to B and C alternately as left to left **Quads**. This way you are maintaining the **Hard End** of the pattern with one hand only! Ten out of ten for sheer style, charisma and brilliance if you pull this one off!

The 'fed' jugglers have an easier time of it, they can do **Four Count** tricks in the feed, there's no need to list all of those here because, as far as the fed juggler is concerned, everything works exactly as if they were juggling ordinary **Every Others**.

However if you decide to break some of the basic rules of the **Feed** you can create some interesting moves.

•B and C can change places (as long as they give A a little warning so that it won't come as *too* much of a surprise. Imagine you are B. When it's your turn to pass, make the throw to A and then instantly gather up your clubs, run around behind C and resume passing on your next scheduled *pass* beat. Obviously C can do this too.

•According to the layout of the **Feed**, B and C never exchange passes, but it can be done. Here's how C throws to B.

Instead of making a normal pass to A, C can make a **Triple** spin pass to B, using **Dip** spin (because B and C are standing

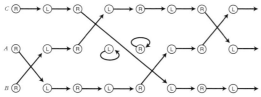

*C and B, the 'fed' jugglers can exchange passes in a **Feed**. Here C throws a **Triple** to B which leaves A, the feeder, holding two clubs for a couple of beats. Use **Dip** spin for these passes.*

side-by-side). The feeder is one club short for a moment and so **Holds through the Gap**.

If B and C both pass these **Triples** to each other at *every* opportunity (on every pass) then they end up juggling seven clubs between them (it's the **Triple-Self** pattern) while A is left holding two clubs and doing nothing.

•**Holding through the Gap** is quite an important principle in **Feeds** especially if, sorry —*when*, a **Drop** occurs. The basic principle is this: if you have only two clubs *do nothing!* Just wait for your next pass *unless* the dropped club is nearest to you in which case, for goodness sake, *pick it up!* Chuck it back to your opposite number on your next *pass* beat.

Losing a club doesn't really matter as long as the timing of the pattern is maintained, you only get catastrophic failure of a **Feed** when somebody loses count or gives up.

•The nine club **Feed** is better juggling practice for the feeder than for the fed so you should all swap around so that you get the valuable experience at the **Hard End**. You can do this by stopping and restarting

in a new arrangement but it's much more fun to change *on the fly*. You should start by standing at the three corners of an equilateral triangle so that nobody has to move when the change takes place. Then, on a pre-arranged count, you simply alter the scheme of the **Feed**. It's far simpler for you to work out the change for yourselves than it is for me to do it for you on paper.

•Also, please never, ever, forget the **Golden Rules of Passing** —the essential guide to club-passing ettiquette and personal safety.

See also **Ten Club Feed**, **Eleven Club Feed**, **One Count Feed**, **W-Feed**, **Typewriter Feed**, **Random Feed** and **Hovey's Nightmare**.

Feed

Finish

A beginning, a middle and an end, that's what every routine needs to have. For a neat beginning you can use a **Three Club Start** or a fancy **Kickup**, for the middle you just pile on a succession of your favourite tricks. For the end you need a positive and flashy **Finish**.

This is an area in which the personal skills and tastes of the individual juggler are the best guide but the COMPENDIUM can nevertheless make a few suggestions. The most important point of all though is this; *never* use a **Finish** that you cannot perform **Five Times in a Row** in practice without a **Drop**.

• Three club jugglers —finish your routine with a high throw at the very least. Toss one club high (as high as you can reliably manage), collect the other two clubs in one hand and catch the high one *just* before it hits the floor.

• Too easy? Ok, turn a pirouette under the high club before the catch.

• Still too easy? Who *are* you people? Right, throw it high, turn a pirouette and make a **Scissor Catch**.

• Here's another one, throw a right self **Double**, while it's in the air make a **Balance** with the other two clubs and catch the **Double** as a **Knee Catch**.

This is a three club version of a four club **Finish** invented by Micky Taylor, who also built the tent in the background. In the four club version, the extra club is gripped in the teeth, **Oral Six** style.

• Here's another; toss a high self **Triple** with your right hand and then collect the other two clubs in the right hand. Catch the **Triple** with your left hand from *behind your back*. Now turn a full pirouette to the *left*, keeping your left hand where it is, so that you are effectively 'unwinding'. When you get all the way around, toss the left hand club up again as a **Triple** and **Scissor Catch** it between the other two clubs.

• In a six club passing pattern the **Right-Left-Triple!** combination is often used as a **Finish**. You and your partner need to count into the move together and it looks great if you both pirouette under the **Triples** before that final catch.

• It's tempting to add an extra 'twiddly bit' to a passing pattern finish. Here's some business that the jugglers from *Ra Ra Zoo* used to use.

After the **Right-Left-Triple!** both you and your partner can arrange matters so that you are holding just one club in your right hand, in perfect synchronisation you both toss your right hand club as a **Single**, then **Reverse Catch** and **Flourish** it, follow this by tapping the nose of the club on the ground and then knock your clubs together (as if drinking a toast) —very cool!

•**Numbers Juggling** routines can be finished elegantly with one of the jugglers gathering *all* of the clubs. You need to jam them under your arm, between your legs and so on because you start to run out of hands very quickly!

A nice sting in the tail is for the gatherer (who looks like they are going to end up with all the clubs) to throw the *last club but one* back to their partner. Make damn sure your partner knows you are going to do this because it's supposed to be a visual surprise to the audience —not your partner when they catch it in the eye!

•The standard, simple, **Finish** to any passing pattern is for all of the jugglers to throw a high self **Triple** and then catch it.

To add a little more spice, as soon as you all catch the **Triple**, gather all of your clubs together and throw them as a unit to your partner (who throws back simultaneously).

In a three person routine you will each toss your collected bunch of clubs in a pre-arranged direction.

•A comic variation would be for two of the three to toss their clubs to each other while the third tosses their bunch offstage. Everybody loves odd-person-out jokes!

Fire Juggling

Dangerous? You bet —that's half the point! The other half is that **Fire Juggling** looks just wonderful! You get to be your own firework, watch those shadows dance and hear the *thwoosh!* of flames turning in the air. It's pure magic.

But first, here's a grim reminder:

Burns really hurt!

I'm not trying to put you off, I just don't want any beginners finding out the hard way. A minor burn to the hand may leave you unable to juggle for a few days, a serious burn can scar you for life —it's simply not worth taking unnecessary risks!

Continued overleaf...

Fire Juggling...

Choice of Fire torch

There is a wide range of fire torches (also known as fire sticks) on the market and all of the ones made by the larger manufacturers are fine from the safety point of view. If you plan to make your own, or use some obscure brand then make quite sure that the metal used in the construction of the 'hot end' is not steel, copper or brass. These materials burn flesh instantly on contact because they are such good conductors of heat. Sensible manufacturers use aluminium which is a very poor conductor and takes a few moments to do any damage —long enough for you to take evasive action and escape unharmed.

The most innovative set of fire torches I have ever seen was improvised from three loaves of french bread which had been dipped, at one end, in paraffin. Bread, incidentally, is a poor conductor of heat!

If you intend to juggle fire in the dark (of course you do!) then I advise you to buy torches with white handles because you will be able to see them more easily in the dark. It sounds so obvious doesn't it?

Choice of fuel

Never, ever, *ever,* use petrol.

I used it once and it was a bad mistake. If you don't end up blown to pieces or seriously burned then you are incredibly lucky. Petrol burns with a very hot flame, it can be highly explosive, and the torches are practically impossible to put out. The thick black column of smoke that rises from your torches doesn't exactly endear you to an audience either. Run your *car* on petrol if you must —but don't juggle with it!

A juggler's last moments.

Paraffin is just about the best outdoor fuel you can use, it burns at quite a low temperature and gives a nice yellow flame without too much smoke. Unlike petrol, paraffin doesn't burn on its own (unless it's very hot) so it's relatively safe to have containers of it in the same general area as your juggling. It may smell nasty but it's fairly harmless even if you drink it (which you shouldn't of course, but these things do happen!).

Methylated spirits (that is, alcohol with a dangerous poison added to put you off drinking it) can be mixed with paraffin for indoor work to reduce the amount of smoke. Meths burns with a cool blue smokeless flame which is useless on its own because it blows out too easily, but combining it with paraffin is useful because the mixture is much less smoky than pure paraffin. The two liquids don't actually mix so your concoction is rather like french salad dressing —it needs a good stir before applying it to the wicks. Also, meths evaporates really quite quickly so you should only apply it immediately before juggling. Be warned that this mixture is much more volatile than straight paraffin so you must keep it in sealed metal containers well away from the action!

It's also possible to buy specially refined lamp oil. This fuel is quite rare in England but readily available in many countries in Europe and around the world. Lamp oil is specially prepared for use in table lamps and lanterns and it is often scented and coloured. It's supposed to be more pleasant than ordinary paraffin and fire jugglers generally assume this is because it is 'purer' or 'more refined'. The unfortunate truth is that lamp oils are the devil in disguise. They contain a deadly mixture of lethal chemicals and additives to make them *seem* purer. These chemicals shouldn't do you any harm when you just burn the stuff, but if you swallow more than a tiny amount of it you are in big trouble. This is a very important point since fire jugglers and fire breathers tend to hang around together late at night and borrow each other's kit. Apart from that —fine!

There are, of course, many other liquids that burn, some are safe and some are not. The best advice is, use paraffin and stick to it. It's the safest and most sensible fuel that there is for the fire juggler.

Accidents will happen

So prepare for them!

You should always have access to clean, cold water, preferably in a bucket. If anybody does get burned then immerse the affected part into cold water immediately and keep it there. Small burns can be cured *completely* by this treatment. If the burn is anything other than a very minor one you should keep it completely clean and seek medical attention. Burns become infected very easily.

If you are performing indoors with fire you will probably have to have your precautions checked by a Fire Officer. You will need sealed metal containers for your fuel, suitable fire extinguishers (CO_2 ones are best) and a metal bin to dump your props in after use. You will also need to be quite sure that you are not working anywhere near cloth drapes or curtains and that someone is acting as a 'spotter', ready to pick up anything that drops offstage before the situation gets out of hand.

Phew! I think you might be ready to start now!

Learning to juggle fire

•Your first experience with fire juggling should be out of doors and in daylight. Start by having a good long *cold* juggle with your new fire torches before lighting them for the first time. Get used to their balance and feel. It's unlikely to be as good as your regular clubs. Make sure that you practise **Wrong End** catches, learning to handle the torch by grabbing the *body* instead of the wick.

•When you feel comfortable with your torches the moment has come to fuel up. The best method is to hold the torch over a metal bowl and pour fuel onto the wick until it starts to drip, at which point it is saturated. This avoids the over-fuelling that is inevitable if you simply dunk the wick straight into the fuel. The trouble with over-fuelling is that the excess paraffin tends to fly off as you juggle, usually into your eyes, causing all sorts of problems. Some fire jugglers routinely dip and over-fuel their torches and then flick the excess off onto the ground which is dreadfully messy, unprofessional and dangerous. Don't do it.

Continued overleaf...

Fire Juggling...

•Move away from your fuel dump and light up your torches. Zippo lighters are the best because they don't blow out in the wind. Let them burn for a few moments and then start to juggle.

It's quite terrifying at first! If you feel out of your depth then don't be shy of simply dropping everything and stepping back, this is *much* better than getting burned! Take it slowly, build your confidence and don't try any flashy tricks yet, just get that **Three Club Cascade** nice and solid.

•During your learning phase you'll probably want to do five or six 'burns' in one session. A 'burn' will usually last for two to four minutes, depending on the state of the wicks —old ones don't burn for so long. Remember that fire torches are not designed to burn continuously and you should let them cool off for a minute or so before re-lighting.

When the flames start to die down you should blow them out, let the wicks cool for a moment and then soak them with fuel again to cool them down some more. Be warned that adding fuel to a hot torch can produce white paraffin-steam which is *highly* inflammable.

•As your confidence grows you should practise a deliberate **Wrong End** catch and recovery, working with a single, freshly lit (therefore relatively cool) torch. It is possible to catch the flaming wick and toss the torch again without being burned (if you are quick) but I seriously advise you to grab the torch by the *body* if you possibly can.

•The next big hurdle is learning to juggle with fire in the dark.

The best way to learn this is to start a practice session just before dusk and keep practising as night slowly falls. This gets you used to the problem gradually.

Juggling with fire at night is an amazing experience, the main revelation is that you can't really see the handles, even if they are white as I advised earlier. You can't see the body of the torch either, just a crazy wheeling flame that floats through the air with its own special interpretation of the laws of gravity. One very important tip is to *listen* to the flame as it snarls through the air.

•Having arrived at the dead of night, with torches flaring before you, it's time to decide what tricks you are going to put into your fire juggling routine. I have some very serious advice for you on this topic.

There is no drop so obvious as the drop of a fire juggler. You can spot a fire juggler dropping from over a mile away —really you can. It looks *awful.* Even worse, while *you* may well have overcome your natural fear of fire, your audience have *not*. When they see a burning torch hit the floor they can find it deeply unsettling and it completely ruins the magic that you are performing for them.

So, don't put in tricks that you can't manage **Five Times in a Row** without a drop. Body moves, like **Back Crosses**, **Under the Leg**, **Alberts** and so on are pretty useless and self indulgent in the dark since you can't really see the juggler. **Doubles**, **Triples**, **Flats**, and **Flourishes**, on the other hand, are all very effective because they make such lovely shapes in the air. The magic of night-time fire juggling is not about jugglers showing off their skills. I'd rather watch a simple cascade, juggled on **Double** spins, than *anything* with a **Drop** in it.

•If you are planning on passing fire in the dark you and your partner(s) should adopt a similar strategy. Make sure that you have built up your confidence as a team by practising through a few dusk sessions. In your final routine, concentrate on the patterns you make in the air rather than on individual showing-off skills.

•I'm assured (by those that know) that juggling a **Five Club Cascade** in the dark with fire torches is not *much* harder than juggling five in daylight. There is so much light from the flames that you can see everything perfectly well.

•Finally, whenever you put your torches away you should make sure that there is a little fuel on the wicks, they'll last much longer that way!

Fish

A **Fish** (according to some) is a throw made in a **Passing Pattern** that resembles a dart player's throw. The club is lifted over the shoulder and tossed overhand, as a nose-first **Flat** to your partner.

•If you throw the club knob-first (or perhaps I should say *tail-first*) then the throw is called a **Javelin** or a **Spear**.

•However, if a juggler asks you to toss them a **Fish** they could also be referring to the famed 'love-em-or-hate-em-but-you-won't-forget-the-name' *Radical Fish* brand of juggling clubs.

See also **Javelin** and **Tomahawk**.

Five Club Cascade

Those who wish to become club jugglers of legendary proportions will know already that a solid **Five Club Cascade** is something they will need to achieve. If this is you then you may well be wondering whether you stand the slightest chance of being able to learn this pattern. Is it something that anybody can do, or are some of us built in such a way that it is just beyond our scope?

You'll find a certain amount of advice about one's *attitude* to the **Five Club Cascade** in the story at the end of this book entitled **Zenith and the Art of Pattern Maintenance**.

From a purely practical point of view the simple answer is that if you can cope with the hundreds of hours of practice in a positive frame of mind then you *will* be able to learn to juggle five clubs. There are however, no shortcuts, you must learn to accept slow progress and avoid treating the process as a battle. Remain relaxed and calm and have fun. You'll get there.

Continued overleaf...

Five Club Cascade...

The **Five Club Cascade** is an extraordinary pattern. Find a five-club juggler (or a video of a five club juggler if you don't have access to the real thing) and watch it for a while. The first thing you notice is the sheer *amount of stuff* in the air. Next you can see the concentrated activity of the juggler's arms, hands and eyes as they work to maintain the tight definition of the pattern. Ignore all this and focus instead on the path of a single club through the pattern. Notice how it seems to be in slow motion; floating lazily upward as it rotates on a gentle **Double** spin, floating down again and then suddenly being *snapped* out of the air by a furiously working hand and flicked back upwards into another lazy flight.

This always reminds me of a factory production line in which the products amble gently down the conveyor belts occasionally being brutally grabbed by mechanical devices that do wild things to them in the blink of an eye before sending them wobbling slowly on down the line.

Juggling a **Five Club Cascade** is a *trick*, like all juggling. You cannot hope to be able to keep five, four or even three objects in the air by simply chucking them up and then dealing with the first to come down again. Instead jugglers have developed special techniques that enable them to *appear* to be able to freely manipulate large numbers of objects in the air; the **Cascades**, **Fountains**, **Showers** and so on.

By developing your skill with these techniques you can extend your ability as a juggler in two fundamental directions. Firstly, by learning a large number of different techniques with say, three balls, you can reach such a level of proficiency that you can *appear* to be able to weave them through the air at will, in any way you wish. The truth however is that you are really just dazzling your audience with a flamboyant sleight of hand that conceals the fundamental *trickery* that is going on as you secretly combine one well-rehearsed move with the next.

The other direction is that of refining one technique, like the **Cascade**, to such a point of perfection that you can use it to keep an improbable and impressive number of objects in the air at once.

This is what the **Five Club Cascade** is all about. Forget any illusions you may have of being able to freely control the paths of five clubs as they spin through the air over your head. That is not an achievable ambition. Concentrate entirely on the *technique* and you will be rewarded with success.

Practice Tips

• The learning process is much like that for the **Five Ball Cascade**ᴱᴮᴶ only *much* harder. Anyone who manages to learn the pattern in less than six months is doing very well indeed, I've been working on it for *years* and my **Five Club Cascade** is still pretty rough!

• Every throw is a **5** In the **Five Club Cascade** and, although **5**'s are normally thrown as **Triples**, most five club jugglers prefer to use **Doubles** because this reduces the amount of spin in the pattern and makes it more manageable.

• It's well worth practising in the presence of other five club jugglers, most of the skill required for the pattern is acquired subconsciously and it's amazing how much good technique can 'rub off'.

• Keep your shoulders dropped and relaxed. Your body weight should be evenly distributed on both feet. If the pattern starts to wander to one side or the other then move so that you remain *under* the pattern, rather than reaching out or stretching your arms awkwardly.

• Don't forget to breathe! It's very common for beginners to hold their breath as they launch into the pattern which means that, should the pattern run for long enough, they will simply end up dropping from asphyxiation.

• Five club jugglers, like all **Numbers Jugglers** become hyper-aware of themselves and their surroundings while practising, developing a sort of mental all-round vision which sounds bizarre until you experience it for yourself. You will find it a great advantage to work in a large clear area on a perfectly flat floor. Stand well, breathe well and pay attention to everything that's going on around you.

• You should proceed with patience and calmness and never allow yourself to become rattled with failure. To learn the **Five Club Cascade** you must be nice to yourself. Make the learning process as enjoyable as possible and always try to finish a practice session on a high note rather than on failure. Use the hypnotist's trick of positive reinforcement by actually *telling* yourself how well you are doing out loud.

• When you **Drop** you should pause for a moment, rather than reaching immediately for the clubs and launching straight back into the pattern. Some jugglers seem to be in a hurry to get as many throws as possible into an afternoon's work. You need *quality* juggling time, not *quantity*. Take it slower and you'll learn much faster!

• It's a mistake to try and impress your friends with your progress because what seems amazing to you just looks like a half baked and unreliable **Five Club Cascade** to them. Your glory will come, but only when the pattern is solid.

• You should also avoid 'rationalising' about the pattern too much. Everybody does this, convinced that they can overcome the problem by 'logic' *'if I throw the first two a little higher then perhaps...'* You know what a perfect **Five Club Cascade** looks like, and in your heart you know that there is no 'great secret' apart from long, patient and steady practice.

• As soon as your pattern starts to get solid on **Doubles** you should start working on the **Triple** spin pattern to keep a hard edge on your practice. **Triples** are obviously harder to control, but this can be traded off against the slower and more even tempo of the resulting pattern.

Continued overleaf...

Five Club Cascade...

•Part of the process of learning to juggle five clubs is that of learning to throw really good, reliable **5**'s. Be sure to check out all of the patterns in the COMPENDIUM that use these throws; **Five-0-Four**, **Five-Three-Four**, **Five Club Gap** and so on.

As your **Five Club Cascade** becomes solid you can start to learn tricks and variations; here are a couple of suggestions.

•You can go into a **Five Club Cascade** on **Triples** from a six club **Two Count** passing pattern. Persuade or bribe your partner to throw *very* steady passes while you attempt this move.

You can't lead straight into the **Five Club Cascade** because you'll run out of clubs. Instead you lead with a self **Double** from the right hand and then start throwing **Triples**, (left hand first). You'll be looking *up* as you catch the last pass from your partner so it needs to be bang on target. They also need to hang on to the last club.

•If you start by passing seven clubs with your partner on **Singles** you can launch into a **Five Club Cascade** on **Doubles** using the same technique.

•Throwing continuous **Back Crosses** on **Triple** spins out of a **Five Club Cascade** is

a very highly regarded trick. A good practice pattern for this is **Triple-Singles** with four clubs, throwing every **Triple** as a **Back Cross**.

•You can throw a three club **Flash** out of a **Five Club Cascade** and do a pirouette underneath before resuming the pattern. Three **Triples** out of a **Double** spin pattern should be sufficient.

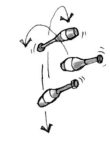

•Five club jugglers often use elaborate starts and finishes to their **Five Club Cascade**s.

For example, juggle a **Three Club Cascade** with two extra clubs placed in **Kickup** position, one on each foot. Kick up one club and go into a **Four Club Fountain**, then kick up the other and go into the **Five Club Cascade**. Juggle for a few moments, then execute a three club **Flash Pirouette**. Finally throw one club high, catch the other four, pirouette once more and catch the high club with a **Scissor Catch** —ta daa!

•If you are a **Balance** expert then you could try juggling a **Four Club Fountain** with the fifth club in a forehead **Balance**. When dramatic tension has peaked you drop the fifth club off your head and into a **Five Club Cascade**.

See also **Five Club Gap, Numbers Juggling, Seven Club Cascade** and **Zenith and the Art of Pattern Maintenance**.

Five Club Gap

A**Gap** pattern is a pattern from which an object is missing. This sort of thing is common in **Passing Patterns**. Usually a **Gap** of this sort is a mistake.

A **Five Club Gap** pattern is a **Five Club Cascade** juggled with one club deliberately missing. This is very good practice for the full **Five Club Cascade**, and is and interesting and useful pattern in its own right.

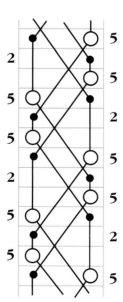

A Five Club Gap pattern (522) in Ladder Notation.

The juggler is Holding through the Gap, that is, throwing only when they have to.

The 2's are the 'holds' that result from this strategy.

•There are two variants of the pattern: one based on the idea of throwing only when you *have* to and the other in which you throw *whenever you can*.

Throwing only when you *have* to is known as **Holding through the Gap** and results in a pattern with a rather unusual throwing order:

right—right-left—left-right—right-left…

Juggle it with **Triple** spins —it's a great exercise. In **SiteSwap Notation** the pattern is written as:

5 5 2 5 5 2 5 5 2 5 5 2…

The **2**'s are holds.

•The alternative is to juggle so that you throw *whenever you can*, and this is just like juggling a **Five Club Cascade** with a hole in it. You may find, unless you are already a **Five Club Cascade** star, that it's quite hard to 'lock into' the rhythm of this pattern. The **SiteSwap Notation** for *this* pattern is:

5 5 5 0 5 5 5 0 5 5 5 0…

The **0**'s are *empty hands*.

Effectively, in this pattern you are throwing continuous four club **Flashes** which immediately suggests a good way of

learning the pattern.

•Juggle a **Four Club Fountain** on **Doubles** and then throw four consecutive crossing **Triples** (a **Flash** of four clubs) before dropping back to the **Fountain**. Written in **SiteSwap Notation** this is:

4 4 4 4 **5 5 5 5** 0 4 4 4…

Building up on this trick will lead you gradually to the full pattern.

•Since one of your hands ends up completely empty in this trick you can **Feed** a club directly into it from the opposite hand which results in the sequence:

5 5 5 1

This is a repeatable sequence and can be juggled as a pattern in its own right, see **Five-Five-Five-One**.

•I hope that the mathematically minded reader hasn't missed the interesting arithmetical progression here, from **55550** to **5551** to **552**. The next in two terms in this series are **53** and **4***, both of which are *very* important patterns.

See **Five-Three** and **Four Club Fountain**.

*Can you see why?

Five Club Gap

Five Club One Count

Here's a **Passing Pattern** that is ideal for absolute beginners. It's a two person pattern that uses five clubs and passes are made from both right and left hands. The term **One Count** means that *every throw is a pass*. It's closely related to the much more advanced **Seven Club One Count**. This pattern is just about the easiest **One Count** that there is!

• Stand facing your partner, you get three clubs and they have just two. You begin with two clubs in your right hand.

*Every throw in this pattern is a pass. You throw diagonal **Singles** (that is right to right and left to left) to your partner and they throw tramline **Singles** back.*

Lead with a diagonal pass from your right hand, to your partner's right hand, this gets the pattern started.

As the pass approaches they toss you a tramline pass back, which triggers you to throw a left to left and so the chain reaction of passes goes around the pattern.

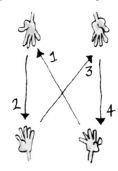

*A map of the sequence of passes in a **Five Club One Count**, only one juggler is making a throw at any given moment.*

The **Five Club One Count** is, as readers of the Encyclopædia of Ball Juggling will realise immediately, a **Domino Pattern**[EBJ], so named because it resembles a chain of falling dominoes. Each throw 'forces' the next as the receiving hand makes itself empty for the catch —just as each toppling domino knocks over the next one.

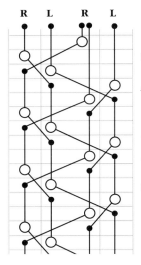

*The **Five Club One Count** looks pretty complex in **Ladder Notation** but take note all those long holds that make it so easy to juggle.*

*Below, for comparison is a **Causal Diagram** of the same pattern which clearly reveals its amazing simplicity.*

*The **Causal Diagram** is read from left to right. You juggle the bottom row (passing right to right and left to left) while your partner juggles the top row (passing right to left and vice versa).*

See also **Passing Patterns, Seven Club One Count**.

Five Count

A **Passing Pattern** in which every *fifth* throw is a pass is called a **Five Count**. It's one beat slower than a **Four Count** and because of the odd-numbered count you make passes from alternate hands.

•A five beat rhythm is not a very natural one to 'lock into' and unlike four time, you won't hear it often in music. It's therefore a very good idea to count off the rhythm in your head (or out loud) until it starts to feel natural.

Pass - two - three - four - five - Pass - two - three - four - five ...

The **Five Count** is the rhythm used for the first four passes of the **Four Four Eight** juggling routine.

You may throw **Syncopations** and, as always, there are millions of possibilities. I'll just list the basics...

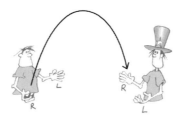

•An **Early Double** can be thrown on any *five* beat, you get a **Gap** on your side of the pattern. Because the **Five Count** is an ambidextrous pattern this could be a right to right *or* a left to left. Be sure to practise both!

•A **Late Double** can be thrown on any *pass* beat. Because you are passing with both hands that could be a right or a left hand throw. Your partner gets the **Gap** this time.

•You can also throw *self* **Doubles** on either the *two*, *three* or *four* beat of the pattern —plenty of scope for improvisation there!

•Experiment with putting all of these **Doubles** together into frantic combinations.

Continued overleaf...

*The **Five Count** and some **Syncopations** that you can throw...*

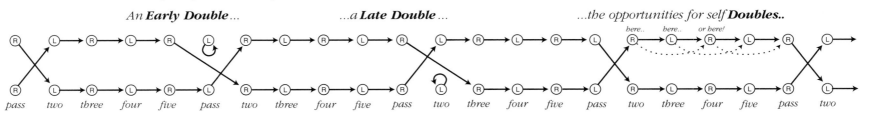

Five Count...

• An **Early Triple** tramline pass can be thrown on the *four* beat, it should arrive in your partner's hand bang on time. It creates a two beat **Gap** in your pattern.

• A **Late Triple** tramline pass can also be thrown on the *five* beat, it arrives in the 'wrong hand' a beat late, just like a **Late Double**. Both you and your partner get a **Gap**.

• You could also throw a *very* **Late Triple** tramline pass on the *pass* beat. This is not shown in the diagram.

• A crossing self **Triple** can be thrown on either the *two* or *three* beats. It has no effect on your partner's pattern.

• A **Late Single** pass is possible, it's thrown a beat 'late' from the wrong hand. You need to set the move up by missing the immediately preceding regular pass, a self **Double** will do the trick:

*Pass - two - three - four - five -**Double**[SELF] - **Pass!***

This is a tricky little throw and your partner is quite likely to miss it the first time that you throw them one.

There are many more possible **Syncopations** for the **Five Count** which you may or may not choose to work out for yourself.

In practical terms the **Five Count** is too pedestrian to suit the tastes of most club-passers so it's unlikely to end up as your favourite rhythm —still, it's nice to know where all those **Syncopations** go, don't you think?

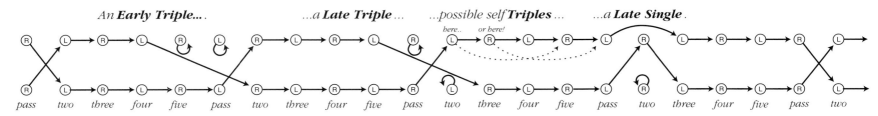

*An **Early Triple**... .*   *...a **Late Triple** ...*   *...possible self **Triples** ...*   *...a **Late Single**.*

Five Times in a Row

When you practise a juggling routine for a show it's important to have some way of deciding whether you'll be able to pull a trick off without a drop while under the additional pressure of working in front of an audience.

• A good rule is to only use tricks that you can achieve in practice **Five Times in a Row** *without* a drop.

So —no cheating, try the trick five times consecutively and if you get through the exercise you'll almost certainly be OK on stage.

It's very tempting to try and use material that is at the absolute frontier of your skills. These are, after all, the tricks that you impress *yourself* with. The trouble is that the audience don't understand this, to them it's *all* brilliant —*unless you drop!*

There's a big difference between dropping because you made a mistake and dropping because, really, you can't quite manage the trick you are attempting.

The **Five Times in a Row** rule should save you a lot of embarrassment!

Five-Two-Two

A surprisingly simple and yet very significant pattern for three objects. The **Five-Two-Two** (**522** in **SiteSwap Notation**) is none other than a **Slow Cascade** on **Triples**.

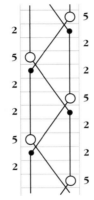

• Juggle three clubs in a **Cascade** making every throw a **Triple** —feel that rhythm! No, I mean *really* feel it, it's one thing to keep three clubs going on **Triples**, it's quite another to do it as elegantly as you can **Cascade** on **Singles**.

• Both hands get long holds (**2**'s) every time a **Triple** is thrown. If you are an ace at **Flourishes** then you should be able to **Flourish** a club on *every* throw.

• I've also seen this pattern used with full arm swings being made with each club before the throw. Sounds easy doesn't it? Don't be fooled —this is a serious trick.

• The exotic and mind-muddling pattern **Mike's Mess** is a distorted **522**. In that pattern the **5**'s are usually thrown as **Double** spins, just as they are in the **Five Club Cascade**.

See also **Slow Cascade**.

Five-Five-Five-One

Closely related to the **Four-Four-One** this pattern relies on the same basic principle —you juggle a pattern with one club missing, and every time the inevitable **Gap** arrives in one hand, you **Feed** a club into it from the other.

If you apply this idea to juggling a **Four Club Fountain** with three clubs you end up doing a **Four-Four-One**. Try juggling a **Five Club Cascade** with four clubs and you end up with the **Five-Five-Five-One**.

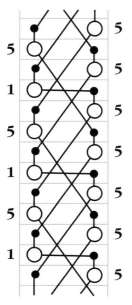

This can be juggled as a solo pattern in its own right, and has a lot in common with the **Five Club Gap** pattern, but you are more likely to see it thrown as a **Syncopation** in a **Passing Pattern**.

• Here's how to throw it in a six-club **Four Count**.

Each **5** is thrown as a crossing self **Triple**. The **1** is a **Feed** —one hand placing a club directly into the other.

Juggle a regular **Four Count** with your partner and then, on the *pass* beat, you throw a three club **Flash** (which means that you have missed the pass). You then catch your partner's incoming pass, **Feed** it under your **Flash** and pass it straight back to them.

Effectively you have been juggling four clubs for a few beats.

• To juggle the **Five-Five-Five-One** as a solo pattern you need to start with four clubs, two in each hand. Lead off from the right into a three club **Flash** on **Triples** and then **Feed** the fourth club from your left hand to your right —that's **5 5 5 1**.

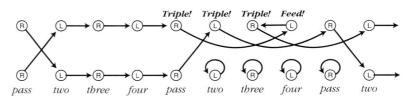

*A **Causal Diagram** showing a quick burst of **Five-Five-Five-One** in a **Four Count**, which amounts to a quick three club **Flash** with a cheeky **Feed** underneath it. The other juggler is left holding two clubs for four beats.*

Now keep repeating that sequence and you are juggling the pattern. Note that every **Feed** is in the *same* direction (left to right) as opposed to the **Four-Four-One** in which you get to **Feed** in both directions.

It is possible to juggle this as a continuous four club pattern but it is more likely to be used as a trick thrown out of a **Four Club Fountain** or **Triple-Singles**.

•There are, in theory anyway, a whole family of patterns based on the same principles as the **Four-Four-One** and the **Five-Five-Five-One**. The five club juggler might like to attempt the *Six-Six-Six-Six-One* (not listed in the COMPENDIUM) in which a **Six Club Fountain** is juggled with just *five* clubs. Once again, as soon as the **Gap** arrives in one hand, the other feeds a club into it. This is a seriously difficult pattern and there's not much point trying it unless you can manage **Three in One Hand** in *both* hands.

See also **Four-Four-One** and **Five Club Gap**.

Five-0-Four

SiteSwap Notation fiends need no more instruction, juggle **504** and you have it. The rest of us might like a slightly more gentle and informative introduction.

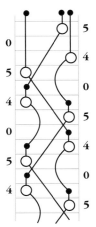

Five-0-Four is an elegant pattern for three objects which looks particularly good with fire torches because it keeps everything well up in the air. You can arrive at the Five-0-Four by adding extra Doubles to a Slow Cascade, alternatively it can be thought of as the pattern Five-Three-Four with one club missing.

The three throws used in the pattern are, as you would expect **5**, **0** and **4**. The **5**'s are crossing **Triples**, the **4**'s are self **Doubles**, and the **0**'s are **Gaps** (empty hands).

•The **Five-0-Four** has a slightly curious rhythm, and the best way to learn the pattern (unless you can sight-read **SiteSwap**) is to start by juggling a **Slow Cascade** of three clubs on **Triples** as a warmup.

The **Triples** take so long to cross the pattern that your hands are actually hanging around doing nothing for most of the time. In **SiteSwap** this reads as:

5 2 2 5 2 2 5 2 2 5 2 2 ...

The **2**'s represent the time that your hands are just holding clubs.

•Now you are ready to add the **Doubles**. Take two clubs in the right hand and one in the left. Remember that every **Double** is a throw to the same hand while every **Triple** crosses the pattern. Lead into the pattern with a **Triple** from the right. Pause for a moment, then follow with a **Double** from the right. Now throw the same sequence from the left —the throwing order is *right-right left-left*. It might take you a few goes to get the pattern to 'click' but when it does there is nothing forced or awkward about the timing. It really is just a **Slow Cascade** with **Doubles** added.

If you are competent with **Doubles** and **Triples** you should be able to master this pattern. Its main difficulty is that it goes against the usual juggler's instinct to throw *only when you have to*. In **Five-0-Four** you are throwing *whenever you can*.

Continued overleaf...

If you find the **Five-0-Four** too knacksome and tricky than you can always practise it with balls first. Just make sure that the **5**'s are thrown to about double the height of the **4**'s.

Once it's solid you can polish up those fire torches and wait for nightfall!

Five-Three

The **Five Three** is a juggling pattern for four objects in which one hand throws **5**'s (**Triples**) while the other throws **3**'s (**Singles**). It's a very popular four-club pattern and it's hardly surprising that club jugglers usually call it **Triple-Singles**.

See **Triple-Singles**.

Five-Three-Four

Named after the **SiteSwap Notation** of its throwing sequence, this solo four club pattern is very similar to **Popcorn**, the **Seven Club Passing** pattern. The **Five-Three-Four** is an infuriatingly complex mixture of **Singles**, **Doubles** and **Triples** and requires perfect control over spin and a good sense of timing. It also happens to be my favourite four club juggling pattern.

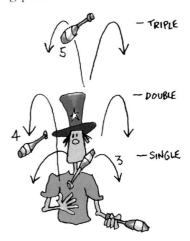

•The throwing sequence is:

5 3 4 5 3 4 5 3 4...

The **5**'s are crossing **Triples**, the **4**'s are self **Doubles** and the **3**'s are ordinary crossing **Singles**.

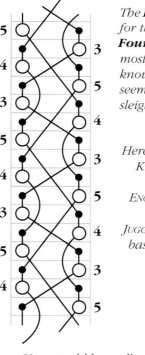

*The **Ladder Diagram** for the **Five-Three-Four** is one of the most elegant charts I know. The pattern seems to fit together by sleight of hand.*

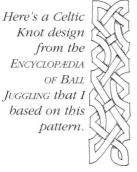

Here's a Celtic Knot design from the ENCYCLOPÆDIA OF BALL JUGGLING *that I based on this pattern.*

• You would be well advised to learn the pattern with balls first —just to get the throwing sequence locked in your mind. The pattern is listed in the ENCYCLOPÆDIA OF BALL JUGGLING under the same name.

• To learn the pattern with clubs I suggest that you begin by juggling a **Four Club Fountain** and practise throwing in the occasional round of **Triple-Singles**. Try juggling:

4 4 4 4 **5 3** 4 4 4...

That's one round of **Triple-Singles** thrown out of the fountain. Practise starting this move from both the right hand and the left hand. The most common difficulty is with the timing of the throws. Make sure that your **Singles** are being thrown low enough. The rhythm of the pattern should not falter —*listen* to the slap of the clubs hitting your hands.

• Next you can go one stage further and throw in rounds of **Triple-Singles** from alternate hands so that the *same club* is thrown as a **Triple** every time. This results in:

4 4 **5 3** 4 4 4 **5 3** 4 4 4 **5 3** 4 4 4 ...

• When that's solid you take the exercise one stage further and you're there. For the full **Five-Three-Four** pattern all you have to do is throw each round of **Triple-Singles** while the last **Triple** is still in the air, resulting in:

4 **5 3** 4 **5 3** 4 **5 3** 4 **5 3** 4 ...

That's the pattern! Good luck with it!

• If you find a partner who can also juggle a **Five-Three-Four** then you simply must try the eight club version of **Popcorn**.

Both of you stand face to face and juggle **Five-Three-Fours**, making every **Triple** a tramline pass to your partner. Since the **Triples** happen on every third throw the pattern is a **Three Count**.

• An alternative (and we are getting ourselves into *very* deep water here) is to use the **Pass-Pass-Self** rhythm, combined with **Five-Three-Four** to create a *mega-poptastic* eight club pattern.

From a **Fast Start** you will be juggling:

Triple^{PASS}-Single^{PASS}-Double^{SELF}-Triple^{PASS}-Single^{PASS}- Double^{SELF}

Words fail me!

See also **Popcorn**.

Five-Three-Four

Flash

A **Flash** is the act of throwing all the clubs in a pattern once (and catching them again). There are two slightly different meanings to the term, depending on whether you are a mere mortal or a **Numbers Juggler**.

If somebody says that a juggler is throwing a 'three club **Flash**' they usually mean that all three clubs have been thrown up so that *both hands are empty for a moment*, as you must do to perform a **Flash Pirouette**.

If a **Numbers Juggler** claims to be '**Flashing** six clubs' they mean that they are able to throw all six and catch them again —*once!* For a **Numbers Juggler** to 'qualify' with a pattern it's generally agreed that they must run the pattern long enough for each object to complete a full cycle of the pattern, this requires a burst about twice as long as the simple **Flash**.

Flash Pirouette

J uggle three clubs, toss all of them high into the air and turn once with the grace of a ballet dancer before catching the lot —you have just turned a **Flash Pirouette**.

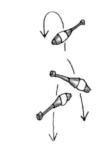

•More likely you have just dropped everything, made yourself dizzy and cricked your neck into the bargain! The **Flash Pirouette** is a trick that truly deserves the applause when it's pulled off.

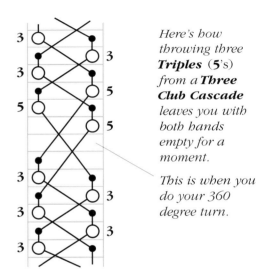

*Here's how throwing three **Triples** (**5**'s) from a **Three Club Cascade** leaves you with both hands empty for a moment.*

This is when you do your 360 degree turn.

•First you'll need to develop a really good **Flash**. Just throwing three **Triples** is not quite enough because they don't give you *quite* enough time to make the turn. Three **Quads** are better, but then you have the extra spin to contend with. Some jugglers upgrade just the *first* **Triple** to a **Quad** to gain a little extra time.

•Others use *pattern compression*. This heavy sounding term simply means reducing the spacing of the clubs in *time*, making the three throws of the **Flash** happen in rapid-fire succession:

Bam - bam - bam - bambambam!

Practise your **Flash** long and hard until you manage to increase the time for which both hands are completely empty to the absolute maximum without losing control of the throws.

•Next, you need to work on the **Pirouette** itself. Skilled exponents of the **Flash Pirouette** snap around at incredible speed. The turn must not interfere with the throwing of the **Flash** and it must be a complete three hundred and sixty degree rotation —getting most of the way around is simply not good enough. It's important not to force the move. Use control rather than brute force, it's very easy to pull your neck out of joint by trying too hard!

Notice how dancers turn a **Pirouette**, they keep their eyes locked onto a fixed point for half of the turn and then snap their heads around quickly, locking back onto the same spot. This technique is the answer to dizziness. The dancer usually chooses a spot directly ahead, but jugglers take a higher viewpoint, right through the tangle of turning clubs in the air.

It's quite nerve-racking building up to a **Flash Pirouette** (*not this one...not this one...NOW!*) so it's a good idea to use a standard routine so that you are working to a rhythm. For example, juggle three right hand throws of a **Three Club Cascade** and then throw a **Triple** spin **Flash**, three more rights and throw just one **Triple** and **Pirouette** underneath it, three more rights and throw two **Triples** and **Pirouette**, and finally three more rights and throw the full **Flash Pirouette**.

•A four club **Flash Pirouette**, while certainly possible, is hardly ever seen, it's *very* difficult. An equally impressive (and much more learnable) move is to juggle **Four Club Synch Doubles** and throw just *two* clubs high, while you **Pirouette** holding the other two.

•Five club jugglers can throw a three club **Flash Pirouette** while hanging on to two clubs. If the **Five Club Cascade** is being juggled on **Double** spins the pattern is already 'compressed' and three **Triples** should do the trick.

Flats

When a club is thrown with no spin at all you are throwing a **Flat**. When you throw a succession of no-spin throws to your partner in a **Passing Pattern** it's a *block* of **Flats** (hold on —it gets worse) and when you throw a really high one with no spin, it's a *high rise* **Flat**.

Vertical **Flats** *in a* **Three Club Cascade**.

•Easy? Sorry, **Flats** can be very difficult indeed. Try throwing **Flats** in a **Three Club Cascade**. Just throwing one isn't too much of a problem, but try to make *every* throw a **Flat** and you will be struggling.

Continued overleaf...

Flats...

*Horizontal **Flats**.*

There are two distinct styles used in the **Cascade**, the most elegant and impressive is to make every throw a *horizontal* **Flat** though throwing *vertical* **Flats** is considerably easier.

•**Flats** make a nice contrast from the usual spinny, turning feel of club juggling and it's good to throw them in for visual contrast (rather like playing a *blue note* in music). Four club jugglers can try throwing every *third* throw of a **Four Club Fountain** as a **Flat** instead of a **Double** spin, or use **Flats** instead of **Triples** in **Triple-Singles**.

•**Flat** passes are good too, how about throwing a **Right-Left-Triple!** combination to your partner using three **Flats**?

Flat Spins

Clubs are almost always spun in the vertical plane, so for contrast you can use **Flat Spins** where clubs turn in the air like helicopter blades, in fact the resemblance is so strong that **Flat Spins** are often called '*helicopter spins*'.

•These throws are very hard to make because your wrists just aren't built for it! They are also very hard to catch. This isn't all bad —they make ideal throws for **Volleyclub** players to chuck over the net.

There are two possible directions of **Flat Spin**, and you'll find that your right hand can throw most easily so that they turn clockwise when viewed from above (and contrariwise for the left hand of course).

•I've seen a **Three Club Cascade** juggled with *every throw* a perfect **Flat Spin**. It looks like a swarm of helicopters taking off —this is a difficult trick to master but well worth the effort.

See also **Helicopter**, **Dip** and **Over the Top**.

Flat Spin compared to *Normal* spin.

Flourish

Of all the 'twiddly bits' you can add to your club juggling, the **Flourish** is the one that oozes with the most debonair dexterity.

There is more than one way of twirling a club in your fingers (rock'n'roll drummers and baton-twirlers usually have a few suggestions) but what follows is a description of the juggler's favourite technique.

•Practise the move with a single club before trying to **Flourish** while actually juggling.

Take a club in your right hand in a **Reverse Grip**; your hand is palm downward and the handle of the club is gripped between thumb and the base of your forefinger.

Now swing the club so that the nose is pointing upwards and you are holding it as if you were about to paint a wall. This is the starting position —what follows is supposed to be a single flowing movement, but it's fine to fumble your way through a couple of times while you make sense of the words.

Swing the club downward and let its momentum carry it back up again, passing *inside* your arm, so that it's made a full turn, your hand needs to turn *palm-upwards* to keep hold of the club.

Now allow the club to 'fall' between your index and middle fingers, releasing it from your thumb. As the club starts its second revolution it's gripped between these fingers. This time it turns *outside* your arm.

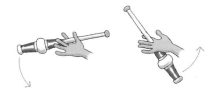

As the club nears the end of its second turn your hand needs to turn palm-downward again and you finish with the club's nose pointing forwards. You'll find that the club is, more or less, back in a **Normal Grip** —you have just **Flourished** a club.

It doesn't feel like much the first time you struggle through it. Most jugglers, when taught this move, are convinced that it isn't the **Flourish** that they've been wanting to learn, but some simpler version. After you've spun a hundred **Flourishes** you'll start to get the idea. Don't forget to practise this with your *left* hand too!

*A **Flourished** pass.*

FLOURISH!

•Now that you have the basic movement you should practise making a **Flourish** as you would in a running pattern. Here's a one-club exercise.

Start with a club in your left hand and toss it, as a **Single** to the right where you make a **Reverse Grip** catch (i.e. catch the club *high* with your hand palm-downward). Now execute a snappy **Flourish** and toss the club back to the left hand where you repeat the process.

Beginners tend to make the **Reverse Grip** catch then pause for thought before making the **Flourish**. It takes quite a bit of practice before you can do the whole thing in one flowing movement and actually *use the momentum of the catch* to get the **Flourish** going.

•When you can do that, you are ready to **Flourish** in the middle of a pattern, we'll start with the solo **Three Club Cascade**.

To execute a **Flourish** in this pattern you need to gain a little extra *hold* time. One way of doing this is by throwing a self **Double** in the *left* hand while you do the **Reverse Grip** catch and **Flourish** with the right. There's a little coordination problem here, especially for the beginner, because you need to be making the **Reverse Grip** catch at *exactly* the same time as the **Double** is thrown.

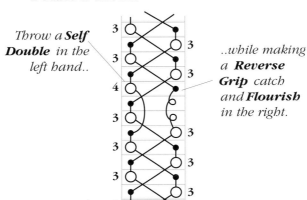

Throw a Self Double in the left hand..

..while making a Reverse Grip catch and Flourish in the right.

•Some beginners find this altogether too much to cope with so here's another method.

Juggle a **Three Club Cascade** and throw a right to left **Triple**, making the *next* right hand catch a **Reverse Grip** catch. The **Triple** may be a harder throw to make but at least all the action is now in the right hand.

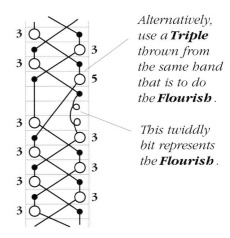

Alternatively, use a Triple thrown from the same hand that is to do the Flourish.

This twiddly bit represents the Flourish.

Choose whichever of these two methods you prefer and practise the **Flourish** to death!

•The **Flourish** combines very well with **Over the Shoulder** throws (and **Slapovers**) because at the end of the **Flourish** the club has the perfect position and momentum to flow from one trick to the other.

•Using the **Double** technique to buy time for the **Flourish** you'll find that working the trick on alternate sides creates a wonderful pattern which looks particularly good if you are working with fire torches.

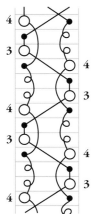

Throw a left self **Double** and **Flourish** in the right hand.

Now catch the **Double** and do a **Flourish** on the left and keep going. Every **Double** is caught in a **Reverse Grip** and **Flourished** before being tossed up as another **Double**.

You'll find that two of the three clubs are being **Flourished** while the third just hops from hand to hand on **Singles**.

•You can take this up one more 'gear' and **Flourish** *every single club* in the pattern. To do this you need to be juggling a **Slow Cascade** (on **Doubles**) to get enough hold time. This is very advanced juggling.

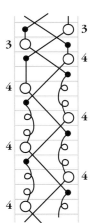

Start with a regular **Three Club Cascade** and then change up into the **Slow Cascade** by leading with a **Double** (a **4**) from the right hand immediately followed by a **Reverse Grip** catch.

As you **Flourish** that club, your left hand replies with a **Double**, makes its first **Reverse Grip** catch and **Flourishes**.

Now just keep going, every throw is a **Double** and every catch is a **Reverse Grip** and **Flourish**. Unless your **Flourishing** is very solid, you don't stand a chance!

•Using the **Triple** spin technique you can execute *two* **Flourishes** for each **Triple**, the action of each is staggered from the other by one beat —it looks brilliant!

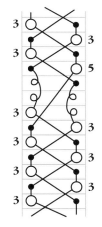

Juggle the **Three Club Cascade** and launch a right to left **Triple** (a **5**) and make both a left hand and a right hand **Reverse Grip** catch.

Flourish both of these clubs, catch the **Triple** and resume the **Cascade**.

•Your **Flourishing** skills can be put to good use in **Passing Patterns** too. To buy time for the trick you throw a **Syncopation** (like an **Early Double**) and having **Flourished** the club you have the option of throwing it either as a normal pass or as a **Slapover**. Here are a few basic moves to get you going. I'll assume in each case that you are juggling six clubs with a partner.

Continued overleaf...

Flourish...

• To make time for a *right* hand **Flourish** in a **Four Count** you can either throw an **Early Double** pass (on the *four* beat) or a left self **Double** on the *two* beat. The second of the two is the most elegant because the **Flourished** club gets thrown as a pass directly after the move.

• Again in the **Four Count**, if you throw an **Early Triple** pass (on the *three* beat) you have time to **Flourish** *both* of the clubs you are holding. See the similar solo exercise on the previous page.

• Still in a **Four Count**; throwing a right self **Double** on the *three* beat gives you time to make a *left* hand **Flourish**. This is slightly complicated because the club you need to **Reverse Grip** catch is the incoming pass from your partner. It's a skill worth learning!

• In a **Two Count** you make an **Early Double** pass to give you time to **Flourish** in the right hand. The **Flourished** club is passed straight out to your partner at the end of the move. For major thrill points you can make that throw an **Over the Shoulder** pass.

Thrown continuously this is my favourite **Two Count** trick. Your partner receives, alternately, **Early Doubles** and **Over the Shoulder** passes.

• If you are looking for ways of incorporating **Flourishes** into your passing work then **Causal Diagrams** are a very helpful way of looking at the problem. Wherever you see a *hold* (indicated by an arrow pointing at its own tail) —*there* is an opportunity to make a **Flourish**.

Foot Lift

Here's an easy foot **Pickup** for those of you who haven't quite mastered a proper **Kickup**. The advantages of the **Foot Lift** are that you can do it 'blind' and it is totally reliable. It's ideal for adding an extra club to a running pattern, say for a change from **Three Club Cascade** to **Four Club Fountain**.

• Place a club on the floor and roll it onto your right foot (using your left foot) so that its point of balance (usually about halfway up the shoulder of the club) is located behind your toes. Ideally the knob will be pointing to the right.

Whenever you see a 'hold' in a ***Causal Diagram*** *there is time for a* ***Flourish***.

The time needed to execute a ***Flourish*** *in a* ***Two Count*** *can be gained by throwing an* ***Early Double***.

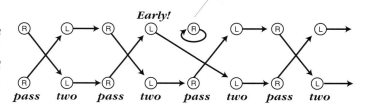

pass   two   pass   two   pass   two   pass   two

The **Foot Lift** is executed by simply lifting your right foot so as to place the club directly into your waiting right hand.

•In a real-life juggling situation you make the **Foot Lift** at the same moment as your right hand throws.

Juggle a **Three Club Cascade** and manœuvre the fourth club into **Foot Lift** position. Now lead into a **Four Club Fountain** from the *left* hand.

As you throw the first **Double** from the right hand you *simultaneously* **Foot Lift** the fourth club into the right hand.

No problem!

See also **Seven Club Pickup**.

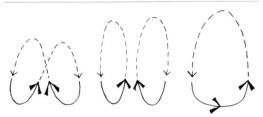

Cascade, *Fountain* and *Shower*
Just in case you didn't know the difference.
Cascades *work with odd numbers,*
Fountains *with even numbers and*
Showers *are tricky with any number.*

Fountain

The **Fountain** is the fundamental pattern for even numbers of clubs (or other objects) as opposed to the **Cascade** which is the basic pattern for odd numbers and the **Shower** which is the *non-juggler's* fundamental pattern for any number of objects.

In a **Fountain** each hand juggles half of the objects in the pattern completely independently —thus for a **Four Club Fountain** each hand juggles its own **Two in One Hand** pattern. Each hand throws alternately and what is *not* immediately obvious to the observer is that the objects being juggled *don't cross the pattern*.

For the vast majority of club jugglers the only **Fountain** pattern that they will have any dealings with is the **Four Club Fountain** since very few of us ever progress to the level of the **Six Club Fountain** (where each hand juggles **Three in One Hand**). The utter limit appears to be the *Eight Club Fountain* which serious **Numbers Jugglers** occasionally have a stab at. There is no such pattern as the *Two Club Fountain* since *two* clubs is exactly the right number for holding one in each hand and doing nothing at all.

Four Club Fountain

Even numbers of objects can be juggled in **Fountain** patterns and odd numbers fit the **Cascades** so the series of 'pure' patterns for ascending numbers runs from **Three Club Cascade** to **Four Club Fountain** to **Five Club Cascade** to **Six Club Fountain** to **Seven Club Cascade**. After that we enter realms of fantasy and vague rumour.

Continued overleaf...

Four Club Fountain...

• The **Four Club Fountain** is **Two in One Hand** juggled in both hands at once. The hands throw alternately. The two individual **Two in One Hand** patterns are juggled 'rolling out' —that is with throws on the *inside* and catches on the *outside*.

While this is certainly the simplest and most basic four club pattern many jugglers prefer the pattern **Triple-Singles**.

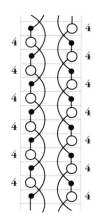

*The **Four Club Fountain** is actually two completely independent **Two in One Hand** patterns, juggled out of phase with each other. Audiences often fail to realise that the clubs never cross from hand to hand.*

In the **Four Club Fountain** every throw is a **4** and these **4**'s are almost universally thrown as **Doubles** by club jugglers. For the beginner the main problems are collisions and a weak left hand. Practise **Two in One Hand** mercilessly with your weak hand if you want to succeed with the **Four Club Fountain**.

Another common ailment is a lack of rhythm between the two hands —one side of the pattern starts to run a little fast and starts to 'catch up' with the other. This happens because there is no direct communication between the two hands as there is in a **Cascade** or other crossing pattern —apart from your brain. Keeping a smooth and even tempo is vital if you are ever to feel comfortable with the **Four Club Fountain**.

To start the pattern place two clubs in each hand and go for it! I usually advise beginners to make the first throw from their *weaker* hand so that their full concentration can be devoted to it.

The pattern is considerably harder than the **Three Club Cascade** but when compared to the **Five Club Cascade** it's like riding a tricycle. A month's hard work should see you a long way to a solid pattern.

• There are a vast number of tricks and variations that you can throw in a **Four Club Fountain**. To start with, you'll realise that since the clubs don't actually cross there is really no need for your hands to throw alternately, you can make *simultaneous* throws instead. This pattern is called **Four Club Synch Doubles** and has its own entry in the COMPENDIUM.

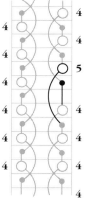

*To change from a running **Four Club Fountain** to **Four Club Synch Doubles** you throw one self **Triple** instead of a **Double** (a **5** instead of a **4**). The **Triple** takes a beat longer to arrive back in the throwing hand and this one beat delay takes your hands into the synchronised timing.*

To change back again you just repeat the process, throw a **Triple** from one hand (the other is simultaneously throwing a **Double** of course) and you'll drop back into the staggered timing.

Some jugglers *force* the change from one pattern to the other by kludging the rhythm of their juggling for a few throws, I said nasty things about this tatty way of doing things in the ENCYCLOPÆDIA OF BALL JUGGLING. It's inelegant and clumsy —don't do it!

•The **Four Club Fountain** can also be juggled on **Singles**. These throws need to be very floaty and precise. They look especially good if you juggle the pattern in four columns, each club bobbing up and down in its own position while your hands dart back and forth underneath them. The equivalent ball juggler's trick is **Pistons**[EBJ].

•Height and spin fanatics will, of course, practise taking the pattern up into **Triples** (and possibly beyond) which looks wonderfully wild —especially with fire torches.

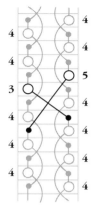

*One 'round' of **Triple-Singles** thrown in a **Four Club Fountain** causes two clubs to swap sides.*

•Chucking in one 'round' of **Triple-Singles** into a running **Four Club Fountain** is a useful trick.

Juggle the **Fountain** on **Doubles** and then throw a right to left **Triple** *immediately* followed by a left to right **Single**. The key to this trick is to get the throw heights correct, most jugglers manage to get the **Triple** right (about twice the height of the **Doubles**) but many get the **Single** wrong by throwing it too high (it should be about *half* the height of the **Doubles**). When the trick is thrown properly there is no break in the regular rhythm of clubs slapping into your hands.

•Try right *and* left handed rounds of **Triple-Singles** and when you get smooth with the trick you are ready to learn the awesome **Five-Three-Four**.

•Similarly a 'round' of **Six-Three-Three** can be used to good effect. You wham up a right self **Quad** (a **6**) which gives you time to make two throws of a **Three Club Cascade** (two **Singles** or **3**'s) underneath it before resuming the fountain.

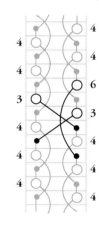

*One 'round' of **Six-Three-Three** thrown in a **Four Club Fountain** is a dramatic trick. The **6**, that is a **Quad**, needs to be nearly three times the height of the **Fountain**.*

Continued overleaf...

•You can use a self **Quad** to give yourself time to execute a **Flourish** in a **Four Club Fountain**.

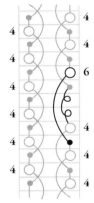

*Juggle the pattern and throw a right self **Quad**, making the next right hand catch a **Reverse Grip**, now **Flourish** the club before resuming the fountain. Your left hand juggles its **Two in One Hand** pattern unmolested throughout the move.*

•Another way of making time for a **Flourish** is to throw two crossing **Triples** out of the fountain.

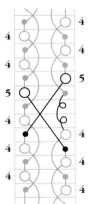

*For a right hand **Flourish** you'll throw a right to left **Triple** followed by a left to right **Triple**. Your right hand makes a **Reverse Grip** catch right after its **Triple** and that's the club you **Flourish**.*

•**Back Crosses** don't work in a pure **Four Club Fountain** because there are no crossing throws in the pattern. Instead you use a 'round' of **Triple-Singles**, making the **Triple** the **Back Cross**.

•Expert **Back Crossers** can throw a **Flash** of four consecutive **Back Crosses** out of the **Fountain**. This works because you are actually going into a **Five Club Gap** pattern for those four throws.

•If you make a **Wrong End** catch in a **Four Club Fountain** you will probably find it easiest to recover using a *two and a half* spin throw to get the handle back into your hand. This is such a stunningly useful throw that you should practise it by deliberately **Wrong Ending** clubs in your **Fountain**.

•When you **Drop** you can (usually) manage to hang on to three clubs and drop down into a **Cascade**. This is a great opportunity to use your **Kick Up** skills to dramatic effect.

While juggling the **Cascade** you 'cheat' the dropped club onto your favourite foot in preparation for the **Kick Up**.

Timing is everything, the **Kick Up** is made as the *opposite* hand leads into the **Four Club Fountain** with the first **Double**. So, if you are kicking up with the right foot, you throw the first **Double** from your left hand more or less simultaneously with the kick. This is a very difficult move and requires a totally reliable **Kick Up** but it impresses the hell out of everybody —they all wish *they* could do it too!

*Two **Over the Top** style throws in a **Four Club Fountain**, these throws are made in a sideways plane.*

• Another area worth exploring in your **Four Club Fountain** is that of altering the plane in which your clubs spin by using **Dip** and **Over the Top** style throws.

• Working along the same lines you can experiment with **Reverse Spins** and the **Over the Shoulder** throws.

• You can make use of your **Four Club Fountain** skills when juggling a six-club **Four Count** passing pattern.

Juggle a **Four Count** and then annoy your partner by missing a pass and launching instead into *exactly* four throws of a **Four Club Fountain** after which you make another pass to resume the **Four Count**.

Your partner is left holding two clubs during your bit of showing off.

Now, since you are juggling four clubs and your partner is just hovering around waiting you can juggle four clubs for as long or as short a time as you wish but it's good practice to stick to four throws (or a multiple of four) since in that way, you stay 'on time' with the general scheme of a **Four**

Count. This is not crucial if there are just two of you passing but if you are standing at the easy end of a nine club **Feed** it becomes *very* important.

• The trick is not limited to the **Four Count**, it can be thrown in any passing pattern of the three-clubs-per-juggler variety. In all cases it's good practice to keep to the scheme of the pattern, so if you go into a **Four Club Fountain** while passing a **Three Count**, you should throw a multiple of *three* throws before passing out again.

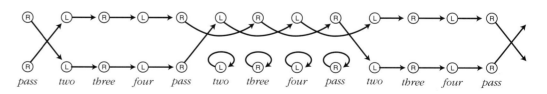

*A juggler showing off their **Four Club Fountain** skills in a **Four Count** passing pattern. They launch into the **Fountain** on the pass beat and juggle it for exactly four throws before dropping back into the regular pattern. Their partner is left holding two clubs for four beats.*

Four Club Fountain

Four Club Synch Doubles

The *purest* pattern for four clubs is the **Four Club Fountain** (see the previous entry) in which both hands juggle **Two in One Hand** patterns while making alternate throws.

Four Club Synch Doubles is the same pattern juggled with *simultaneous* or *synchronous* throws.

•The human body is better suited to alternate-sided movements like walking than it is to the frog-hopping and parasynchronous action of **Four Club Synch Doubles** but the pattern does have the advantage of enabling the juggler to precisely match the **Double** spins, causing two clubs to rise and turn as if they were a single object in the air which is a powerful visual effect.

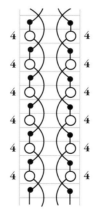

•It looks very good if you toss in the occasional pair of **Triple** spin throws for contrast, or even a **Triple** spin **Flash** in which two successive pairs of throws rise as **Triples**, leaving your hands empty for a moment.

•You can change the shape of the pattern so that it is juggled in four columns, throwing one pair of **Doubles** to the left and the other pair to the right.

This pattern is called **Spreads** and has its own entry in the COMPENDIUM. It's very difficult to learn but well worth the effort.

• You can throw **Back Crosses** in **Four Club Synch Doubles**. Throw one club behind the back with the right hand while making the simultaneous left hand throw travel a little to the right, thus allowing two clubs to swap from one side of the pattern to the other.

• A **One Eighty**, or half pirouette is easy in **Four Club Synch Doubles**. Toss a pair of clubs high, as **Triples** and turn about-face underneath them before resuming **Four Club Synch Doubles**.

• The relationship between the two strangely similar and yet awesomely different methods of juggling four clubs (**Four Club Fountain** and **Four Club Synch Doubles**) is reflected in two possible ways of juggling a six-club **One Count** passing pattern.

Since the clubs do not cross from side to side in a **One Count** it doesn't actually matter whether the hands are juggling in or out of synch. When juggling a **One Count** with your hands throwing in synch you can toss in a round of **Four Club Synch Doubles** whenever you like, it looks very good if you and your partner take it in turns to throw a pair of self **Doubles** followed by a pair of passes.

Four Count

Sometimes, indeed *often*, called **Every Others** —the **Four Count** is a passing rhythm in which every *fourth* throw is a pass.

The **Four Count** is the world's most popular rhythm for club passing. It allows you to make passes *only from the right hand*, and it's *four time* like nearly all popular music. You get to throw three selfs between each pass and this gives you loads of time to juggle tricks and jazz the pattern up. Once you become comfortable with the **Four Count** it's as easy as walking.

The **Four Count** is the beginning of serious creative club passing for nearly every club juggler —it is the **Three Ball Cascade**[EBJ] of club passing.

In some ways it's a shame that jugglers have chosen the **Four Count** as the 'main thing' in club passing because it is most certainly *not* an ambidextrous pattern and jugglers quickly develop such good passing skills in their right hands (and catching skills in their left) that they find it very awkward to work with more balanced patterns like the **Three Count** in which passes are made from *both* hands.

Continued overleaf...

Four Count...

In any case, if you meet a juggler from some foreign land who indicates, by sign language, that they'd like to pass clubs, you can do an **Up-Down-Go!** and launch into a **Four Count** confident that they will almost certainly reply in the same rhythm.

Apart from being internationally understood, passing clubs is just about the most fun you can have as a juggler. You *have* to learn this!

• You need six clubs and a partner. Stand face to face, two or three metres apart, two clubs in the right hand and one club in the left.

Do an **Up-Down-Go!** and launch straight into the pattern with a tramline pass from your right hand, to your partner's left.

Now continue so that every other right hand throw is a pass, hence the popular name **Every Others**.

All of the throws are normal **Singles**. The most common mistake (apart from just generally *dropping* things) is to make the passes higher than the selfs. This messes up the rhythm terribly and is a significant, but often unnoticed, cause of problems. A well juggled **Four Count** should produce a completely even rhythm, which you can *hear* from the slap of the clubs hitting the juggler's hands in perfect four-time.

• The first thing to learn, after you have managed to get the **Four Count** more or less solid is how to handle a **Drop**.

Here's the secret:

You don't stop juggling when you drop!

A **Drop** creates a **Gap** in the pattern, leaving one juggler with two clubs and the other with three. The juggler with three keeps going while the juggler with two **Holds Through the Gap**. When 'three-clubs' makes their next pass the situation is reversed, so the two jugglers end up taking it in turns to keep the pattern going.

'Two-clubs' has the opportunity to pick up the dropped club (if it's near enough) and then throw it back into the pattern on the next *pass* beat. If neither of you are anywhere near the dropped club you have

Always keep that **Four Count** *running —even when you* **Drop!**

to move to whole pattern over to it, still juggling, until one of you can make the **Pickup**.

The most important thing is to keep the **Four Count** rhythm going in your head (see the **Golden Rules of Club Passing**). Once you have recovered from your first **Drop** you can keep passing all day! The whole wonderful world of club passing lies before you just waiting to be explored.

- Next you must learn to throw **Syncopations**. These are **Doubles** and **Triples** and so on that you can throw without disrupting the underlying rhythm of the pattern.

Nearly all **Syncopations** involve making a throw of a greater weight than normal, and this creates a **Gap** in the pattern. Somebody's hand, somewhere, ends up idle for a beat or two. Sometimes a **Syncopation** is used specifically to create that **Gap**, to allow a juggler to perform a trick, like a **Flourish**. But often **Syncopations** are thrown for their own sake, just to paint pretty patterns in the air.

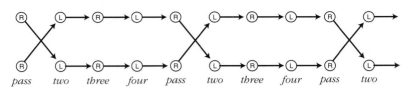

pass   two   three   four   pass   two   three   four   pass   two

A good way of explaining, understanding and inventing **Syncopations** is to use **Causal Diagrams**. They may sound frighteningly technical but they are really very simple and friendly animals that help enormously when you want to actually *understand* what's going on as well as just juggling the tricks!

The two lines of L's and R's running from left to right in a **Causal Diagram** represent the throws made by you and your partner. Every fourth throw is a pass, represented by arrows crossing the chart. All the other throws are selfs. You can tell that every throw is a **Single** because each arrow moves just *one beat* to the right.

Causal Diagrams are a very straightforward way of representing the basic scheme of the pattern and they are *very* much simpler than the **Ladder Notation** because instead of tracking the path of every single object in the pattern they simply track the 'chain reaction' of throws.

*A **Causal Diagram** (left) and some **Ladder Notation** (below). Both diagrams depict a **Four Count**.*

***Ladder Notation** is useful if you want to know where everything is, but **Causal Diagrams** are a simpler way of describing what you do.*

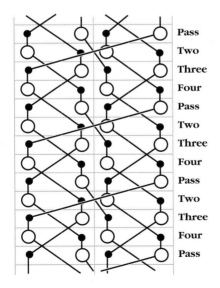

Pass
Two
Three
Four
Pass
Two
Three
Four
Pass
Two
Three
Four
Pass

Continued overleaf...

Four Count...

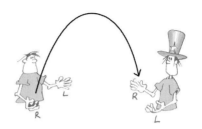

• The first **Syncopation** to learn is the **Early Double** pass. This pass is thrown on the *four* beat, from your left hand, *diagonally* across the pattern to your partner's left hand. The pass is made a **Beat** earlier than a regular pass, but because it's a **Double** instead of a **Single** it still arrives at the right time.

A handy tip is that the **Early Double** is thrown with the club that you have just received from your partner. Concentrate on getting a nice high floaty **Double**, it should drop into your partner's hand exactly 'on the beat'.

• Next comes the **Late Double** pass. This throw is made on the normal *pass* beat, in place of a regular pass. It travels diagonally from your right hand to your partner's right hand, arriving one beat late and in the 'wrong' hand. The first time you are thrown one of these you'll probably drop in confusion, but after a couple of tries you'll find that it's perfectly catchable.

It's useful to know that having received an **Early Double** pass you throw it *straight back* to your partner.

• You can throw self **Doubles** as well. A right to right self **Double** can be thrown on the *three* beat. It's just like going into **Two in One Hand** for one throw.

A left to left self **Double** can be thrown on the *four* beat. Neither of these tricks affects your partner's pattern in any way.

Some fancy **Doubles** *in a* **Four Count**, *all thrown by the juggler in the top line. In* **Causal Diagrams** *an arrow pointing to its own tail is a hold.*
An **Early Double** *...* *...a* **Late Double** *...* *...a left self* **Double**,

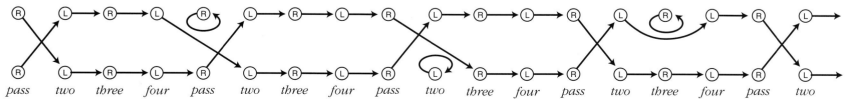

• You can throw one 'round' of a **Four-Four-One** while passing a **Four Count**. You throw a left self **Double**, followed by a right self **Double** followed by a left to right **Feed**. Here's how it fits into the **Four Count** rhythm:

*Pass - **Double** - **Double** - **Feed** - pass - two...*

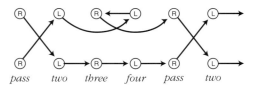

*Note that in **Causal Diagrams** a **Feed** appears as an arrow pointing to the left.*

The move starts right after the *pass* beat. The club that gets 'fed' is the pass you have just received from your partner —you pass it straight back out again. It's elegant to take the **Feed** behind your back.

• For the next level of **Syncopations** you need to throw **Triples**.

Note that every **Double** is thrown from right to right, or left to left. Hence they are always either *diagonal* passes or *selfs*. The **Triples** on the other hand always travel from right to left (or vice versa), so they are either *tramline* passes or *crossing selfs*.

The first **Triple** to learn is the **Early Triple** pass. This is made on the *three* beat. After you throw it you have a nice long **Gap** on your side of the pattern. It's very important to get the height of this pass right (even more important than getting the spin right). Watch to see when it arrives at your partner's left hand —if it's either early or late it's *your* fault!

• Now try the left to right **Triple** pass. This is thrown on the *four* beat (just like the **Early Double** pass). It's caught like a **Late Double** as it arrives in the 'wrong' hand a beat late. Both you and your partner get a pause, or **Gap**, in your pattern.

Continued overleaf...

*Triple passes in a **Four Count** thrown by the juggler in the top row.*

*An **Early Triple** ...*   *...and a **Late Triple** .*

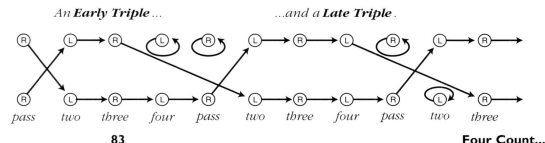

Four Count...

• A right to left *self* **Triple** can be made to work but only if you throw *two in a row*. Effectively you are going into the four club solo pattern **Triple-Singles** for four beats before resuming the **Four Count**. You lead into this move on the *pass* beat:

*pass - two - three- four -**Triple** -**Single** -**Triple** -**Single** - pass - two - three - four...*

Your partner is left waiting with two clubs while you show off.

• A left to right self **Triple** can be thrown on the *two* beat, this has no effect on your partner's pattern.

• You can also throw a right to left **Triple** pass on the *pass* beat (not shown in the diagram) which arrives in your partner's left hand two beats late, it's a *very* **Late Triple**, but as long as your partner keeps to the **Four Count** scheme, and they make their next pass at the proper time, it will work perfectly well.

Most **Syncopations** can be mixed together, pretty much at random, and the pattern will not crash (i.e. two clubs arriving in the same hand at the same time). This gives jugglers the freedom to improvise and jazz up their juggling with no need for previous rehearsal.

Some combinations, however, fall foul of juggling logic. For example, passing an **Early Double** and *immediately* following it with a **Late Double** will crash the pattern unless your partner is made of very stern stuff! You have to be pretty determined to throw a combination like that because it doesn't *feel* right. You are unlikely to throw it by mistake!

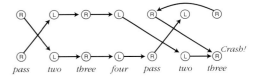

*An **Early Double** followed by a **Late Double** will cause the pattern to crash as two clubs arrive in your partner's right hand at the same time. The **Late Double** causes the right hand to become empty (unnecessarily) which is why this move feels unnatural and also accounts for the backwards-pointing arrow.*

***Triple** selfs in a **Four Count** thrown by the juggler in the top row.*

*Two 'rounds' of **Triple-Singles** ...*   *...and a left self **Triple** .*

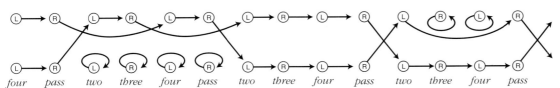

The **Early Double**, **Late Double** combination crashes the pattern because you have made two incompatible throws. A different sort of crash occurs when a **Syncopation** from your end of the pattern clashes with one from the other end.

•For example; you can throw one round of **One-Up Two-Up** in a **Four Count** by throwing an **Early Double** to your partner and then tossing two *simultaneous* self **Doubles** before resuming the regular pattern —a great trick to throw if you are juggling fire.

The move is 'illegal'* because you are making two *simultaneous* throws and you'll discover (sooner or later) that if your partner tosses you a **Late Double** while you are in the middle of the move you won't have a hand to catch it with.

•Here's another popular 'legal' move, the **Right-Left-Triple!**

You throw a **Late Double**, followed by an **Early Double**, followed by an **Early Triple**. Each **Syncopation** must be thrown on its proper beat, but if you are familiar with all three you'll be able to 'feel' your way through the move with no trouble.

•Moving up a level, you can throw an **Early Quad**, from your left hand to your partner's left, on the *two* beat. The **Early Quad** is great when 'tacked on' to the end of a **Right-Left-Triple!**

Listing every possible **Syncopation** of the **Four Count** would be like trying to list every tune that you can make from a musical scale of eight notes —it simply cannot be done. You have to invent your own moves and pick up what you can from other jugglers.

Remember also that **Syncopations** are only one way of playing with the pattern, you also have all the possibilities of **Tomahawks**, **Behind the Back** throws, **Flourishes** and so on.

Have fun with the **Four Count** (thousands already do) but don't avoid the more ambidextrous odd counts since these involve passing from *both* hands and will make you a better and more ambidextrous juggler.

See also **Three Count**, **Two Count**, **One Count**, **Syncopation**, **Early Double**, **Late Double** and any entry with a **Causal Diagram** in it!

---

*By the terms 'legal' and 'illegal' I am certainly not trying to suggest that there is anything 'wrong' with one move or 'right' with another. I just find it amazing that such a bewildering array of 'legal' **Syncopations** can be thrown without crashing the pattern no matter how they are combined. The 'illegal' moves are sometimes interesting and useful because they always add something new or unusual to a pattern —rather like a cleverly placed sharp or flat in music.

*The **Right-Left-Triple!** combination thrown in a **Four Count** with an **Early Quad** tacked on for good measure.*

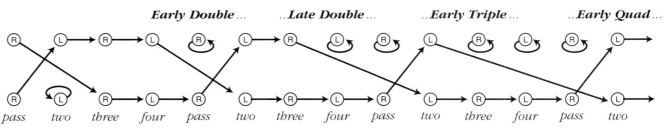

Four Count

Four Four Eight

Here's the double-handed version of the **Three Three Ten**. The **Four Four Eight** is a passing routine for two jugglers and six clubs and involves passing with both hands. The sequence of passes starts slowly, gets faster and finishes with a burst of **One Count** passing (also known as **Ultimates**).

• Stand facing your partner, three clubs each, two in the right hand and one in the left. Together you do an **Up-Down-Go!** then a **Slow Start**. You follow this with four passes of a **Five Count**, four passes of a **Three Count** and finally eight passes of a **One Count**. The full count is:

(Up down) - go! - and - two - and -pass!
One - two - three - four -pass!
One - two - three - four -pass!
One - two - three - four -pass!
One - two -pass!
One - two -pass!
One - two -pass!
One - two -pass!
Pass - pass - pass - pass - pass - pass - pass - pass!

You can optionally toss up a self **Triple** and pirouette underneath it at the end of the routine.

See also **Three Three Ten**.

Four-Four-One

In this pattern three clubs are juggled in what looks, and feels a lot like a four club juggling pattern. Any club juggler who is competent with **Double** spins should be able to learn the **Four-Four-One** without any trouble. As well as being juggled as a full blown pattern it can also be thrown as a trick, both in solo juggling and **Passing Patterns**. This is an important pattern.

The name of the trick comes from the **SiteSwap Notation** for its repeating sequence of three throws —**4 4 1**. The **4**'s are self **Doubles** and the **1**'s are **Feeds** (one hand placing a club directly into the other).

• Start with three clubs, two in the right and one in the left. The right hand throws a **Double** straight up, then the left hand throws a **Double** straight up, then the right hand **Feeds** its club directly into the left hand. Now repeat the sequence from the left —left self **Double**, right self **Double** and left to right **Feed**.

This sequence of six throws now repeats:

4 4 1 4 4 1 ...

It is almost as though you are juggling a **Four Club Fountain** with only three clubs, every time the **Gap** arrives in one hand, you **Feed** a club into it from the other. It's excellent practice for budding four club jugglers.

• You can throw just three throws of a **Four-Four-One** out of a running **Three Club Cascade** —just lead straight into it. Do two **Doubles** and a **Feed** and then drop back down to the cascade again.

3 3 3 4 4 1 3 3 3 ...

- For extra thrill points the **Feed** can be made **Behind the Back** or **Under the Leg**.

- You can throw a 'round' of **Four-Four-One** as a **Syncopation** in a **Four Count**. You lead into the move on the *two* beat. An interesting feature of this move is that, like an **Early Double**, it returns your partner's passed club immediately —useful for the old *'I don't want to juggle with that scruffy club —you have it!'* gags.

See also **Five-Five-Five-One** and **Four-Four-One**[EBJ]

Forced Pass

A **Forced Pass** is special kind of throw made in a passing pattern as a response to an 'illegal' **Syncopation** made by your partner.

Usually when you are passing clubs with someone you do what *you* want to do, but there are times when your partner throws something so bizarre that you are *forced* to throw something equally bizarre right back at them.

The simplest kind of **Syncopation** is the **Early** pass, in which only your end pattern is modified. A slightly more complicated **Syncopation** is the **Late** pass which modifies your partner's actions (by creating a **Gap** in their pattern).

The **Forced Pass** is the next level of subtlety —either you or your partner is **Forced** to take evasive action (by making an additional pass) in order to prevent the pattern from crashing.

For a full explanation of this fascinating (if rather technical) concept, see **Syncopation**.

Gap

A **Gap** (sometimes called a 'hole') is a space in a juggling pattern that *could* be occupied by a juggling club but isn't.

Learning to juggle **Gaps** is crucial to mastering club juggling and while the art of juggling with *nothing* sounds paradoxical, it turns out to be very easy to do —after all it's just not possible to **Drop** a **Gap**!

Continued overleaf...

Gap...

• The basic **Gap** exercise is to juggle a **Three Club Cascade** with only two clubs. You should keep to the rhythm and tempo of a normal cascade, *imagining* the missing third club. This missing club is the **Gap**.

Beginners find this slightly weird at first since two clubs are not enough to 'force' their hands to juggle.

• Extend the exercise by juggling three clubs in a **Cascade** and then quickly sticking one club between your legs in the **Khyber Pass** position with your right hand. Keep juggling with the remaining two clubs until the **Gap** reaches your left hand (two

throws) and then grab the **Khybered** club with your left hand and resume your **Three Club Cascade**. Playing around with this sort of **Gap** manipulation is a very good way of improving your general coordination skills.

• A **Drop** in a **Passing Pattern** creates a **Gap**. The usual strategy (if the jugglers are going to attempt a recovery) is to allow the **Gap** to travel around the pattern until it is close to the dropped club —this allows the nearest juggler to execute a **Pickup**.

There two ways of moving the **Gap** around the pattern. One is **Holding Through the Gap** or throwing *only when you have to*. The other is *throwing whenever you can**.

---

*There is also a third option, which is to be seriously stamped on in club-passing situations because it messes the pattern up altogether and is totally lacking in style, grace or any merit whatsoever. It is this: a juggler, on finding that there is a **Gap** in the pattern instantly converts the pattern into a new one by **Feeding** a club into the **Gap**. For example, you are juggling six clubs with a partner as a **Two Count**. You drop a club on the floor and it's lying at your feet. Your partner, on discovering the **Gap** converts their end of the pattern into a dreadful rendition of a two club **Shower** (an ugly pattern at the best of times) by **Feeding** every club they catch into their right hand and then passing them straight back to you. There is now no **Gap** left. Nasty! The best thing to do is to start showering them with **Triples** which will create a new **Gap** and hopefully break their thumbs.

Here's an exercise to familiarise you and your partner with the two sensible ways of handling a **Gap**.

• Find a partner and start with just *five* clubs between the two of you. You get three and your partner gets two. Stand face to face about two and half paces apart.

Juggle a **Three Club Cascade** for a few throws and then make a right hand pass to your partner's left hand. This stops your pattern and starts theirs. Now they juggle a few throws of **Three Club Cascade** before passing back to you and so you continue.

When you are warmed up you increase the speed a little —every time you get passed the extra club you juggle just long enough to throw just one right to yourself, the *second* right hand throw is the pass. When both you and your partner are doing this you are juggling exactly the same pattern you would be if you were both **Holding Through the Gap** in a **Four Count** with one club dropped.

Notice that the **Gap** makes its way around the pattern much more quickly than the real clubs. **Holding Through the Gap** is an ideal technique for recovering a **Drop** because you don't have to wait for ages for the **Gap** to meet up with the dead club.

• The alternative strategy is to pretend that the **Gap** is a real club, in other words *'throw whenever you can'*. With this technique the **Gap** moves around at the same rate as the real clubs.

• Practise juggling **Three Around** with a partner. You need just three clubs and you juggle so that every left hand throw is a self, while every right is a pass. The three clubs chase each other around, playing follow-my-leader through the four hands.

Three Around is a six-club **Two Count** with three **Gaps** in it. If you add a fourth club you are left with two **Gaps**, add a fifth and there's one **Gap** left, add the sixth and there are no **Gaps** at all. Beginners will need to stop the pattern to add each new club but experts can execute the **Pickups** in a running pattern.

See also **Drop, Pickup, Seven Club Pickup.**

Gladiators

This is the name given to one of my favourite juggling games. It's a regular feature of the games at every juggling convention along with the *Five Ball Endurance*, *Long Distance Passing*, the **Big Toss Up**[EBJ] and **Volleyclub** tournaments.

• Find as many jugglers as you can (anything from a dozen or so to a couple of hundred). Everybody gets three clubs and they all start to juggle.

The last one left juggling is the winner.

Rules? —those *are* the rules.

It's not good form to seriously injure an opponent but you can do pretty much whatever you like to destroy everybody else's pattern. This high quality game is not to be confused with an unaccountably popular and rather tacky leotard-clad steroid-based form of TV entertainment.

For a full rundown on both the methods and madness of this game with tips on how to win, see **Combat Juggling Techniques**.

Glowing in the Dark

The club-juggler's favourite way of **Glowing in the Dark** is to juggle with fire torches. This is hot, dangerous, exciting and spectacular. Alternatively you can use luminous clubs which glow with a surreal soft green light. This is cool, clean and safe and *doesn't* stink of paraffin.

Many of the good brands of juggling club come in luminous versions and since they look perfectly fine in daylight, the *only* disadvantage is the slightly higher price.

You can charge your luminous props up under bright light or use a 'flash bin' which is a box lined with silver foil into which you drop your props, close the lid and then let off a camera flashgun inside. This charges them up instantaneously.

The best method of all is to use ultraviolet lamps or tubes which are placed between you and the audience and left on throughout your performance as these keep the props glowing constantly.

With UV lighting you can also use fluorescent materials on your costumes and props to create some truly dazzling visual effects.

Golden Rules of Club Passing

NEVER LOOK AWAY.

NEVER LOSE COUNT.

NEVER SAY 'SORRY'.

The rules above have been developed by general consensus over many years of hard juggling by jugglers from all over the planet. Here are a few more tips.

• If your partner seems to be throwing too high, it's probably because you are throwing too low. Conversely, if your partner is throwing too low, then you are probably throwing too high.

• The same applies to spin, direction, angle and every other aspect of juggling style (with the possible exception of *attitude*). This is because you instinctively try to correct what you see as your partner's faults. This means that if the whole pattern crashes in ruins it is most likely *everybody's* fault.

• **Passing Patterns** are about cooperation and communication. With the single exception of **VolleyClub**, they are *not* about competition.

Club passing is a truly international language that is understood by a rapidly growing number of people who are all united in their love of pure fun.

So be polite!

Half Shower

Half Showers are dealt with in some depth in the ENCYCLOPÆDIA OF BALL JUGGLING. They don't feature quite so much in club juggling but they are worth knowing about nevertheless.

A **Half Shower** is a solo pattern that falls somewhere between a full **Shower** pattern and a **Cascade** or a **Fountain**. Each hand makes throws of different weights.

•In a **Cascade** of three objects both hands throw **3**'s. In a **Shower** of three one hand throws **5**'s while the other throws **1**'s. To juggle a **Half Shower** one hand throws **4**'s while the other throws **2**'s (that's **Doubles** and **Vamps**). In each three-object pattern the throw numbers add up to 6 (see **SiteSwap Notation** for more about this). Because the three-object **Half Shower** uses even numbered throws you know that both hands are throwing *simultaneously*.

•The four-object **Fountain** uses **4**'s from both hands. The four object **Shower** uses **7**'s and **1**'s and there are *two* possible **Half Showers**. One is **5**'s and **3**'s (better known as **Triple-Singles**) and the other is **6**'s and **2**'s (simultaneous throws, **Quads** and **Vamps**).

•With five objects you can **Cascade**, using **5**'s from both hands, and **Shower** with **9**'s and **1**'s (never seen it!) and there are no less than *three* distinct **Half Showers**; **6**'s and **4**'s, **7**'s and **3**'s, and finally **8**'s and **2**'s.

The only one of the three that is likely to be of any practical interest is the **7**'s and **3**'s pattern —**Quins** and **Singles**.

See also **Triple-Singles**.

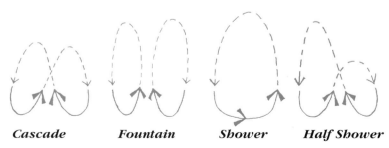

Cascade   *Fountain*   *Shower*   *Half Shower*

Half Spin Pass

Chuck one of these to your partner in a **Passing Pattern** and they'll find it completely weird and disturbing. It is, however, a completely catchable throw.

•You've probably never noticed this, but a normal **Single** spin pass actually turns *one and a half* times. At the moment of the throw it's pointing more or less straight down, and when caught it's pointing more or less straight *up*.

The **Half Spin Pass** simply uses the minimum amount of spin necessary to get from A to B. It feels very like throwing a **Flat**. It *looks* as though your passing pattern has gone into slow motion for a moment.

As soon as your partner has got used to the **Half Spin Pass** chuck them a couple of **Butterfly Passes** to keep them on their toes!

Half Spin Pass

Hand Across

This is an American term for a **Feed**, the action of passing a club directly from one hand to the other.

See **Feed**.

Hard End

The **Hard End** of a **Passing Pattern** is the end at which all the drops and problems seem to be happening. You may think that your partner is not quite up to scratch and that it's all *their* fault.

• Shame on you! Change places and see how *you* like it at the **Hard End**.

Having Problems?

Here is the place to come in the COMPENDIUM when everything is going wrong. A quiet corner among these busy pages where helpful advice and words of comfort are offered to jugglers who are finding it hard to cope. Maybe your **Double** spins aren't working too well. Perhaps your thumbs are bruised, your **Five Club Cascade** is giving you gip, your **Three Club Start** just smashed you in the teeth and your **Kickups** seem anatomically impossible.

You are, in short, a failure. You feel like giving up and doing something *useful* with your life instead. Good plan. Why not grab the paper and see if there are any good movies on? Go and have some *fun* for a change!

But no, you want to persevere, to try a little harder, perhaps even *achieve* something. Fear not, dear reader, the COMPENDIUM is here to help.

I refer you immediately to the entry for **Having Problems**[EBJ] in the ENCYCLOPÆDIA OF BALL JUGGLING, but perhaps you do not have a copy of that book in which case you now have even more problems than you thought you did a moment ago.

Learning to juggle is difficult, if it wasn't then there's a good chance that you would never have bothered to get interested in the first place. The fact that you are desperately frustrated at being wholly unable to make your body do a simple juggling trick that your brain understands perfectly well is a classic illustration of the first of the Buddha's Four Noble Truths —*all life is suffering*. To paraphrase in the modern idiom —*life's a bitch*.

Juggling is like life. You know what you *want* to do (fast cars, big houses, impress your friends and so on), you know what you *should* do (get up early, eat good food, think carefully before opening your mouth etc.) and somehow you still manage to get it all wrong.

Your problem is that you can't manage a juggling trick —it's driving you nuts. The solution is to give yourself a jolt, change tack, view the problem from a new perspective, see the wood for the trees and have a bit of fun for a change. The secret is to *sidle up to the problem and catch it unawares*.

• Give up working on the trick you are stuck on immediately. Learn this one instead.

Take two clubs, one in each hand. Toss both clubs simultaneously and catch them, each in the throwing hand —one club is to perform a perfect **Single** spin while the other is to do a **Reverse Spin**.

Gotcha! 99% of jugglers find this *completely impossible* on the first attempt and yet you'll be able to do it after just a little practice. Be sure to learn it both ways around (so that each hand gets to practise the **Reverse Spin**).

• With this new and incredible skill wired into your consciousness you may return to work on whatever was stumping you before. You'll find that the quick stretch you have just given to your 'learning muscle' has done wonders for your general coordination and dexterity.

Head Flip

The method of 'throwing' a club from a *nose*, *chin*, or *forehead* **Balance** in order to return the club to the pattern.

See **Balance**.

Head Roll

The **Head Roll** is fairly similar to the **Helicopter**. In a **Three Club Cascade** the juggler places a club against the side of their head and allows it to roll over their cranium to a catch in the opposite hand.

• The club is placed, nose up, against the side of the head and given a slight push by the placing hand. The weight and momentum of the perfectly placed club cause it to roll over the head in a surrealistic uncanny style.

The best clubs for this trick are the larger round-bodied type, like the 'American Classics'.

Head Roll

Helicopter

The **Helicopter** is the unlikely trick in which the juggler spins a club on top of their head as if it was impaled on a spike.

•This trick, like the **Kickup** is 'one of those', a move that can only be mastered through long practice, during which your hands and head develop an uncanny familiarity with the feel of the trick.

You juggle a **Three Club Cascade** and, instead of making a right hand throw you *place* the club on your head, knob to the right, and give the handle a quick push forward.

This sets the club spinning and after one rotation your left hand reaches up and intercepts the handle, taking the club off your head and resuming the **Cascade**.

Gosh!

•Keen **Helicopter** pilots develop the trick by adding extra spins. Complete aces can manage as many as four turns of the club reliably.

Flat Spins, and the **Lovegrove Loop** are sometimes called **Helicopters** too.

Hits

There is no direct counterpart in ball juggling to this trick, except perhaps the **Flick Off**[EBJ]. As you juggle a **Three Club Cascade** a club is 'batted' back to the throwing hand by striking it with another club.

•Juggle a **Three Club Cascade** and throw a slow and lazy **Single** from the left hand, a little higher than normal.

Instead of catching this club you strike its handle from below with the club in your right hand, so as to reverse its spin and send it back to the left hand.

It's best to strike it so that the held club's centre of gravity (on the shoulder of the club) hits the *handle* of the airborne club. Go for control rather than force, otherwise you may damage your clubs! You can send the hit club on its way with either **Single** or **Double** spin.

•When you start to develop some control over the move you can try throwing a series of **Hits**, say three consecutive left hand throws **Hit** back to the left hand.

•A very dramatic variation on this theme has a club dropped from the left hand, as a **Flat**, straight down the centre of your pattern and then **Hit** from behind your back, **Trebla** style, with the 'batting' club between your legs.

This is a very cheeky fake drop and recovery. To learn the trick you will need to practise the **Hit** in *front* of your body until it is completely solid and then go for the full move. For best effect try to **Hit** the club up as a **Flat**. Avoid putting any spin on it.

•Clubs aren't built for this sort of work and it's very hard to see how one can *learn* to be accurate. The best advice is to use the Zen archer's technique of focusing entirely on *where you want the club to go* rather than on *what you do to get it there*.

The ultimate **Hit** trick is to smash a passed club back across the pattern to your partner. The accuracy required here is extreme and yet, with the right attitude, you can succeed every time. May the Force be with you!

See also **Tennis** and the **Devilstick Trick** for more impact-based tricks.

Hovey's Nightmare

During my research for the ENCYCLOPÆDIA OF BALL JUGGLING and the COMPENDIUM OF CLUB JUGGLING I came across a whole series of similar juggling patterns called variously 'Ovy's', 'Ogie's', 'Hoagie's', 'Hogleby's', 'Oby's', 'Odie's', 'Oddy's' and 'Oggie's' Nightmare. The one unifying feature of these patterns seemed to be that they were all *different!* OK, they were all passing patterns, and they all involved left and right hand passes, but that was about as far as the resemblance went. In the ENCYCLOPÆDIA I decided to list a pattern which I called **Ogie's Nightmare**[EBJ] and while it's an interesting pattern, I was completely wrong and have therefore, unintentionally, managed to confuse matters even more.

I am indebted to the American club-passing 'guru' Martin Frost who resolved the whole problem in an article in JUGGLER'S WORLD (winter 1993-1994 issue).

Hovey's Nightmare was created by a juggler named Hovey Burgess way back in 1970, long before I first learned to juggle and probably long before you did too.

Hovey's original idea was to create a **Triangle** pattern in which each juggler passes sequentially to each of the six hands in turn, repeating the cycle every six beats. Each pass was to involve just two jugglers (i.e. no *triangle* passes) while the other juggler throws a self.

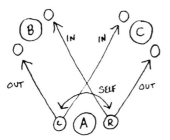

In a **Triangle** there are six directions in which a club can be thrown, two possible *outside* passes, two *inside* passes and two *selfs* (I'm not including *diagonal* passes here). Martin Frost has worked out that there are eight distinct ways of sequencing a pattern that results in each juggler making all of these throws every six beats. Six of them have each juggler throwing the same sequence of throws (though out of phase with each other) and two have different sequences for different jugglers. **Hovey's Nightmare** falls into the last category. No wonder there's been all this confusion!

• Here's how to juggle the genuine and original **Hovey's Nightmare**.

Arrange yourselves in a **Triangle**, three clubs each, two in the right hand and one in the left. Name yourselves A, B and C.

You all start juggling together with a right hand throw, throwing these sequences, starting from the right hand.

A: I I O O S S
B: O S S I I O
C: S O I S O I

I = Inside
O = Outside
S = Self

If you find this a problem you are not on your own! When Hovey Burgess and his partners worked on the pattern in the 70's they only managed to get through it a couple of times!

• Here's one of the other variants, this one was developed by Martin Frost and has all three jugglers working the same sequence, but out of phase with each other:

A: I I S O O S
B: O S I I S O
C: S O O S I I

• As I said before, there are eight variants in all. I'll leave working out the rest as an exercise for the reader!

See also **Triangle**.

Holding Through the Gap

When a club is dropped out of a juggling pattern a **Gap** is created and the juggler (or *jugglers* if it is a **Passing Pattern**) can continue to juggle with the remaining clubs.

The **Gap** then moves around the juggling pattern in one of two ways; the jugglers can either continue to throw *whenever they can* or they can throw *only when they have to*.

Throwing *only when you have to* is called **Holding through the Gap** and is the usual technique to use when you **Drop** in a **Passing Pattern**.

If you throw *whenever you can*, keeping the the original scheme of a pattern, the **Gap** travels around the pattern like an invisible club, causing your hands to become empty from time to time as it passes through them.

When you are **Holding through the Gap** your hand realises, as the **Gap** approaches, that there is no need to throw the club it is holding, and so it hangs on to it for a couple of beats.

•Juggle a six-club **Four Count** with a partner and drop a club accidentally *or* on purpose (it's up to you!). Now continue juggling and throw only when you have to, keeping to the basic four count rhythm. You'll find that instead of juggling:

Pass - two - three - four ...

You are now juggling:

*Pass - **wait** - **wait** - **wait** - **wait** - two - three - four - ...*

Holding Through the Gap like this is standard practice when a **Drop** occurs in a **Passing Pattern** because all of those *'waits'*, during which you are just holding two clubs, give you plenty of opportunity to bend down and pick up the missing club.

•You'll also find that the **Gap** travels around the pattern a lot faster if you **Hold Through the Gap** instead of *throwing whenever you can*.

For an interesting comparison between **Holding through the Gap** and *throwing whenever you can*, see **Five Club Gap**.

Hot Potato

This is a style of juggling in which you try to keep the clubs out of your hands for as much time as possible —as if they were hot potatoes!

•The way to do this with three clubs is to make every throw a **6** (technically these are **Quads** but many jugglers use **Triple** spins here) and throw *as often as you can*, in other words don't **Hold through the Gap**.

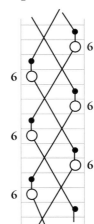

*In **Hot Potato** the actions of the two hands do not overlap, the right hand doesn't make a catch until after the left has thrown and vice versa.*

This is quite a tough rhythm to 'lock into', it may help you to realise that this pattern is actually **Three in One Hand** juggled so that your hands take it in turns to make the throws. It's a great exercise and very satisfying when you get it. **Hot Potato** is worth learning because it just oozes skill and flair when it's performed.

See also **Slow Cascade** and **504**.

How many clubs should I buy?

This is a tough question. After all, juggling clubs are expensive items. After careful consideration I have decided that the best answer is —*none!*

Get *somebody else* to buy them for you! Explain that juggling is fundamentally a good thing for you to be doing. It'll keep you off the streets and out of trouble —the fact that you will probably end up *on* the streets with some mad street show is conveniently ignored for the sake of this argument.

Now the question is transformed into something far easier to deal with —*how many clubs should I get somebody else to buy for me?*

• For basic three club juggling you need four clubs to leave yourself room for improvement. If you don't *have* four then you'll never *learn* four. Anyway, by virtue of natural rotation they'll wear out 33% slower so they won't cost any more in the end.

Of course if you can already juggle four, you'll need *five,* and since this is only one short of a complete matched set for a six-club two person **Passing Pattern** you might as well go the whole hog and get six.

The trouble is, if you can juggle four clubs on your own you'll almost *certainly* be up to the level of **Seven Club Passing** so maybe you should get *seven* just to be on the safe side.

Dreadful isn't it? Still, at least if you do get seven you'll never run out of clubs for solo work.

You are very unlikely to need eight, since nobody ever really learns to juggle eight clubs, and if you are planning to pass eight clubs with a partner —isn't it time *they* got some clubs of their own?

Hup!

Now, you may *think* that **Hup!** is just a silly noise that circus types make in order to spice up their routines along with *Hey!* and *Ho!* and other enthusiastic exclamations. But you may also end up with a club in your eye.

• **Hup!** means '*Stop!*'

In other words, **Hup!** is a *simple* way of saying, 'There is a complex juggling problem happening right now, possibly in the region of air directly over your head and I really don't have time to go into all the details at this precise instant in time, perhaps we should all stop juggling for a moment and try again.'

See also **The Golden Rules of Club Passing** and **Up-Down-Go!**

Javelin

A **Javelin** throw is a **Fish** thrown backwards. You make a pass to your partner, throwing the club overhand as a **Flat** that travels knob-first. It's also called a **Spear**.

Juggling Clubs

Sometimes called 'batons' or 'skittles' by non-jugglers, **Juggling Clubs** are one of the very few pieces of human technology that are designed for throwing, catching and *nothing else*.

Well perhaps that's not *quite* true, **Juggling Clubs** are also designed to be dropped repeatedly without falling apart.

Juggling Clubs are *hand tools*, and jugglers are quite rightly very fussy about the balance, feel and look of their props. For this reason there is a wide range of clubs on the market. Some jugglers seem convinced that their favourite brand is the best and that all the others are all rubbish or at least sub-standard in some way. To be fair to the club manufacturers it must be said that the vast majority of clubs are very well made, despite the occasional appearance of a lemon with a handle on it. The 'ideal' club is just a matter of personal choice. I've changed my mind again and again over the years about which club is my favourite and have spent a good deal of juggling time with most of the major styles. In the end I think that the best club for *you* is the one that happens to be your current favourite.

A juggling club is fundamentally a top-heavy stick. The off-centre balance is crucial to the 'feel' and handling of the club. If you try juggling with plain sticks of wood you'll see what I mean. In former times jugglers have worked with hand made clubs of their own design ranging from simple weighted sticks to elaborate constructions using papier mâché and split bamboo. Some clubs were turned on lathes from solid wood and then cut in half before being hollowed out and stuck back together again. Today's new wave of jugglers tend to use the 'European Style' club which is a complex construction of wood, plastic and rubber.

While writing the COMPENDIUM I wrote to 'H' at BEARD JUGGLING EQUIPMENT and asked if he could give me some insight into the design and manufacture of juggling clubs. H's reply was so thorough and informative that I have included it here in full.

Notes on the Design and Construction of Clubs
by 'H' of Beard Juggling Equipment

Central Dowel

This is almost universally wooden, although some manufacturers have experimented with plastic and fibreglass. The wood is selected for resilience and straightness of grain. Tropical hardwoods are out for obvious reasons, and price is another consideration. Even a small increase in the cost of materials can significantly affect the final retail price of the club. So really exotic and expensive woods are out of the question.

The best woods are White Oak or Ash. At BEARD, we have a preference for North

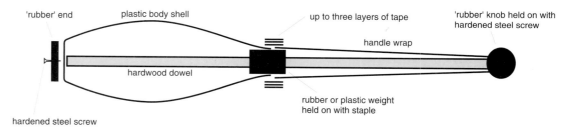

'rubber' end — plastic body shell — up to three layers of tape — 'rubber' knob held on with hardened steel screw — handle wrap — hardwood dowel — hardened steel screw — rubber or plastic weight held on with staple

Juggling Clubs...

American Ash, it is very consistent and strong so we can use a thinner section. In spite of careful selection the density of the wood varies, the moisture content will also vary with storage and drying conditions so dowels are selected by weight. A variation of plus or minus five grams is usually very difficult to notice.

The wood tends to split if screws are driven straight into the ends so the dowels have to be drilled out first. This gives rise to another problem, drilling a straight hole in the bloody things. A normal drill bit will follow the grain and tend to drill a hole at an angle so special sharpening methods are used for the drill and a special jig prevents the drill bit from bending and ensures that the hole is central.

Body Shell

There are two ways of producing the plastic body; rota-moulding or blow-moulding each with their own advantages and disadvantages.

Rota-Moulding

A thin-walled mould is used, into which polyethylene granules are placed and the mould is heated while being rotated in two directions so that the melting plastic coats the inside of the mould, hopefully evenly! The mould then has to be cooled before the body shell can be removed. This is quite a time consuming process so it's best suited to short production runs. This is the more low-tech method of moulding and it's a lot cheaper to set up than blow-moulding.

Rota-moulding is used by RENEGADE, TODD SMITH, DUBÉ (I think) and MEDIUM AIR in Australia. At BEARD we have three machines which we use mostly for making balls. As far as we know only BEARD and RENEGADE have in-house moulding facilities, having built our own machines.

Blow-moulding

This is a much more hi-tech and expensive process to set up, but the cycle time (the time it takes to produce one unit) is much faster. A thick tube of hot plastic, called a *parison*, is extruded so that it drops into an open ended heavy mould. The machinery then clips off the parison and seals the ends of the mould, inflating the parison so that it is forced into the shape of the mould where it sets immediately because the mould is cool. The mould then opens and, in theory, a completed body shell pops out ready for the cycle to begin again.

In practice the machine needs to be tuned, there are about fifty different adjustments to make and the first part of a production run consists mainly of mutated and gnarled abominations. Once the whole thing is running properly you need to churn out something like fifteen to twenty thousand units before the economics start to work in your favour. The finish and seam lines are superior to rota-moulding and it's possible to get thinner wall sections although tight corners can be problematic because of the stress induced in the plastic.

Blow-moulding is used by HENRY'S, BEARD, AJA, FREAKS and SPOTLIGHT. The moulds are horrendously expensive!

Choosing exactly the right type of plastic is difficult —high strength must be combined with the right 'feel'. Polyethylene is the most common, though polypropylene is sometimes used. Both of these types can be recycled.

Handles

There are many different types of handle and the type used will depend on the end user that the club is aimed at and the price bracket that the club will fall into. Beginners get a soft chunky handle with expanded foam underneath it, as in the BEARD Beach Club, or a simple blow-moulded one like the very cleverly designed handle on the HENRY'S Delphin Club. Wrapped handles are for serious hobby jugglers and performers. The spiral wrapped handle with a smooth outer coating, as first used by RENEGADE, is increasingly popular because it's cheaper to make but it requires very careful construction to ensure that it doesn't shred your hands.

Spin and balance

This depends very much on the personal preference of the juggler. It's affected by the handle weight, body weight, overall weight and the weight weight (that is, the weight of the balance weight included in most designs). Most composite clubs (as opposed to one-piece clubs) use rubber or plastic for this central weight to give the club its characteristic balance. Moving it closer to the handle will give a more centrally balanced, faster-spinning club (like HENRY'S Circus Clubs). A heavy body weight will give a more top-heavy spin with better control like most of the American clubs.

Recently, club designers have started to dispense with with the separate weight and integrate this into the body shell (Radical Fish, TODD SMITH'S Satellite, and the BEARD Technic Range). This can only be done by carefully adjusting the wall thickness during the moulding process (or by crossing your fingers and hoping). The shape of the body is also a factor and a few, such as the RENEGADE Fat Head, Radical Fish, and MORE BALLS THAN MOST'S infamous Nikita club go to ridiculous extremes (some say) to find a new 'feel'. The thing to avoid here is the 'sledgehammer effect' as achieved with the Nikita in which the handle whips round and smashes you in the gob no matter how you throw it.

Knobs and ends

These have two functions, to protect the end of the club from repeated drops, to differentiate between different models and allow for use as a swinging club (er, make that three uses). Most clubs use a foamed plastic called EVA (ethylene vinyl acetate) for softness and toughness. HENRY'S use a microcellular rubber and some others use a simple moulded rubber but this tends to be heavy and adversely affects the balance.

Adhesives

The polyethylene used for most club bodies has a very low surface energy (i.e. it's non-stick) and it is notoriously difficult to get anything to stick to it. Many things have been tried like hot-melt and cyanoacrylates (super-glue) but the best solution by far is to use double sided tape and rubber or acrylic based adhesives with a screw and washer as backup. Most European manufacturers use this method to affix the top to the body.

Central Join

This is the real bastard. Joining the solid body to the flexible handle and the springy dowel is a difficult technical problem. It can be overcome with good design of the body shell and balance weight at the point where it connects to the dowel. At BEARD we use two different types of glass cloth tape to absorb the continuous and sudden flexing.

Overall weight

The current trend in Europe is towards a lighter club, between 210 and 230 grams. The reason for this may be that a lot of people juggle indoors or it may simply be a result of advances in materials and design. The original American clubs* were often over 250 grams and felt very heavy.

At BEARD we get almost no requests for heavier clubs though the lighter they are the harder it is to get a good feel and balance.

Assembly

Operation 1: Fit weight onto dowel to correct position and secure with staple.

---

*There were no European manufacturers of juggling clubs at the beginning of the 1980's so the few jugglers around in those days tended to bring them over from the United States or make their own, some readers may remember the fashion for making clubs from MOTHERCARE kiddies skittles —C.D.

Operation 2: Fit dowel/weight assembly into body shell and stick on the end, securing it with screw and washer.

Operation 3: Fit the handle wrap and staple into position, tape the join with strong tape.

Operation 4: Fit the knob and secure with screw and washer.

Operation 5: Decorate with amazingly flashy foil and fit finishing tape.

Operation 6: Stick a BEARD label on it.

God it sounds easy! The logistics of the whole operation are horrendous. At BEARD we make almost everything ourselves on machines and jigs that we also make ourselves. We hold some five hundred different components in stock and use eight thousand square feet of factory space and employ twelve people to produce our equipment. Training someone to make the full range takes about three months!

'H' —BEARD JUGGLING EQUIPMENT.

Juggling Information Service

If you have access to the Internet (the incredible global linkup of computers, people and ideas that you can hook into for the price of a local phone call) then you should immediately type the following gobbledegook into the appropriate box on your screen:

`http://www.hal.com/services/juggle/`

This will connect your machine to the **Juggling Information Service**. This is a very well run operation and an absolute gold mine of information for the juggler. Think of it as a virtual juggling convention!

The great thing about the jugglers on the Internet is that they all do something *real* as well as using computers. This is largely an anorak free zone!

While you are about it you should also subscribe to the lively newsgroup `rec.juggling` where you can ask questions and receive answers and make comments on just about anything to do with juggling.

Khyber Pass

This is another of those flashy throws that is often seen in **Every Others** passing routines. It's quite closely related to the **Scoop Pickup** but for this trick, you don't need to **Drop** first!

•Juggle a normal **Four Count** passing pattern with your partner.

Immediately after the pass you *place* the club in your left hand between your thighs, knob pointing forwards.

With the two other clubs held one in each hand you grip the knob of the clenched club and swing it forwards causing it to execute a perfect **Single** spin pass to your partner. Elegance indeed!

•If you are an ace at the **Scissor Catch** you might consider flashing the trick up even more.

Start by placing the club between your legs at the *same time* as you do a **Circus Grip** stop in your right hand. (Look it up). Now place your left hand casually on your hip as you **Scissor** the clenched club across to your partner before resuming your **Four Count** with a nasty little **Multiplex** from your right hand. You get extra points for stuff like this!

•The **Khyber Pass** is especially impressive if you happen to be **Fire Juggling** at the time. The position of the **Khybered** club is such that flames lick dangerously over your behind for a few moments. The **Scissor** throw emphasises the comic idea of the torch being too hot to handle.

Kick Up

The **Kick Up** is the classic recovery from a **Drop**. It's such a great move that jugglers have developed it into a trick performed for its own sake, rather than just saving it for when disaster strikes.

•The classic **Kick Up** is quite difficult to learn because it seems *quite* impossible the first time that you try it. It will help you a lot to wear rubber edged shoes, (like most 'trainers') because these give an all important extra fraction of 'grip' on the club.

*A club ready to **Kick Up**, the crucial points of contact between you and the club during the kick are marked.*

Lay a club across your right foot so that the handle lies on the arch of your foot. The central tape on the club should be directly over the right hand side of your shoe.

Now roll your foot over to the left and raise your toes —this should feel like a stretching exercise! You are ready to **Kick Up.**

A Kick Up into a Three Club Cascade. The right hand throws so as to be ready for the catch.

The action of the kick should be aimed to drive your heel towards your right shoulder, keeping that awkward twist of the foot at full stretch all the way. The **Kick Up** works (when it *does* work!) because you are maintaining two points of contact with the club, the shoulder of the club rests on the edge of your foot while the knob gets 'caught' on your shin.

The beginner's **Kick Up** often fails because the club slips out of this delicate arrangement. When you get the action right you should be able to lift the club quite slowly and under control, merely adding power to the kick is *not* the answer!

Have patience with this move —it is not going to be solid by teatime! Make a point of using a **Kick Up** every time you drop a club in practice. Try to work on both sides evenly, it's a shame to get a solid **Kick Up** on the right but never learn it on the left!

•Once you can **Kick Up** from a 'cold start' you should start to work on putting **Kick Ups** into a running pattern. You **Drop** a club directly onto your foot (as a **Flat**) in mid-juggle and immediately kick it back into the pattern.

It's possible to do this in one flowing movement and some jugglers devote hundreds of hours to perfecting the trick.

A deliberate Drop sending a club into Kick Up position.

•To add some colour to this trick you can drop the club with a **Dip** spin onto the foot. You may well find that this is more reliable than a **Flat** drop because the spin on the club helps it to 'lock in' to the **Kick Up** position. Some jugglers use a **Helicopter** spin which looks even more impressive! In each case the *right* hand drops to the *left* foot and vice versa.

Flat, **Dip** *and* **Helicopter** *drops onto the foot. When thrown correctly the* **Dip** *and* **Helicopter** *drops cause the club to 'snuggle' into a perfect* **Kick Up** *position on your foot.*

• *Polished* **Dip** *droppers actually place the club against their leg, just above the knee and give it a quick spin as they let go.*

The club seems to crawl down their leg into the **Kick Up** *position.*

• *Another method of dropping a club into* **Kick Up** *position is to jam it between your legs from behind (like a* **Khyber Pass** *but pointing the other way) and let it drop.*

You'll find that you can control the fall of the club so that it ends up perfectly placed for the **Kick Up**, even without having to look, which can be very useful in **Passing Patterns**.

The stepover **Kick Up.**

• Next you could learn the *stepover* **Kick Up**, a classic move that has been well-used over the years.

Place the club that you are going to **Kick Up** across your right foot in the 'wrong' direction —with the nose of the club on the *inside*. Now step right over the club with your left foot and **Kick Up** from this legs-crossed position. The two all important points of contact with the club are the inside edge of your right foot and the calf of your left leg. After the **Kick Up** you have made two steps to the left (like a 1960's rock'n'roll guitarist) and you can repeat the whole move —travelling across the stage to your right as you go —a great stage exit!

Kick Up...

•Here's another one.

Cheat the dropped club so that it is lying between your feet, jump and turn through one hundred and eighty degrees, quickly grab the club between your ankles and hop it across to your partner.

•I've also seen a juggler toss a dropped club back into the pattern by grasping it between their feet and going into a quick handstand as they throw the club over their head to their partner!

•It's very common to see jugglers using a **Kick Up** to pass a club from the floor directly to their partner. These can fairly unpredictable to catch, especially if you are being used for 'target practice' by someone who hasn't quite got the trick solid.

Kicking up a fourth club to move up from **Three Club Cascade** *to* **Four Club Fountain**.

•One way of starting a **Four Club Fountain** is to begin with a **Three Club Cascade** and **Kick Up** the fourth club.

Timing is everything!

Place club number four into **Kick Up** position on your right foot and start to juggle the **Cascade**. Lead into the **Four Club Fountain** with a **Double** from the left hand and, more or less simultaneously, **Kick Up** from the right foot.

Your **Kick Up** needs to be very reliable to pull this one off as you don't get a chance to look down during the move!

•Alternatively you can **Kick Up** a fourth club, but drop another down simultaneously so that you stay in the **Three Club Cascade**.

Juggle a **Three Club Cascade** with a fourth club ready in **Kick Up** position on the right foot. Simultaneously **Kick Up** from the right foot while dropping a club from the left hand *back onto the right foot*. You end up back where you started! This not only *looks* very skillful —it actually *is!* I've seen the trick worked with two extra clubs, one on *each* foot with drops and **Kick Ups** mixed into a bewildering display of pure skill.

•Five club jugglers can also use a **Kick Up** to switch from the **Four Club Fountain** into a **Five Club Cascade**. The **Kick Up** is made *simultaneously* with the first **Five Club Cascade** throw and from the same side.

•Next come the **Multiplex Kick Ups**, in which more than one club is kicked up at a time. These **Kick Ups** are not generally very useful for recovering from drops because the clubs need to be carefully pre-arranged on your foot (by hand).

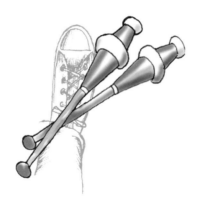

For a two club **Kick Up** place the first club on your right foot as normal, the second club is laid on top with its nose to the *left* of the first. Pay very close attention to the positioning. The knob of the lower club needs to be in contact with the handle of the upper one. The upper knob traps against your shin during the kick, the lower knob gets trapped against the *handle* of the upper club.

When you try the kick, concentrate on the upper club (it should feel like a normal **Kick Up**) —if the lower club flies out at some random angle then it was not placed correctly.

Both clubs should rise with identical spin, and you catch one in each hand.

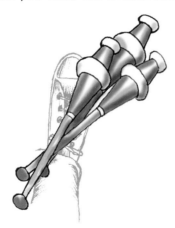

•The three-club **Kick Up** is also possible, though it requires such a careful setup that you would be very hard-pushed to put it into the middle of a flowing routine. It's best used as a starting move.

The best way to think of the arrangement is as a two club **Kick Up** with the third club lying *underneath* and projecting further out than the other two. Once again, you should concentrate of the top club as you kick. The two upper clubs should rise as **Single** spins while the lower club (because it's projecting out further) will do a **Double** spin. The whole arrangement is caught like a **Three Club Start**.

See also **Toe Kick**, **Drop Kick**, **Slap Kick** and **Summertime Pass**.

Kick Up

Knee Catch

'How do you *do* that crazy mad thing with that juggling club?' they ask —to which the only sensible answer is, '*like this!*'

•Juggle a **Three Club Cascade** and toss one club straight up as a self **Double** from your right hand. While it's in the air you turn slightly to your left, raise your right leg and catch the club behind your knee. Not on the first attempt, or the second, but after days and days of *practice*.

This is a good finishing trick for a comic three club routine, it has that special 'Marx Brothers' flavour.

The thing to remember about finishing tricks is that they are worse than useless if you get them wrong. Spend one whole month during which you finish every bit of three club practice with a **Knee Catch** *before* you take it out onto street, stage or screen.

•In a **Passing Pattern** you can throw a club from a **Knee Catch** grip to your partner. To make a pass with a club jammed behind your right knee you turn almost one hundred and eighty degrees to the left and straighten your leg quickly, like a Kung Fu kick, propelling the club to your partner as a **Flat**.

See also **Elbow Throw**, **Finish** and **Five Times in a Row**.

Ladder Notation

A good deal has been said about **Ladder Notation**[EBJ] in the ENCYCLOPÆDIA OF BALL JUGGLING. It is the system of juggling notation that has been used to produce the ladder-like charts throughout this book.

Of all the systems of notation that have been devised for the juggler, **Ladder Notation** is the closest to musical notation but, for obvious reasons, it's not intended to be sight-read.

Ladder Notation was invented quite independently by various different people, including myself, in the early 1980's. Many inventions throughout the ages have occurred like this; the time arrives for an idea to come into being and it just magically *does*. The inventors should not be pleased that they have had the idea so much as being pleased that the idea has had *them!*

A ladder chart does not, at first glance, resemble a juggling pattern, and just like **SiteSwap**, you can't tell whether the pattern is being juggled with balls, clubs, rings or flamingos. Neither is there any indication of **Spin**. All you get is *left, right, throw, catch,* and the passage of time.

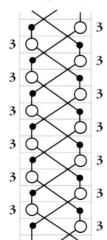

Here's a **Cascade** of three. The chart is read from top to bottom and the rungs of the ladder divide the passage of time into **Beats**. The right and left hand sides of the ladder correspond to the right and left sides of the juggling pattern. The numbers are the **SiteSwap** values of each throw.

The path of each object in the pattern is represented by a line that crisscrosses from side to side, being thrown and caught on

the way. A white circle is a throw and a black dot a catch. If you examine the chart carefully you'll see that it does give a very accurate picture of the happenings in a **Cascade** of three objects. Most important of all it shows you *how* and *why* the juggling pattern works. It may not be as concise as **SiteSwap** but it tells you a whole lot more.

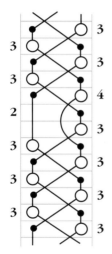

Here's a chart of a **Cascade** of three objects interrupted by a simple trick, one hand throws to itself and then the cascade resumes. The normal cascade throws are **3**'s or **Singles** to the club juggler. The self throw is a **4** or **Double**.

Looking at the **SiteSwap** numbers of the throws you will spot the self **Double** marked as a **4** and the long hold in the left hand as a **2**. Note that the weight of a throw according to **SiteSwap** is *one more* than the number of **Beats** the object actually spends

in the air. This is because **SiteSwap** takes no account of *hold times*. **4** simply means that the object will be ready to throw again *four beats later*. Actually, it spends three **Beats** in the the air and one **Beat** in the hand.

Ladder Notation is pretty difficult to use for **Passing Patterns** because you end up with a spaghetti of crisscrossing lines that looks considerably more complex than the juggling it is trying to represent. It's easier to use **Causal Diagrams** for that sort of thing. **Ladder Notation** tracks the *path of each object* in the pattern while **Causal Diagrams** track the *sequence of throws*.

Ladder Notation is the ideal tool for the illustrator or animator who wishes to draw juggling patterns accurately, placing every object in the correct position. I used **Ladder Notation** sketches for this purpose with almost every single cartoon drawing in the ENCYCLOPÆDIA OF BALL JUGGLING. In the COMPENDIUM I have used more artistic freedom in an attempt to convey the *feeling* of club juggling. Juggling clubs are simply not seen as *point* objects and completely accurate drawings, while they might freeze the instant correctly, do not communicate movement very well.

Ladder Notation...

Ladder Notation can be used by the juggler as a 'calculator' for working out new tricks and patterns 'on the back of an envelope' before committing them to gravity. When doing this it's best to follow a few simple rules that prevent you from charting anything too impossible.

•The normal *hold time* or *dwell* of an object in the hand is one beat. More is possible, less is *very* unlikely.

•The normal *empty time* of hand after a throw and before the next catch is also one beat. Again, more is possible but less is very rare.

•From the first two rules it follows a hand is very very unlikely to make a throw more often than once every two beats. Almost all juggling patterns are like this — either the hands take it in turns to throw (one throw per beat) or they throw in unison (two simultaneous throws every two beats).

•It's perfectly OK to throw two or even three objects at once, this is a **Multiplex**. On the other hand *catching* two or more objects at once is virtually impossible.

•You need to keep the airtime of your throws within reasonable limits. Few jugglers are solid beyond **Quads** (**6**'s in **SiteSwap** —five beats of airtime). Most practical juggling is done using two beat to four beat throws (**3**'s to **5**'s).

Armed with those basic guidelines, a pencil and some handy envelopes to scrawl all over you should, after a little practice, be able to create some brand new patterns of your own.

Have fun!

See also **Notation**, **Causal Diagrams** and **SiteSwap Notation**.

A **Late Double** is a diagonal throw made on the regular pass beat.

Late Double

A **Late Double** is a **Syncopation** that you can throw in a **Passing Pattern**. Most jugglers learn this trick right after they have mastered the slightly simpler **Early Double**.

Instead of making a normal **Single** pass you throw a **Double** pass diagonally across the pattern. The throw seems to break the rules because it arrives *a beat late* in the *wrong hand* but it turns out that these two wrongs make a right and it is a very useful and elegant variation.

Unlike the **Early Double**, which only alters *your* end of the pattern, the **Late Double** causes a forced response at your partner's end. You need to learn to throw it, your partner needs to learn how to respond to it.

The first time you are thrown a **Late Double** you will almost certainly drop it.

Sounds complicated? Not a bit of it. Two moderately competent club passers can have this trick solid in fifteen minutes flat.

•In a right handed **Four Count** you make the throw on the *pass* beat and that's all there is to the trick as far as *you* are concerned —the rest of your pattern is unchanged.

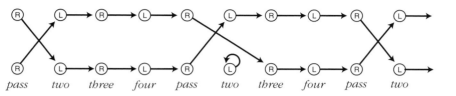

pass   two   three   four   pass   two   three   four   pass   two

*A **Causal Diagram** of a **Late Double** being thrown in a **Four Count** by the juggler represented by the top row. The **Double** arrives one **Beat** late and in the 'wrong' hand, causing the receiver to **Hold through the Gap** in the left hand.*

*A charming oddity of **Causal Diagrams** is that holds appear as arrows pointing to their own tails.*

For your partner it's a slightly different story, their left hand (which was expecting a normal pass) now **Holds through the Gap** that the **Double** has created, then their right hand catches the **Double** and *passes it straight back* as a normal pass. The first time you see a **Late Double** heading your way you will probably fumble and drop in confusion —nearly everybody does! After a couple of goes at it you'll get used to the idea and it will feel perfectly natural.

Both you and your partner can throw **Late Doubles** to each other on any *pass* beat and the pattern will still hold together. When you get used to the idea you should

mix in some **Early Doubles** as well and you'll paint some really pretty patterns in the air.

•You can throw **Late Doubles** in the **Two Count**, **Three Count** and **Five Count** —in fact, in any 'count' that uses **Singles** as its normal passing throw. In each case the **Late Double** is thrown on the *pass* beat.

•The **One Count** is *almost* an exception to this rule. If you want to throw a **Late Double** in a **One Count** you need to throw *two in a row* to avoid crashing the pattern.

•**Late Doubles** can be thrown in almost any **Passing Pattern** of the three-clubs-per

juggler type. They are often chucked around in **Feeds** by both feeder and fed to spice things up a bit (or even a lot).

•Finally it should be noted that **Late Doubles**, like any other **Double**, don't *have* to be thrown with **Double** spin although they usually are —it's the airtime that counts. You can use floaty **Single** spins, snappy **Triple** spins or even **Flats** if you wish.

•For your next trick you should check out the **Early Triple**.

See also **Syncopation**, **Causal Diagrams** and **Early Double**.

*If you want to throw a **Late Double** in a six-club **One Count** you'll need to throw two diagonal **Doubles** in a row to avoid crashing the pattern. One on its own simply won't work. Both you and your partner get to **Hold Through the Gap** as two clubs cross the pattern dramatically. This is a wild trick that feels really good both to throw and to catch.*

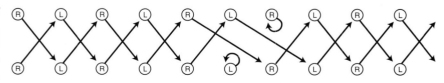

Late Double

Late Single

The **Late Single** is an obscure and largely unknown **Syncopation** for patterns of the three-clubs-per-juggler persuasion. It's a moderately advanced trick so I'd leave learning it until you are skilled enough to throw **Syncopations** in a **Three Count**. Being obscure, its most common use is to surprise your partner into dropping a perfectly catchable throw. A **Late Single** can be thrown in any regular count (except the **One Count**) and is a **Single** pass, made one beat late, and aimed at the 'wrong' hand. It's therefore caught exactly like a **Late Double**.

• In a **Four Count** you throw a **Late Single** pass on the *two* beat, one beat *after* the regular pass. You have to *miss the regular pass* to make that throw. This is a non-trivial juggling problem.

The neatest method is to throw a right to right self **Double** on the *pass* beat (throw the club straight up, to yourself, instead of to your partner) and then throw the **Late Single** on the *two* beat immediately afterwards.

There's a strong possibility of a collision between your outbound **Late Single** and the incoming pass from your partner. You avoid this by throwing your pass *inside* theirs, just as you would if you were juggling a **One Count**.

For most people this move goes 'against the grain' and some furious coordination is required of the head-patting and stomach-rubbing variety.

• Catching the **Late Single** is exactly like catching a **Late Double** (or any other **Late** pass) except that it's a little harder to spot what is going on in time to react. Your partner will probably be caught by surprise the first time this unexpected pass is made so it's best to warm them up with a few **Late**

Doubles before throwing them their first **Late Single** —unless you *want* them to screw up!

• There is a technically easier method of setting yourself up for the **Late Single** which has an unconventional elegance that I simply adore.

Juggle the **Four Count** and after making a pass you stop your pattern dead, with two clubs in the right hand —*Clack!*

Freeze like this for two beats and then throw the **Late Single** to your partner (one beat *after* their pass) and resume your cascade.

THEY JUGGLE:
Pass -two-three-four-*pass* -two -three-four-*pass* ..

YOU JUGGLE:
Pass -two-***clack!*** -wait-wait-**Pass**-three-four-*pass* ..

The secret is to concentrate on the timing of the move. The most common mistake is that of throwing the **Late Single** too early, typically at the *same time* as your partner's normal pass —it must be thrown one beat *after* their pass.

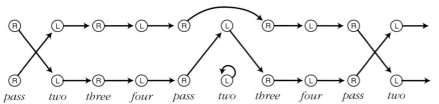

*Throwing a **Late Single** pass in a **Four Count**.*

*The regular pass is missed by throwing a self **Double**.*

pass two three four pass two three four pass two

•If you and your partner take it in turns to throw **Late Singles** using the *clack* technique you'll find yourselves juggling to a very hypnotic rhythm punctuated by the sound of clubs clacking together. It may be easy but it's awesome juggling!

•**Late Singles**, as I said earlier, can be thrown in **Two Count** and **Three Count** patterns but not in **One Counts**.

In the **Three Count** you throw a self **Double** so as to miss the regular pass and throw the **Late Single** on the *two* beat.

Since the **Three Count** is an ambidextrous pattern you have two versions to learn —left-handed and right-handed.

•In the **Two Count** it's a little more hectic but at least there is only one side to learn it on!

Once again, throw a self **Double** on the *pass* beat and the **Late Single** on the *two* beat. Note that the **Late Single** is followed immediately by a normal pass —so it feels as if you are juggling **Pass Pass Self** for a moment.

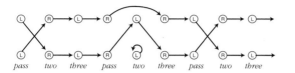

*A **Late Single** in a **Three Count**.*

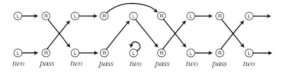

*A **Late Single** in a **Two Count**.*

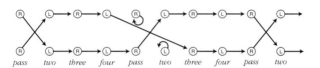

*A **Late Triple** in a **Four Count**.*

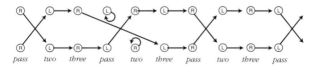

*A **Late Triple** in a **Three Count**.*

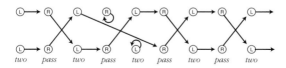

*A **Late Triple** in a **Two Count**.*

Late Triple

Continuing the theme of 'late' passes we come naturally to the **Late Triple**. Once again, this is a pass that arrives in the 'wrong' hand a beat late.

Both you and your partner get a short **Gap** as a result of this throw.

•In a right-handed **Four Count** it is a left to right tramline pass made on the *four* beat and it's useful to remember that you make the throw with the club you have just received from your partner.

The pass is caught exactly like a **Late Double** or a **Late Single**, just remember to pass it straight back again.

•In a **Three Count** the **Late Triple** is thrown on the *three* beat and there are two versions to learn; right-handed and left-handed.

•In the **Two Count** the throw is made on the *two* beat, right after a regular pass.

See also **Early Double**, **Late Double** and **Early Triple**.

Late Triple

Long John Silver

I was browsing through a bookshop the other day when I came across an amusing manual of juggling tricks that listed a trick which it described as (and I quote) "...*without a doubt, one of the most æsthetic, nay, ethereal finishes ever to have been devised.*" It was none other than the **Long John Silver**.

Many jugglers have come up with the idea of using a juggling club as a comic pirate's pegleg but I know for a certain fact that the juggler who devised the full **Long John Silver**, (complete with parrot and telescope), was one cryptically named *Radical Cheney* and that the trick was not originally conceived as a finish.

You can perform the **Long John Silver** solo, or in an **Four Count** passing pattern. The technique is basically the same in either case.

•The solo pirate starts with a **Three Club Cascade** and then executes a left-to-right **One and a Half Spin** immediately followed by a right-to-left **Triple**. On catching the **One and a Half Spin** by its **Wrong End** in the *right* hand the juggler deftly places the club in pegleg position below the right knee. As the **Triple** descends, the left hand clears itself for the catch with a left to right **Single**.

*The **Long John Silver** being assembled from a **Three Club Cascade**. In a **Four Count** passing pattern the technique is similar but that **Triple** is a pass to your partner.*

Finally, the **Triple** is moved into *parrot* position (behind the right shoulder) and the **Single** is moved into *telescope* position (held before the eye).

It all happens in the blink of an eye!

•In a **Four Count** passing pattern you can execute virtually the same move *and* recover without breaking the **Four Count** rhythm.

Starting from the *pass* beat; you make a normal pass and then follow it immediately with a left-to-right **One and a Half Spin**. This is immediately followed with an **Early Triple** pass to your partner.

You now have time to pegleg the **One and a Half Spin** before catching your partner's next pass. It is at this point that you have exactly *four beats* to get Polly and the telescope in position, crack a nautical joke or two, and then resume your normal **Every Others** passing pattern.

•Even when you have the knack of executing a deft **Long John Silver** things can go wrong. It's quite common for the pegleg to be badly placed and drop out from below your knee. If this happens to you in performance my advice is to fall over *with* it which gets a big laugh every time.

Lovegrove Loop

The **Lovegrove Loop** is sometimes called the **Helicopter** although the two tricks are almost completely unlike each other. The only feature common to both is the horizontal rotation of a juggling club.

In the **Helicopter** a club spins as if impaled on a spike sticking out of the top of the juggler's head. In the **Lovegrove Loop** a club is swung around wildly at arm's length in the style of a highland chieftain taunting his enemies with the *severed head* of their king. It's a suitably terrifying move to use during the 'display' phase of **Combat Juggling**.

• Juggle **Two in One Hand** with **Double** spins in your left hand while holding a third club in your right. Watch the timing of the clubs carefully and then swing the *severed head* club from right to left right through the **Two in One Hand** pattern. Continue the swing through a full three hundred and sixty degrees and back through the **Two in One Hand** pattern again. You get one full swing of the head for each left hand throw.

It's all about confidence and timing.

• The **Lovegrove Loop** can be juggled in both left and right handed versions and you should learn both. Right-handed jugglers will find the left-handed swing a bit clumsy to begin with. Having mastered both symmetries you can work on mixing right handed swings with left handed ones. Changing direction on *every* swing produces a pattern that makes **Chops** look like kindergarten stuff.

The **Lovegrove Loop** is a close relative of the ball juggling pattern, **Seeing Stars**[EBJ].

Mike's Mess

This pattern is named after *Mike Day* who worked it out using pen and paper and an innovative form of juggling **Notation** he had developed to describe the **Mills' Mess** and other patterns where the hands cross and uncross as they juggle*.

When juggled with clubs, **Mike's Mess** looks quite uncanny and it's almost impossible for the eye to follow.

The pattern uses three clubs and is a *distortion* of a **Slow Cascade** juggled on **Double** spins —it's the same throws and catches, you just tangle your arms around while you do it. It's best to learn this one in stages.

• Warm up with a couple of minutes of **Slow Cascade** on **Doubles** to get the rhythm into your head.

• Now juggle the same **Slow Cascade** but make every throw an **Under the Hand** throw. This means that you make the left hand throws from a left-under-right position and the right hand throws from right-under-

---

*If you want to find out more about Mike Day's *'Mills' Mess State Transition Diagram'* you'll find it explained (by me) in the appendix of the *second* edition of the ENCYCLOPÆDIA OF BALL JUGGLING and (by Mike himself) in the pages of the **Juggling Information Service**.

Mike's Mess...

left. You'll probably find yourself going into a **Chop** pattern here automatically —very good, but it's not **Mike's Mess**!

•Stop juggling for a moment and put one club down so that you are holding just one club in each hand. It's time to practise the movement that puts the magic into **Mike's Mess**.

Swing the right hand club over the left arm and then downward as if paddling a canoe on the wrong side. Keep the momentum going so that the club rises past your left ear, swings back to the right and continues under the left hand club at which point it is released as an **Under the Hand Double** spin. *That's* the movement you do before each throw in **Mike's Mess**. It's very like a move that **Club Swingers** call a *'cross*

and follow'. The word *follow* refers to the fact that the *right* hand club starts its move as the left hand moves **Under the Hand** for the throw, hence the two clubs seem to be *following* each other.

Practise it on both sides until it's completely solid.

•The complete pattern is the **Slow Cascade** juggled **Under the Hand**. Each switch from left-over-right to right-over-left being achieved with a *cross and follow*. Every throw is made at the end of a *follow*.

It's might be tricky to get the knack of **Mike's Mess** but it's *nothing* compared to my job —trying to explain the damn thing on paper!

Mills' Mess

The original three-ball trick known as the **Mills' Mess**[EBJ] was invented by Steve Mills. It is dealt with in some depth in the ENCYCLOPÆDIA OF BALL JUGGLING and it has been an inspiration to thousands of jugglers who have developed countless variations on the theme (including the previous entry **Mike's Mess**).

This is the famous pattern in which the juggler's hands cross and uncross constantly as they weave three objects through the air.

The question is, 'Can this awesome pattern be juggled with clubs?'

The answer is, 'Yes!'

Juggling a **Mills' Mess** with clubs is perfectly possible —but it's *absolutely essential* that you learn the pattern with balls first. I refer you to the ENCYCLOPÆDIA OF BALL JUGGLING for full instructions and at least three different ways of getting your head around the pattern.

•When using clubs the **Mills' Mess** can be juggled either with **Single** or **Double** spins, take your choice! **Singles** simplify the pattern considerably (there's less chance of a **Wrong End** catch messing things up). On the other hand, **Doubles** slow the pattern down enough to give you time to think

The 'cross and follow' that puts the magic into **Mike's Mess**.

about what you are doing. My personal preference is **Singles** —but that's just me.

To start the pattern place two clubs in your right hand and one in your left. Cross your hands so that your right hand is under the left. There's the sequence of six throws that make up the pattern and with a little luck you'll be able to translate your expertise from the ball-juggling pattern to the clubs without any real trouble. However, if you get stuck just learn this sequence *one throw at a time* and you are guaranteed to get there in the end!

•When your **Mills' Mess** runs for a few rounds you'll see that the curvaceously polished flight paths of the clubs in a smooth **Mills' Mess** is something that cannot be described in words —it can only be fashioned in the hands of an *artist!*

To develop this creamy edge you must spend many long hours with the pattern in search of the path of minimum effort, which also happens to be the path of maximum gloss.

•Complete juggling fiends have been known to actually pass clubs between two running **Mills' Messes**! The obvious choice of pattern for this would be a **Three Count** since the timing of the **Mills' Mess** matches a **Three Count** precisely (they both have a six **Beat** cycle).

See also **Mike's Mess**.

1: Starting with hands crossed left over right, the right hand throws **Under the Hand** *and moves to uncross.*

2: The left hand throws its club towards the centre of the pattern and moves to catch throw number one.

3: The right hand, now uncrossed throws its club towards the centre of the pattern and moves to catch throw number two.

4: The hands now cross right over left as the left hand throws **Under the Hand** *and moves to catch throw number three.*

5: The right hand throws its club towards the centre and moves to catch throw number four as the hands uncross.

6: The left hand, now uncrossed, throws its club towards the centre and moves to catch throw number five.

Mills' Mess

Mixed Object Juggling and Working with Everyday Objects

Mixed Object Juggling is the art of working with a number of different objects rather than using a matched set of clubs, balls or rings. This leads to the theme of working with everyday objects rather than specialised props. Three **Juggling Clubs** are a set of carefully designed throwing objects. A loaf of french bread, a leather jacket and a live hedgehog are something else altogether.

There are three main classes of objects used in **Toss Juggling**[EBJ] and each is represented by the three 'idealised' types of juggler's prop.

A ball, a club and a ring —the three idealised juggler's props.

Ball-type objects

Balls, beanbags, rocks, snowballs, small furry animals, rolled-up socks and anything else that is thrown without regard to **Spin** and caught in a fist-like grip.

Ring-type objects

Juggling rings, hula hoops, rolls of gaffer tape, plates, frisbees, some hats. These are all thrown with flat spin and caught by the edge.

Club-type objects

Juggling clubs, fire torches, knives, sticks, hammers, spoons, rolled-up newspapers, tennis rackets and so on, all thrown with end-over-end spin and caught in a handle grip.

Chinese jugglers shun the western preference for purpose built clubs, rings and balls; working almost exclusively with everyday objects. You won't see a Chinese juggler working with clubs —tennis rackets are far more likely.

• A good exercise for the **Mixed Object Juggler** is that of juggling a cascade with a ball, a ring and a club. This gets your hands used to applying the different **Toss Juggling**[EBJ] techniques simultaneously and it's very satisfying to learn.

• Juggling two clubs and a football leads to a all sorts of possibilities that you can use to build an interesting and entertaining routine. My favourite move is to juggle the three objects and then spin the football on your finger while juggling **Two in One Hand** with the other hand (see **Spinning Ball**[EBJ]).

• Another trick is to keep the football in the air 'keepie-uppie' style, by bouncing it on your forehead while executing snazzy **Club Swinging** moves with the other two clubs.

•A popular game at juggling conventions is the *'Shoe, Shirt and Shilling'* contest. The idea is that everybody takes off a shoe and their T-shirt, adds a coin to the set and the last person juggling in the winner. It's usually allowable to tie a knot in your shirt.

The coin is a *ball* type object, the shoe is a *club* type object and the shirt falls into no category known to juggling science. I mention this competition here for reference only —it's very bad form to practise these things beforehand.

•What really takes **Mixed Object Juggling** into entertainment is creative imagination. Take the wonderful *'Frying Pan, Egg and Fire Torch'* routine. The juggler does a quick show with these three objects (effectively two clubs and a ball) and finishes by tossing the egg high into the air and catching it in the frying pan while holding the fire torch beneath —breakfast!

Don't slavishly copy ideas like this, come up with your own. Audiences are very impressed when they see you working with real everyday objects —and even if you can't manage your greatest juggling feats with them, they'll love it!

*The grand finale of a **Mixed Object Juggling** routine.*

***Mopping your Brow** .*

Mopping your Brow
(and tilting your hat)

Here's a snappy trick for the beginner. Forget **Back Crosses**, **Mills' Mess** and the **Five Club Cascade**. Why go to all that trouble when your audience will be just as impressed when they see you casually **Mopping your Brow** with one of the clubs in your juggling pattern.

•Juggle a **Three Club Cascade** and throw a self **Double** in your right hand (as if you are going into **Two in One Hand** for a throw), while your left hand is **Mopping your Brow**.

•If your wear a hat you can do a slightly more elaborate version of this trick, casually adjusting the angle of your hat while juggling three clubs.

It's cool to use the *thin* end of the club to tilt your hat so the sequence goes as follows:

Start by throwing a **One and a Half Spin** from the right hand (so your left hand will catch at the **Wrong End**) and make the *next* right hand throw the self **Double** as before. Now tip that headpiece to a rakish angle using the club in your left hand (careful not to poke your eye out) and resume your **Cascade**.

Mopping your Brow

Multiplex Throws

A **Multiplex** is the action of throwing more than one object at once. One example of this is the **Three Club Start** —three clubs are tossed up together from one hand. Since it takes a bit of fiddling about to get the three clubs arranged in your hand, the **Three Club Start** is almost always used to start a show. The two club **Multiplex** however, is a throw that can be slammed into the middle of a routine with no hesitation whatsoever.

• Start by practising the **Multiplex** throw on its own, with just two clubs. You'll find that you need to use a **Circus Grip**, rather than a **Normal Grip** to avoid the clubs fouling each other as they turn in the air and flying unpredictably.

Form a neat **Circus Grip** in the right hand and toss both clubs together so that one is caught in each hand. It's daunting at first, but very soon you'll be tossing **Singles**, **Doubles** and perhaps even **Triples** with complete confidence.

Armed with this new skill you are ready to learn how to throw a two club **Multiplex** in a running **Three Club Cascade**.

• While juggling a **Three Club Cascade** gather two clubs in the right hand in a **Circus Grip** (it's important to get this bit right, so see **Circus Grip**). You can now throw them both up simultaneously as **Singles** or **Doubles** to restart the pattern.

• In the plain vanilla version of this trick the entire pattern stops dead for a moment as the two clubs clack together in the right hand. To avoid this pregnant pause, the really smooth juggler throws a quick **Hopstop**[EBJ] in the *left* hand as the clubs are being gathered in the right.

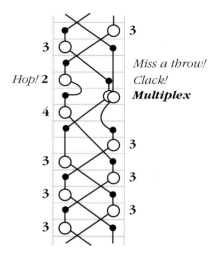

*A **Ladder Notation** chart of a **Single** spin **Multiplex** being thrown in a **Three Club Cascade**. Notice the cheeky **Hopstop**[EBJ] in the left hand that covers what would otherwise be a pregnant pause.*

The **Hopstop**[EBJ] is simply a little self throw which has no purpose other than keeping the rhythm going and making the trick look more elaborate than it really is. It makes the whole move flow with polished and professional grace.

•To spice the move up enormously you can throw the **Multiplex** behind your back, **Under the Leg** or **Under the Arm**.

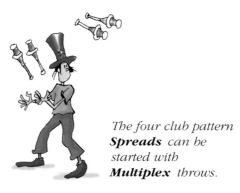

*The four club pattern **Spreads** can be started with **Multiplex** throws.*

•A great way to start the four club pattern **Spreads** is to use two **Multiplex** throws. You start with two clubs in each hand, held in **Circus Grips**. Throw up the right hand pair first, the the left hand pair (using **Triples** to pile on the agony a little) and then go straight into **Spreads**.

•A two club **Multiplex** can be thrown **Tomahawk** style —over your head. Use a **Circus Grip** as you would for a normal **Multiplex** throw.

•When juggling a six-club **Two Count** with a partner you can make a **Multiplex** pass —two clubs to your partner in one throw!

Juggle the **Two Count** and then miss a pass by gathering two clubs in your right hand. Then throw both, as **Flats** across the pattern. You should aim to get the clubs to split so that one lands in each of your partner's hands.

As long as they have not been **Holding through the Gap** they'll find that the **Multiplex** is perfectly catchable.

*The moment you realise your partner is about to throw you a **Multiplex Tomahawk** pass.*

•Instead of making the **Multiplex** pass with **Flats** you can use a **Tomahawk** throw. Each club spins with a **Double** on its way to your partner. The technique is much the same as for throwing a **Multiplex** to yourself **Tomahawk** style.

Continued overleaf...

Multiplex...

•A stupendous trick is to throw a *three club* **Multiplex** to your partner while juggling a **Two Count**. This is very like throwing a **Three Club Start** except that it's your *partner* that catches the clubs and you have to set up the move *while the pattern is running!*

It's a very busy trick and there is absolutely *no time* for the slightest fumble. Your partner does not **Hold through the Gap**, they just keep passing as normal throughout.

Juggle a **Two Count** with your partner and instruct them to watch carefully and keep passing to you *no matter what happens*.

*The grip for a **Three Club Start** (or three club **Multiplex**) is a **Circus Grip** with the third club laid underneath.*

Begin by throwing your partner an **Early Double** while you gather two clubs in your right hand in a **Circus Grip**. *Catch your partner's pass.*

Place this club between and underneath the two gathered clubs as for a **Three Club Start**. *Catch your partner's next pass.*

Throw the caught pass to yourself as a normal left to right **Single** —Aieaargh! (Yes

you *are* holding three clubs in your right hand at this moment.)

Throw the three club **Multiplex** to your partner, two **Doubles** and a **Triple**, and *catch your partner's next pass.*

Gasp in disbelief as they rise into the air, your partner passes their last remaining club to you *without* looking in your direction, they are totally concerned with catching the **Multiplex**.

Juggle a *self* while they sort out the descending chaos and then resume passing —big WOW!

It's a tremendous move and the trickiest moment of all is the moment at which you throw the **Multiplex**. You'll find it quite tricky to throw the **Doubles** far enough to reach your partner without the **Triple** landing miles behind them. A good way to sort this out is to practise throwing **Three Club Starts** to you partner while standing passing-distance apart. The secret is to get your hand right 'underneath' the throw with a scooping motion, it also helps if you step well forward while you toss them.

Neck Grip

Here's some more total stupidity for the club juggler. The **Neck Grip** is the action of holding a club between your chin and your shoulder like a busy person talking on the 'phone.

• Juggle a **Three Club Cascade** and slam a club into a left hand **Neck Grip** with your right hand, then take it out again with your *left* hand to continue the juggle.

• I've seen no less than *six* clubs juggled in a **Three Club Cascade** with the three 'spare' clubs being slammed into and snatched out of various body grips.

• You can catch a **Triple** pass directly into a **Neck Grip**. You need to raise your arm to guide the club into position and the move is therefore nicknamed the *Superman Catch*.

See also **Stevie Spangle Shuffle**.

Nine Club One Count

This nine club **Passing Pattern** (for just two jugglers) is the third in an increasingly difficult series of two person patterns that begins with the **Five Club One Count** (beginner's stuff) and moves on to the **Seven Club One Count** (suitable for eight-club passers) and ends here. This is a very advanced pattern.

Numbers Jugglers would normally use a **Two Count** to juggle nine clubs, passing **6**'s from their right hands (thrown as **Triples**) while throwing regular **Single** selfs from their left hands. The resulting pattern is much like seven clubs on **Staggered Doubles**, but taken up a couple of notches. This isn't very ambidextrous but at least you only have to concentrate on making good throws with one hand and good catches with the other.

The **Nine Club One Count** on the other hand is completely ambidextrous with the work of throwing and catching shared equally by all four hands. Every throw is a pass with the very unusual **SiteSwap** value of **4.5**.

Like the two easier patterns in this series, one juggler makes *diagonal* passes while the other throws *tramlines*. It's a **One Count** so *every* throw is a pass. The pattern is usually juggled on **Double** spins. Correction, the pattern is not usually juggled *at all*, but when it is, **Doubles** are a good choice.

• Stand face to face, you get five clubs to your partner's four, you have three in the right and two in the left and you will be making the diagonal passes while they throw tramlines.

The start is similar to the **Seven Club One Count**, you lead from the right and your partner starts, also from the right, exactly *half a beat later*. After that it's just a matter of finding the rhythm!

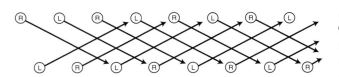

*A **Causal Diagram** of the **Nine Club One Count**. The two jugglers stagger their throws by half a beat, each pass is directed two and a half beats along the chart, so **Doubles** seem to be the most sensible choice.*

Normal Grip

The **Normal Grip** is the exact mirror image of the **Circus Grip**. It's the standard way of holding two clubs in one hand before you start to juggle.

•Hold the first club and place the second club on top of it so that the body lies to the *left*. To start juggling from a **Normal Grip** you throw the *top* club first.

The **Normal Grip** is the preferred grip for the beginner —a much safer bet than the **Circus Grip** because the first throw is far less likely to smash you in the teeth.

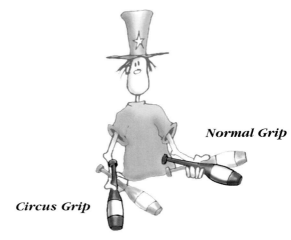

Normal Grip

Circus Grip

*How the last club is gathered for a **Circus Grip** (the previous club on the inside) and for a **Normal Grip** (the previous club on the outside).*

•When you stop juggling, catching two clubs in one hand, you can engineer matters to arrive in either grip. For a **Normal Grip** you make the final catch with the 'already held' club on the *outside*, for a **Circus Grip** the 'already held' club is kept on the *inside*. Not a lot of people know that!

See also **Circus Grip**.

Notation

If there were such a thing as a perfect system of **Notation** for the juggler, something like musical notation perhaps, then books like this COMPENDIUM OF CLUB JUGGLING and the ENCYCLOPÆDIA OF BALL JUGGLING and George Gillson's excellent BEYOND THE CASCADE would have been far simpler to write.

Alas, no perfect system has been devised and even if there was one, it's obvious that sight-reading a juggling routine from a music stand would be out of the question.

Nevertheless some very ingenious **Notations** have been devised. In putting the COMPENDIUM OF CLUB JUGGLING together I have tried to rely mainly on words of explanation and cartoon drawings which, I hope, *anybody* can understand. To supplement these I have used three different systems of **Notation**, each with its own strengths and weaknesses.

Ladder Notation

This system reduces each object in a juggling pattern to a line that crisscrosses down a chart with a ladder-like framework. Each line gives a complete history of that object as it moves from throw to catch to throw and so on. The lines are similar to the trails of light that would be left in the air if you were to watch a juggler from above by night as they rolled past you on a skateboard while juggling with three luminous balls.

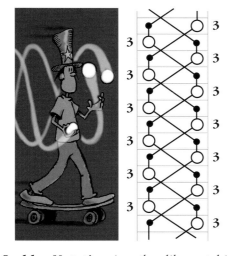

Ladder Notation *is rather like watching the skateboarder from above, the lines show you exactly where the balls have been. The chart shown here represents a **Cascade** of three objects.*

The strength of **Ladder Notation** is that it shows you exactly how a pattern works and where everything is at any given moment of time. It is the best system to use if you are an animator or illustrator who

wishes to draw accurate pictures of juggling patterns. It can handle such complications as **Gaps**, **Multiplexes**, **Drops** and **Pickups** with no trouble at all.

On the down side, **Ladder Notation** doesn't give a very clear indication of the *heights* of throws (only pictures and diagrams do that) and the tracing of every single object in a **Passing Pattern** can produce charts of bewildering and unreadable complexity.

SiteSwap Notation

This is a mathematical **Notation** that reduces a juggling pattern to a completely abstract form —a series of numbers. **SiteSwap Notation** is based on a stunningly simple idea that works incredibly well —let's call a throw from a **Three Ball Cascade**[EBJ] a **3** and throw from a **Four Ball Fountain**[EBJ] a **4** and see what happens!

This idea immediately creates a thoroughly sensible system for naming different weights of throw that anybody can understand. On top of that you can record complex patterns like **Five-Three-Four** as a simple **534**!

Many simple mathematical rules have been discovered that make **SiteSwap**

Notation the mathematical-gamers dream and many new juggling patterns have been discovered using it as a pattern calculator. You'll find a good example of this in the appendix of the ENCYCLOPÆDIA OF BALL JUGGLING in which I list 1093 juggling patterns generated by a computer that had been instructed with the basic rules of **SiteSwap Notation**.

The main failings of **SiteSwap** result from its simplicity. It is only interested in *throws*, completely ignoring the concept of a *catch* and it assumes that the hands always throw alternately*. This causes it to become very unwieldy when applied to patterns in which the hands throw in synch and it's a total nightmare when applied to **Passing Patterns**, **Multiplexes**, **Drops** and **Pickups**.

These problems don't mean that there is anything fundamentally *wrong* with **SiteSwap** or that somebody could come up with a better way of transcribing juggling patterns as numbers, it's more an indication of the fundamental complexity of juggling itself. **SiteSwap Notation** has made an

---

*I could get shot down in flames for this statement by a **SiteSwap** guru. The truth is even *worse* —**SiteSwap** does not know *how many* hands are in a pattern at all, it simply assumes that there is one throw per **Beat** and how ever many hands are involved take it in turns to throw.

Notation...

enormous contribution to the Art of Juggling and is constantly inspiring both jugglers and mathematicians to have new and significant ideas and to invent some really wild patterns.

Causal Diagrams

This system, invented by Martin Frost, incorporates ideas from both **Ladder** and **SiteSwap Notation**. Instead of tracking the movement of *objects* in a pattern, the **Causal Diagram** charts the sequence of *throws*, showing how one throw triggers another as the juggler 'clears the hand for the catch'. The resulting diagram looks similar to **Ladder Notation** except that, for a given pattern, the **Causal Diagram** is far simpler, and more accurately charts the 'feeling' of juggling the pattern.

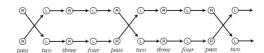

*A **Causal Diagram** of a **Four Count** passing pattern. Reading from left to right it's plain that every fourth throw is a pass.*

Notation gurus point out that a **Causal Diagram** is a like a **Ladder** chart of a pattern that has had **2** subtracted from each of its **SiteSwap** numbers. So it seems that juggling **Notations** can be as intertwingled as the patterns they represent!

* * *

As well as being invaluable tools for recording juggling patterns on paper, juggling notations enable you to try out new ideas on paper *before* committing them to gravity. The *Ten Club* **Triangle**, *Eight Club* **Popcorn** and the **Four-Five-0** are three patterns that would not have appeared in this book if they hadn't been worked out 'on the drawing board'.

For a more detailed look at these systems see **Ladder Notation**, **SiteSwap Notation** and **Causal Diagrams**.

Numbers Juggling

Numbers Juggling is the quest to get just *one more* object into the air. Anybody who progresses beyond five balls or four clubs is likely to be called a **Numbers Juggler**.

I WISH!

Numbers Juggling consumes some jugglers with a passion that is beyond reason or logic and the dedication that is required to excel in this area is indescribably immense.

Numbers Jugglers like to reach mountainous peaks of juggling that few, if any, have trodden before and I'm told that the view from the top is pretty spectacular —personally I'm knocked out by the view from my vantage point just a little way above base camp.

In ball juggling it's generally agreed that **Numbers Juggling** starts with the **Five Ball Cascade**[EBJ] but the corresponding pattern for clubs, the **Five Club Cascade** is very much harder to juggle —*very* few human beings progress beyond this level. Hence **Numbers Juggling** for the club juggler is a very hard road indeed.

The **Seven Club Cascade** seems to be pretty much the limit of human capability but saying that (especially in print) is like waving a red rag at a bull to the **Numbers Jugglers**. Anthony Gatto, at the time of writing, is known to be working on eight clubs (using a **Fountain** on **Triple** spins should you care to have a go yourself). The fact that this level is being explored already raises the awesome question of *nine*.

To become a serious **Numbers Juggler** you must crack the **Five Club Cascade**. Your success, or lack of it, will determine your further progress towards those unattainable double figures.

In America, the INTERNATIONAL JUGGLER'S ASSOCIATION holds serious competitive events for **Numbers Jugglers** and this, coupled with the well-known American attitude to excellence and super-achievement, has been the motivation for some very exceptional jugglers and some truly awesome juggling. It's easy for those who do not participate in **Numbers Juggling** to dismiss it as an obsessive and pointless activity but that attitude is often based on jealousy and perhaps a touch of regret —*'if only I'd worked a little harder then I too might be able to do that!'* You can't argue with a **Six Club Fountain**, it's a major achievement and that's all there is to it!

Two person **Passing Patterns** are also fertile ground for the **Numbers Juggler**. Seven clubs between two jugglers is your starting point and presents no serious problems. Eight is quite a lot harder but it's only when you get up to nine and beyond that you are becoming *specialists*.

Working on numbers patterns with three or more jugglers is very difficult —it's hard enough to match the skill and temperament of two jugglers let alone three or four.

Never forget that **Numbers Juggling** is only one of an infinity of possible approaches to juggling, albeit a very impressive one. If it isn't for you, that's fine. Follow the path that suits you best, invent your own style, and remember that **Numbers Jugglers**, while they may end up capable of feats that nobody else can achieve, are unlikely ever to invent anything truly *new*.

On the other hand, it's very good for your learning muscle to be constantly exercised by attempting the impossible. If you are having a hard time with a three club trick then a short blast with four clubs can blow the cobwebs out of your brain. Even if you don't plan to be a **Numbers Juggler** you should always own at least one more club than you can comfortably manage to juggle just to give yourself the option of pushing yourself to the limit from time to time.

See also **How Many Clubs Should I Buy**, **Zenith and the Art of Pattern Maintenance** and **Zen and the Perfect Juggler**[EBJ].

Numbers Juggling

One Count

In a **One Count Passing Pattern** every single throw is a pass —you throw no selfs at all. It's passing taken to the limit. The **One Count** rhythm is also referred to as **Ultimates** or **Thunder Showers**.

- Stand facing a partner, three clubs each. You do an **Up-Down-Go!** and start to pass. *Every single throw is a tramline pass.* You'll find this pretty difficult at first so here's a few tips that should help.

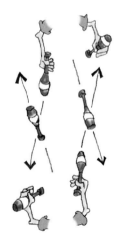

*In the **One Count** your passes should travel from inside to outside, thus avoiding collisions.*

Collisions

Passes should be made from the inside to the outside —your pass should travel *inside* your partner's pass to you. Also, the final destination of your pass should be 'wide' of your partner's shoulder by a few inches.

Limp lefts

Jugglers with a right-handed bias can find that their left hand passes tend to be weak and limp in the ambidextrous **One Count** .

A good tip is to focus strongly on the target points of your throws, switching your attention from right to left as you juggle. Like the Zen archer you should be completely focused on the 'target' of your actions, not on the motion of hand and arm that produces the throw.

Poor timing

The **One Count** is similar to the **Four Club Fountain** in that the two sides of the pattern are quite independent. This can result in one side being juggled at a different speed to the other which is almost always a disaster. Timing is controlled by the heights of your throws, so while you shift your focus from left to right you should also be imagining your passes rising to consistent heights. Floating them a little higher than normal passes will slow the **One Count** down and make it a more manageable pattern.

It's their fault, my end is fine!

Nonsense. This is the worst attitude you can possibly have when passing clubs. A **One Count** is not an occasional exchange of props between two individual patterns, it is a completely interconnected system. Saying that it's the other person's fault is like blaming your left hand for your inability to juggle a **Five Club Cascade**.

Once you have the basic pattern running you can throw **Syncopations** in the **One Count** as with other rhythms. Being symmetrical, any trick that can be thrown on one side can be thrown on the other as well.

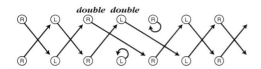

double double

•Diagonal **Double** passes are possible, though you must throw *two in immediate succession*. Effectively you are throwing two **Late Doubles** in a row.

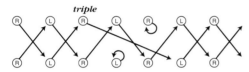

triple

•Tramline **Triple** passes are also allowable, on either side of the pattern at any time. After you throw a **Triple** pass the throwing hand *waits* to be cued by a pass from your partner before throwing again.

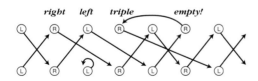

right   left   triple   empty!

•The **Right-Left-Triple** combination also works in a **One Count**. You throw it exactly as you would in a **Two Count**, the two **Doubles** and the **Triple** are thrown on three consecutive beats. Don't be confused

by the backward pointing arrow in the **Causal Diagram**, it just means that the right hand ends up empty for a beat!

•You can tack a **Quad** onto the end of the **Right-Left-Triple** sequence if you like. If you do this you'll find that four clubs end up on the right hand side of the pattern, so your first throw after the **Quad** will be a right to left **Single** *self* which will restore the pattern's balance. Sounds complicated? —not really, your juggler's instinct will guide you through this one!

•If you should **Drop** a club in a **One Count** one side of the pattern will 'freeze' because there are only two clubs left in it. You need to manœuvre yourselves so that the dropped club lies below an idle hand before making the **Pickup**.

An alternative strategy, if you don't want to move your pattern, is to move the **Gap** from one side to the other by throwing a **Late Double** or an **Early Double**.

•A very popular variation on the **One Count** is to juggle the pattern with *simultaneous*, rather than *alternate* throws. None of the **Syncopations** for the regular **One Count** can be used in this pattern.

•Instead you can play around with making simultaneous tramline **Double** passes instead of **Singles**.

•Alternatively, throw two simultaneous self **Doubles** instead of passes, effectively going into a **Four Club Synch Doubles** for one throw.

•One very elegant combination is for both jugglers to throw two self **Doubles** followed by two **Double** passes every time.

See also **One Count Feed**, **Seven Club One Count**.

One Count

One Count Feed

One Counts are **Passing Patterns** in which *every throw is a pass*. Here's a nine club, three person **Feed** pattern in which the feeder juggles a **One Count** while the fed jugglers juggle **Two Counts**.

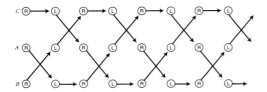

*A **Causal Diagram** of the **One Count Feed**. The feeder (**A**) is represented by the central row, and feeds **B** and **C**, who juggle **Two Counts**.*

•Arrange yourselves in the standard vee formation for a **Feed** with three clubs each. There are two possible ways of juggling the feed, depending on whether the feeder juggles *'ins'* or *'outs'* (see **Triangle**). In either case one of the fed jugglers will be passing a *right-handed* **Two Count** while the other works *left-handed*.

•Some **Syncopations** are possible but you should avoid any **Late** passes as these are guaranteed to crash the pattern. The **Early Double** and **Early Triple** should keep the feeder on their toes!

One Eighty

A **One Eighty** is a half **Pirouette**, the juggler turns through *one hundred and eighty degrees* while juggling. You can turn a **One Eighty** with one, two, or a whole **Flash** of clubs in the air above you.

•The easiest **One Eighty** is thrown from a **Three Club Cascade** and begins with a right self **Double**. While this club is in the air you turn about-face to your right, then catch it and resume the **Cascade**.

Note that the right 'self' **Double** was not actually a 'self' at all because it ended up in

your *left* hand as a result of your turning underneath it. It's rather like **Back to Back** passing, except that you are passing to *yourself.*

•Most jugglers find it easiest to turn to the *right* when throwing from the right hand but to add a little more elegance to the move you should turn to the *left*, and by concentrating on your footwork you can make the **One Eighty** into a very neat piece of choreography.

Start your practice with just one club in your right hand. Step forward with your right foot and simultaneously throw the right self **Double** while turning (on your toes) to the *left*. Catch the club when you are facing in the opposite direction (your left foot is forwards now). This move is quite giddying on the first attempt but after a few tries it starts to make sense. When it's solid you can start working it into a **Three Club Cascade**. Notice that the club is thrown straight up —not backwards over your shoulder. Turning *away* from the **Double** like this ensures that you actually do make it through one hundred and eighty degrees and keeps everything neat. Make sure you practise the mirror image too!

•You'll notice that the **Double** is caught as a **Reverse Spin** as a result of your about-face. It's quite neat to use a **Reverse Spin** throw to initiate the move, which is then caught with *normal* spin.

•Try executing a **One Eighty** that's started with an **Over the Shoulder** throw instead of a normal **Double**, or, even better, use a **Flourish** followed by **Over the Shoulder** as the lead throw.

•A radical alternative is to throw *all three* clubs into the air, as for a **Flash Pirouette**, and turn one hundred and eighty degrees underneath them. Note that in this move instead of using three *crossing* **Triples** you'll need to throw the clubs *vertically* —so they don't cross at all.

*When throwing a three club **Flash Pirouette** (a full 360 degree turn) the clubs cross, but for a **One Eighty** they go straight up.*

•An easier alternative (and for some reason a trick that's rarely seen) is to throw just *two* of the three clubs as vertical **Triples** and make the turn.

•Four club jugglers can do a nice **One Eighty** when juggling with simultaneous throws. Juggle **Four Club Synch Doubles** and toss a pair of clubs high, as **Triples**. Turn a **One Eighty** before making the catch.

See also **Flash Pirouette**.

One-Up Two-Up

Here's a good trick to work on as soon as you can juggle a competent **Three Club Cascade** and have started dabbling with **Doubles**.

It's the same trick as **One-Up Two-Up**[ERJ] for ball juggling but is made a little more tricky by the added dimension of **Spin**. First one club is thrown up through the middle of the pattern with a **Double** spin, then the other two clubs are simultaneously thrown on each side of the pattern, also with **Double Spins**.

•Assuming that you are a beginner, I'd recommend that you spend a little time getting used to throwing two simultaneous **Doubles**. Start with one club in each hand and toss them both up at the same time, aiming to get their flight paths to match

One-Up Two-Up...

perfectly. Each club falls back into the throwing hand. These throws should rise about as high as your arms can reach upwards.

•Now try the whole trick from a cold start. Take two clubs in the right hand and one in the left. The first throw is a **Double** from the right hand straight up the middle. When this peaks you throw the other two clubs, one on each side, also with **Double Spins**. Now catch the first club in your right hand again.

As the pair of **Doubles** peak you throw the first club again, as a **Double**, in between the descending pair. Now catch everything and you are back where you started.

For a beginner this can take quite a lot of getting used to, all those **Double** spins, simultaneous throws and collision problems. Don't force the issue, if it just seems too hard then have patience, try the first exercise again, do some simpler **Double** spin practice and try it again tomorrow. You will get there in the end.

•When you have succeeded with throwing a **One-Up Two-Up** from a cold start you can try to juggle the move from a running **Three Club Cascade**. You'll note that the previous exercise is actually *One-Up Two-Up One-Up*. The extra *One-Up* on the end of the move is not strictly necessary, it's just a lot easier that way. The secret of the trick is to get a good separation in height between the normal **Singles** of the cascade and the **Doubles** of the **One-Up Two-Up**.

Theory dictates that **Doubles** should rise to two and a quarter the height of **Singles** but the height to which a spinning club rises is very difficult to judge. A good guide is to set the ceiling of a **Single's** airspace to the level of the top of your head, and a **Double's** airspace to the height you can reach to with arm raised and fingers outstretched. Once you can juggle a solid **One-Up Two-Up** from a running cascade you should let your natural sense of rhythm be your guide to the height of your throws.

•Next you should go for continuous **One-Up Two-Ups**. You'll notice that when you do this you are really juggling **Two in One Hand** in your right hand while the left hand tags along for the ride. Work on juggling the 'middle' club with alternate

hands in the interests of symmetry and ambidexterity.

•You can then start to play games with the 'middle' club by altering its route through the pattern, for a start, it doesn't have to be thrown up the middle at all. You can throw it on the far right with the right hand, and on the far left with the left hand or even run it around the other two clubs in a figure of eight.

•If you are a more advanced juggler you can try throwing the 'middle' club as a **Back Cross** on each throw.

•By throwing the paired clubs as **Triples** for one throw, instead of **Doubles** you should be able to put a full pirouette into the pattern while holding the third club.

One-Up Two-Up is excellent practice for those who intend to move on to **Four Club Juggling**.

Oral Six

Dreadful name, great trick. In **Oral Six** a full set of six clubs are slammed across a **Passing Pattern** one after another from a mouth grip.

•Juggle a six-club **Two Count** with your partner and place an incoming pass into your mouth with your left hand. Your teeth grip the handle and the club's nose points to the right.

Now slam the club, **Tennis** style, with the club in your right hand so that it travels to your partner as a **Flat** pass. You *must* loosen the grip of your teeth just beforehand!

When you can do this with *every* incoming club you are juggling **Oral Six**.

Thanks to 'Gentlemen Jugglers', Rod & John for this one!

Over the Shoulder

Easier than **Behind the Back**, harder than standing on one leg; an **Over the Shoulder** throw is usually a right to right, or left to left **Double** that turns with **Reverse Spin**.

•Practise the throw with just one club until you start to get a feel for where it is heading. Use a **Double** spin.

The beginner tends to look to the *side* when throwing **Over the Shoulder**, trying to keep an eye on its whole flight. The expert looks *up*, waiting for the club to appear out of nowhere.

•Now add some **Over the Shoulder** throws to your **Three Club Cascade**. They fit into the pattern just like self **Doubles**, the pattern 'freezes' for a moment, waiting for the club to drop back in.

•If you can **Flourish** a club you'll find that an **Over the Shoulder** throw can be tacked onto the end of the **Flourish** creating a very spectacular move.

•You can make a *very* low and tight **Over the Shoulder** if you begin the move with a **Wrong End** catch and give the club **One and a Half** spins instead of a **Double**. The club practically wraps itself around your shoulder, missing it by millimetres.

Because the throw is so low it arrives back in the throwing hand very quickly, you need to keep the other two clubs out of the way during the move by juggling a couple of throws of **Two in One Hand** in your left hand while throwing the trick in the right.

•Highly skilled four club jugglers can throw **Over the Shoulder** in a **Four Club Fountain**.

See also **Behind the Back, Under the Arm, Under the Leg**, and **Slapover**.

Over the Shoulder

Over the Top

Over the Top for the club juggler is not quite the same animal as **Over the Top**[EBJ] for the ball juggler.

In both cases an object is thrown right over the top of the juggling pattern but the club juggler uses *side spin* to achieve this so it feels very different.

•Begin with just one club, held in the right hand. Hold the club with your palm upwards and the nose pointing away from you to the right. Now toss the club upwards (the action is *almost* as if you were going to hit yourself on the head with it) and allow it to make a **Double** spin before being caught in your left hand. The club falls into a very satisfying catch in the left hand.

The **Over the Top** throw has opposite spin to the **Dip** throw.

•Having learned the basic throw you should try all the possible combinations of **Over the Top** throws in the **Three Club Cascade**; every right, every left, same club every time and finally, every club on every throw.

•An interesting pattern results from making continuous **Over the Top** throws from the right hand with throwing continuous **Dips** from the left. Use **Single** spin **Dips** and **Double** spin **Over the Top** throws for this.

Overhead Feed

Before juggling this pattern you need to assemble three jugglers, nine clubs and a little experience with the **Double Return** technique. The **Overhead Feed** is pretty much like a normal three person, nine club **Feed** except that the three jugglers stand in a line, instead of the normal vee formation and so some of the passes need to be made over the head of the juggler in the middle. It's a right-handed passing pattern.

•I'll call the three positions in the pattern the *feeder*, *Piggy-in-the-Middle* and the *Backstop*.

*The setup for an **Overhead Feed**.*

The feeder stands facing *Piggy-in-the-Middle* and the *Backstop*. The feeder starts with four clubs, *Piggy* gets three and the *Backstop* gets two.

The feeder will be juggling a **Two Count**, passing alternately to the other two jugglers —**Singles** to *Piggy* and **Doubles** (over *Piggy's* head) to the *Backstop*.

Piggy will be juggling a **Four Count**, passing singles to the feeder.

The *Backstop* juggles a **Four Count**, passing **Doubles** over *Piggy's* head to the feeder.

The start is simple. The feeder leads with a **Double** to the *Backstop* followed by a **Single** to *Piggy* and then just keeps on feeding the two jugglers.

As far as *Piggy* is concerned this is just a regular **Feed** except that passes are whizzing low overhead in a potentially threatening manner. For the *Backstop* it's slightly different, they are playing **Double Returns** with the feeder —the feeder *leads* and they *follow*.

•This pattern is identical in layout to a **Dropback Line** and you can switch from one to the other easily as long as you all

rehearse the change. It's the *Backstop* who leads the change, and you all need to know what's happening. The *Backstop* starts to count off passes, 'one - two - *three!*' Everybody does something slightly different on '*three!*' so here's the 'script'.

BACKSTOP: On '*three!*' the *Backstop* 'steals the lead' of the **Double Return** pattern* they are juggling with the feeder.

PIGGY: On the beat right *after* the '*three!*' *Piggy* throws their first **Dropback** to the *Backstop* and they then find themselves juggling a **Double Return** follow**.

THE FEEDER: The '*three!*' is the feeder's cue to stop passing to the *Backstop* and just pass **Singles** to *Piggy*.

That's it! From **Overhead Feed** to **Dropback Line** in three easy steps. There's nothing technically awesome about this change, it's just a matter of a little rehearsal and well worth it for the gasps of awe you'll get when you perform it.

---

*If you're not sure what 'stealing the lead' means then look up **Double Return**.

Likewise, a 'follow' is a bit of **Double Return talk that makes perfect sense when you can do it, moreover it isn't very hard to do!

Overhead Throws

Making an **Overhead Throw** is like throwing a **Tomahawk** to yourself. It takes a good deal of control to throw over your head accurately but the results can be spectacular.

•If you juggle a **Three Club Cascade** making every single throw an **Overhead Throw** you end up juggling the cascade completely over your head. Your arms get *very* tired when practising this!

Continued overleaf...

Overhead Throws...

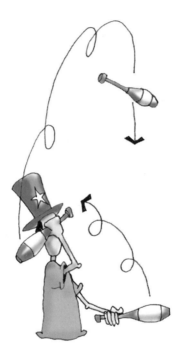

• A very slow and lazy **Half Shower** can be juggled with three clubs, use **Triple** spin **Overhead Throws** from the right hand and normal **Double** spins from the left. As your right hand completes each **Overhead Throw** the **Double** from your left hand should be floating in a perfect catching position.

Pass-Pass-Self

Here's a **Passing Pattern** rhythm that doesn't fit into the **One Count**, **Two Count**, **Three Count** scheme of things. It's 33% short of a **One Count** in that *two throws out of three* are passes. It's sometimes given the more long-winded name *Right-Left-Self-Left-Right-Self* and it can be used for six club passing, **Feed** patterns and **Seven Club Passing**.

• Stand facing a partner, three clubs each. All passes are tramline passes, every throw is a **Single** and you both juggle identical throws in time with each other. Starting together you each make a *right* hand pass, followed by a *left* hand pass, followed by a right to left *self*. Then you throw a *left* hand pass, followed by a *right* hand pass and then a left to right *self*. Thus the count is:

Pass - Pass - Self - Pass - Pass - Self..

—hence the name. This is excellent ambidextrous passing practice and a good deal easier and more balanced than the awesome **One Count**.

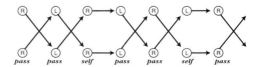

Because of the complex six beat rhythm few jugglers know what **Syncopations** are possible in **Pass-Pass-Self** or when to throw them. The best way to find out is to work them out for yourself, but here, to get you started, are the basics. Bear in mind that the pattern is symmetrical so that any trick that can be thrown on the *right* can also be thrown on the *left* three beats later on. In each of the following **Causal Diagrams** it's the juggler represented by the top row that is throwing the trick in question.

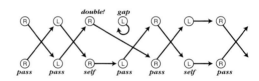

• An **Early Double** pass is easy to make. You throw a diagonal **Double** pass on any *self* beat. You then get a **Gap** in your pattern:

You need to concentrate on the count here, especially if you throw a whole series of these **Doubles** and even more especially if your partner is throwing them back to you!

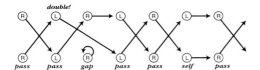

double!

pass · pass · gap · pass · pass · self · pass

•A **Late Double** can be made on any beat immediately before the *self* beat, that's *pass* - **Double** - *self*. Your partner gets the **Gap** this time.

Once again, you must keep the basic count running in your head. The most likely cause of a drop will be confusion rather than technical difficulty.

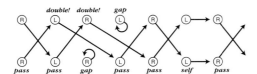

double! double! gap

pass · pass · gap · pass · pass · self · pass

•Two consecutive diagonal **Double** passes can be made, starting on the second *pass* beat. Here you are throwing a **Late Double** immediately followed by an **Early Double**.

•You can tack a tramline **Triple** pass onto the end of that last move if you wish creating a sort of **Right-Left-Triple!** combination. You need to **Feed** a club across your pattern after the move to get back into **Pass-Pass-Self**.

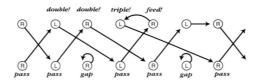

double! double! triple! feed!

pass · pass · gap · pass · pass · gap · pass

The count runs:

*Pass - **Double** - **Double** - **Triple** - **Feed** - Self...*

As usual the Doubles are diagonal passes and the **Triples** are tramline passes and once again you must keep the basic rhythm of the pattern going so that *after* the trick you are still juggling to the same scheme as your partner.

•You can throw an **Early Triple** on its own if you wish

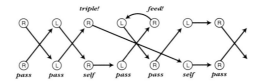

triple! feed!

pass · pass · self · pass · pass · self · pass

Throw it on the *self* beat and then you have to fix your pattern a couple of beats later with a **Feed** as before:

*Pass - Pass - **Triple** - Pass - **Feed** - Self*

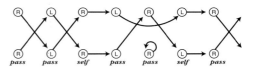

pass · pass · self · pass · pass · self · pass

•A *self* **Double** can be thrown on the first *pass* beat, creating a **Gap** in your partner's pattern due to the missed pass.

* * *

And so on, the possibilities are infinite as usual and you are not going to learn them all from a book. Practise a few of these variations and you will start to get a *feel* for what is possible and what is not. Juggling is not something that you do to a recipe —it's about developing intuitive understanding and *feel* —and that comes only with practical experience.

•The **Pass-Pass-Self** rhythm can be used by the feeder in a three person, nine club **Feed** in which the fed jugglers work **Three Counts**. Developments on this theme lead to such interesting patterns as **Hovey's Nightmare** and other exotica.

Continued Overleaf...

Pass-Pass-Self

• The **Pass-Pass-Self** rhythm can also be used to juggle *seven* clubs between two jugglers.

You start with four clubs, two in each hand. Your partner starts with three, two in the *left* hand and one in the right.

You juggle **Pass-Pass-Self**, throwing each pass as a diagonal **Double** while your partner starts passing one beat later (from the left hand) and throws a curious mixture of throws. The basic scheme is **Pass-Pass-Self** like yours but the first pass is a *tramline* **Single** and the second pass is a *diagonal* **Double** and then an ordinary self is thrown.

Complicated? You bet, but it certainly works because I've *done* it!

Pass-Pass-Self as the rhythm for a two-person, seven-club pattern.

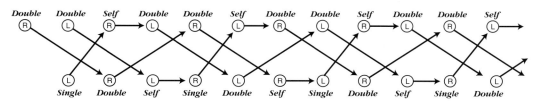

Passing Patterns

The ball juggler thrives on *three ball tricks*, for it's here that the scope for invention and creativity is the greatest. For the club juggler it's **Passing Patterns** that fulfil the same role.

Passing clubs is partly a game, and partly entertainment but most of all it's a social activity and one of the world's most enjoyable non-competitive sports.

When you juggle balls it's far easier to catch one of your own throws than it is to catch a pass, not so with clubs! The handles allow you to catch a pass just as easily as a self throw and so it is that club jugglers have discovered that one of the best ways to add to the complexity and intricacy of their juggling is to add more *jugglers* to their patterns.

You simply *must* learn to pass clubs. Here are some tips together with pointers to other relevant sections of the COMPENDIUM.

• Begin by learning to make a simple pass to another juggler. You need just one club for this. Stand face to face with your partner, about three paces apart holding a club in your right hand.

Swing the club downward, *past* your leg and make a throw, aiming a little to the right of your partner's shoulder. The club turns a **Single** spin (and a little bit more) and is caught upright in your partner's left hand.

Make sure that you do actually swing the club past your leg as you make the throw, it's a common mistake to try and make the throw from *in front* of your thigh. A good pass is a very lazy and relaxed move.

Toss the club back and forth until you both feel comfortable with the basic pass. Don't forget to try some left hand passes as well.

•Now you can add some more clubs. You start with three, and you juggle a **Three Club Cascade** while your partner holds two clubs, one in each hand, and waits.

When you feel ready toss one of your clubs to your partner, as a **Single** spin pass, which causes them to start juggling a **Three Club Cascade** while *you* wait.

They then pass back (when they feel ready) and you can keep going like this, all afternoon if you like, to get your basic passing skills honed.

•Having familiarised yourselves with the basic pass you can move on to useful exercises like **Three Around**, a good basic practice pattern that can be juggled either right or left handed, and the **Five Club One Count**, ambidextrous but also easy.

•These basic exercises completed, you are ready to start work with six clubs. Both of you juggle three clubs (in time with each other) and at agreed intervals you make a pass to each other instead of throwing to yourselves.

Standard passing pattern routines have names like **One Count**, **Two Count**, **Three Count** and so on. A **Two Count** is a routine in which you both juggle in time making

every *second* throw a pass. In a **Three Count** every *third* throw is a pass and so on.

Most beginners start their serious club-passing work with the **Four Count**, commonly known as **Every Others**. Because of its even count, this pattern is usually juggled *right-handed* which is a bit of a shame because it doesn't teach your left hand very much. For more balanced practice you should use the **Three Count**.

•As you develop your passing skills you will learn different routines, including oddities like **Pass-Pass-Self** in which two throws out of three are passes. You'll also learn to juggle multi-person patterns like **Feeds**, **Boxes**, **Triangles** and **Stars**. And then there are the **Syncopations**, 'off-beat' throws that play with the timing of the routine you are juggling, and the mad throws, twiddly bits, jokes, visual trickery and more and more and more!

See also all entries with **Causal Diagrams** in them.

Penguin Catch

The **Penguin**[EBJ] is a ball juggling trick in which the juggler's hands are turned outward for each catch in a **Three Ball Cascade**[EBJ] (the awkward way) like a penguin.

A similar catching style is possible for the club juggler.

•To make a **Penguin Catch** you hang your right arm down and turn your wrist anti-clockwise as far as it will go. Now toss a club from your left hand and catch it in this position.

The club ends up in a **Reverse Grip**. If you now raise it to shoulder height you'll find that it's in the perfect position for a **Fish** pass. Alternatively you can **Flourish** the club back into a **Normal Grip**.

•It is probably possible to juggle three clubs so that *every* catch is a **Penguin Catch**, but only complete fanatics would attempt it (don't you just *love* a challenge!)

•The sequence: **Penguin Catch - Fish** pass is an awesome trick to throw in a **Passing Pattern**.

*A **Fish** pass, being made coincidentally with a 'radical fish' juggling club.*

Philadelphia Line

The **Philadelphia Line** is a club-passing formation of four jugglers. Call them A, B, C and D. They stand in line so that everyone faces into the middle.

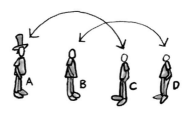

•Usually A and C pass to each other, while B and D pass to each other, all the passes are **Doubles** so that they fly over the heads of B and C in the middle.

•I've seen many different routines juggled in a **Philadelphia Line**, starting with simple **Four Counts** and **Two Counts** and **Three Three Tens** and moving on up to exotic routines in which B and C execute **One Eighties** and passes fly every which way, including long **Triples** from A to D and **Back to Back** passes from B to C.

Don't ignore the possibilities of interlocking two seven club patterns (or **Staggered Doubles**) or adding two more jugglers for a *six-person* **Philadelphia Line**. Four jugglers can spend a very productive and worthwhile afternoon working out a routine based on these ideas. There's some special magic that makes a well-juggled **Philadelphia Line** a one hundred percent guaranteed hit in a live show —there aren't many tricks like that!

Pickups

Often you will be juggling and a club will hit the floor —I say this with the absolute certainty of experience. Non-juggling bystanders may quip, "Ooh look, you've dropped one!", but poor fools, how little they know!

If you happen to be passing when the **Drop** occurs the main thing is to *keep going* and manipulate the **Gap** in the pattern until it arrives at the hand best placed to pick up the dropped club.

Gaps move fastest if you are **Holding Through the Gap** so that will be your normal procedure. In a two person pattern it usually only takes a few seconds for the **Gap** to circumnavigate the pattern. In a large **Feed** it can take quite a while. Just remember that everything will be fine as long as all the jugglers keep their heads and remain slaves to the rhythm.

•In the six club **Four Count (Every Others)** you'll find that **Holding through the Gap** leaves you juggling for four beats and waiting for four beats alternately:

Two-three-four-Pass-**wait**-**wait**-**wait**-**wait**

Those *waits* are you opportunity to move yourself close to the dropped club, ideally so that it lies on the floor under your

right hand and prepare for the **Pickup**.

When the opportunity arrives for the **Pickup** you grab the club off the floor and launch it back across to your partner on the *pass* beat, just as if you were starting the pattern with a **Fast Start**.

If you are new to the art of recovering from **Drops** in passing patterns then I must say two things to you now of great importance:

1. This is where the fun *really* starts.

2. Never forget the **Golden Rules of Club Passing** (unless you *want* to get a club in your eye).

Continued overleaf...

Pickups...

Executing a **Pickup** so that you end up holding two clubs in one hand for a moment may be the easiest method but it's also a bit of a cheat. You should learn to do a *Flying* **Pickup** instead. You can practise this one solo.

•Juggle a **Three Club Cascade** and deliberately drop a club (harder to do than you might expect!). Keep the pattern going with the remaining two clubs while you bend down and pick up the dropped club in mid-juggle.

•You can apply the same technique to the **Pickup** in the **Four Count**. Start by **Holding through the Gap** until you are in position for the **Pickup** (right hand over the dropped club). Now lead your juggling by making a *self* throw from the right on the *three* beat, immediately pick up the dropped club and pass it to your partner. The pattern is restored.

•If you **Drop** in a **Three Count** or a **One Count** you'll find that the **Gap** gets locked onto one side of the pattern or the other. You and your partner need to move until the **Gap** is on the same side of the pattern as the dropped club *before* making a **Pickup**.

•In **Two Count** passing patterns, whether for six, seven or more clubs, it's usual *not* to **Hold through the Gap**. This is because the **Gap** travels around the pattern fast enough anyway.

Quite a high level of skill is required here because it's very awkward to look down and find the floored club at the same time as keeping the rest of the pattern going. In fact with seven clubs (juggled on **Staggered Doubles**) it's impossible! At the precise instant of the **Pickup** you need to be looking *up* to watch one of your partner's passes to you. If you don't do this all you'll achieve is another **Drop**. The secret is to wait until your partner is passing you the **Gap** (i.e. missing a throw) and take that opportunity to look down at the club on the floor.

Look at the club and fix its position in your mind, and a few beats later, when the **Gap** arrives at your right hand you reach for it *blind*, grab it and throw it to your partner.

See also **Seven Club Pickup**.

Popcorn

Of all the seven club passing patterns for two jugglers, this is my favourite. **Triples**, **Doubles** and **Singles** are intermingled into a complex airborne tapestry of spin and synchronisation.

The pattern is a *six count* in which the two jugglers pass out of synch. Every left hand throw is a **Single** self while the right hands juggle **Triples**, **Doubles** and **Singles**. Each juggler's count is a repeating sequence of six throws:

Triple^{SELF} and Double^{PASS} and Single^{SELF} and ...

•Stand facing your partner, you start with four clubs to their three.

You start juggling first, leading off with the **Triple** self (as if you were starting a solo **Triple-Singles** pattern). Your next right hand throw is the **Double** pass and that in turn is followed by your **Single** self. Now just keep juggling that sequence.

Your partner waits until your **Double** pass is halfway over (in true seven club passing style) and then starts their sequence with their self **Triple**. You both end up juggling exactly the same sequence of throws staggered in time by three beats. It's vitally important that you both stay in time and juggle your **Triples**, **Doubles** and **Singles** to the correct heights. Counting the sequence out loud is *not* a good idea since you are working 'out of time' and you'll just end up confusing each other.

• Plenty of practice with seven clubs juggled on **Staggered Doubles** and solo work on the four club **Triple-Singles** pattern will develop the skills you need to master **Popcorn**.

• The solo four club pattern **Five-Three-Four** is strikingly similar to **Popcorn** in its mixed use of **Triples**, **Doubles** and **Singles** and I have used it as the basis for two *eight-club* versions of **Popcorn**.

In the first, you and a partner stand face to face and juggle **Five-Three-Four** patterns in time making each **Triple** a tramline pass to your partner. This is a **Three Count** since every *third* throw is a pass.

• Really adventurous jugglers can upgrade this to a **Pass-Pass-Self** rhythm by throwing both the **Triples** and **Doubles** as passes.

See also **Five-Three-Four**.

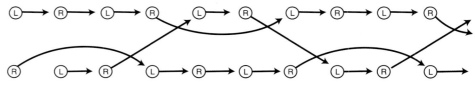

*Seven club **Popcorn**, a six count. The standard pattern.*

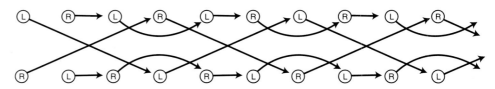

*Eight club **Popcorn**, a three count. Seriously advanced stuff!*

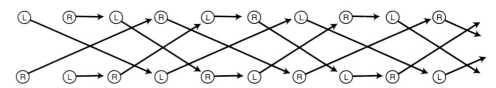

*Eight club **Popcorn**, using the **Pass-Pass-Self** rhythm. World class passing!*

Quad

Shortspeak for *Quadruple*. A **Quad** is so-called by club jugglers because they would normally make the throw with *four spins*.

In practice there is a fair degree of chance involved. An intended quadruple spin may land after anything from three to five spins (including all of the intermediate half-spin combinations).

A **Quad** usually equates to a throw with *five beats* of airtime (which is useful to know if you are messing around with **Ladder Notation**) and its **SiteSwap** number is **6**. In **Causal Diagrams** a **Quad** appears as an arrow moving *four beats* along the chart.

Throwing reliable **6**'s or **Quads** is the upper limit of most club jugglers' ability. Throws of this weight are used for juggling difficult patterns like **Three in One Hand** and **Six-Three-Three**.

Most of the interesting work with **Syncopations** in **Passing Patterns** happens at the lower and easier levels of **Doubles** and **Triples**, there are very few who are adept with **Quads**.

Quin

The **Quin** lies at the outer reaches of club juggling. Once you go beyond the **Quad** in the hierarchy of club juggling throws the talk tends to turn to that of *five-spin*, *six-spin* and *seven-spin* rather than *quintuple*, *sextuple* and *septuple*.

A **Quin** is a throw with *six beats* of airtime and is referred to in **SiteSwap Notation** as a **7**. Throws of this weight are used in the **Seven Club Cascade** which hardly anyone ever learns to juggle. As always it's the *airtime* that's really important when talking about throw weights and you'll find that seven club jugglers will, most often, use *three* spins, when juggling the **Seven Club Cascade**.

You'll rarely see jugglers throwing **Quins** as **Syncopations** in **Passing Patterns** simply because it's so hard to control throws of this power.

One practical use for a throw of this weight is described under **Triple-Singles** where a *wild high one* is thrown out of the regular **Triple-Singles** pattern.

You can also juggle five clubs in a **Half Shower** by using constant **Quins** from one hand and **Singles** from the other.

Random Feed

The **Random Feed** is a **Passing Pattern** based on the same principle as the **Ten Club Feed**. It's a pattern for three or more jugglers. You work with three clubs per juggler and one more 'for luck'.

For a three person **Random Feed** you'll need ten clubs, for four jugglers you'll need thirteen and for five you would need sixteen.

Every pass in the **Random Feed** is a **Double**, just like the **Ten Club Feed**. The big difference is that the 'firing order' of the pattern is *random*. The feeder fires off passes *in any order they like*.

This works because the passes are staggered; you don't have to pass back until the feeder's pass is halfway over to you. It's all about reaction times and keeping your eyes open.

•Arrange yourselves in a **Feed** layout. The feeder starts with four clubs and everybody else gets three.

The most reliable start is for the feeder to start passing seven clubs, on **Staggered Doubles** to one juggler while everybody else waits. Then, with no warning, the feeder starts to swing the passes up and down the line to the fed jugglers completely at random.

• Standing on the receiving end, you wait until the first pass approaches and respond with a **Double** then keep juggling to the overall tempo of the pattern, passing back to the feeder every time they pass to you.

It's perfectly OK for the feeder to send two or more consecutive passes to the same person.

Try it, you'll love it!

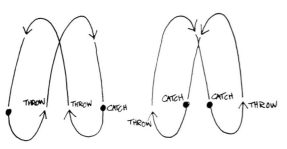

Cascade and *Reverse Cascade*.

Reverse Cascade

Ball jugglers are familiar with the **Reverse Cascade**[EBJ] of three balls which is a time-reversed version of the **Three Ball Cascade**[EBJ].

In the three ball **Reverse Cascade** every throw is made **Over the Top**[EBJ]. If you were to play a film of a **Reverse Cascade** *backwards* then you would find that it looked exactly like a normal **Cascade**.

The **Reverse Cascade** is not a pattern that club jugglers have a lot of use for because it's very unnatural to juggle with clubs and more difficult than the visual effect justifies.

• Take three clubs and juggle a **Three Club Cascade** making every throw *over* the previous one instead of *under*. It feels very awkward but it can be done.

• That pattern was *almost* a perfect **Reverse Cascade** but for complete time-reversal you would need to juggle the pattern with **Reverse Spin**.

If you do this then you will immediately become a legendary figure. The trouble is, only *jugglers* will appreciate the trick!

Reverse Grip

The **Reverse Grip** is simply another way of holding a juggling club. This might sound trivial but by concentrating on subtle variations like this amazing new tricks can be invented.

• Toss a club into the air with a **Single** spin and catch it with your hand in a palm downward position. The club lands between your thumb and forefinger in a position similar to way you hold a pen (the fat end is the 'nib').

This is the **Reverse Grip**. It's the catch you make if you are going to **Flourish** a club. The action of **Flourishing** returns the club to a **Normal Grip**.

• If you point the knob of a **Reverse Gripped** club forwards you'll find that it is in a **Wrong End** grip. To return the club to a **Normal Grip** from here you could use a *half* or *one and a half* spin toss.

See also **Flourish** and **Penguin Catch**.

Reverse Spin

Most throws made by a club juggler turn with normal spin —the far end of the club moves up, while the near end is moving down. This rotation matches the rotation of the human arm as it throws the club upwards and so it is the most natural and easy direction to work with. The opposite of this is **Reverse Spin**, the near end goes up as the far end goes down. This is a less natural way of tossing a club.

• Juggling a **Three Club Cascade** with **Reverse Spin** is awkward but perfectly possible. The rotation is applied to each club by pulling back on the handle with the fingers at the moment of release. Build up to the full **Reverse Spin** pattern by trying all the combinations; a right, a left, *every*

right, *every* left, same club every time and finally *every club on every throw*.

• With practice you can throw **Doubles** and **Triples** with opposite rotation too. An occasional **Reverse Spin** in a **Four Club Fountain** adds plenty of visual spice.

• When you pass clubs, standing face to face with your partner, the clubs in your pattern turn in the opposite direction to your partner's, so every normal pass arrives as a **Reverse Spin**.

This is why passes are caught high with the handle swinging *up* into your hand, rather than low, with the handle swinging *down* into your hand.

• **Over the Shoulder** throws and **Tomahawks** are also **Reverse Spin** throws, but when thrown in a passing pattern they'll arrive with normal spin. They should therefore be aimed to be caught *low*, in the normal solo catching position rather than *high* like regular passes.

• My favourite **Reverse Spin** trick is a quick backwards flip executed with a club that would otherwise just be held in the hand for a moment —a kind of miniature **Flourish**.

Juggle a **Three Club Cascade** and throw a left self **Double**. This gives you time to execute a **Reverse Spin** flip in the right hand before resuming the cascade.

•You can build the trick up into a complete pattern so that you first throw a left **Double** and a right flip, followed by a right **Double** and a left flip.

•An extension to this is to throw a right to left **Triple** which gives you time to execute *two* **Reverse Spin flips**, one in each hand, before the **Triple** is caught again.

This rather difficult move will hone your **Reverse Spin** flipping skills to such a level that you'll be able to put them into your juggling at every available opportunity without even having to think about it.

See also **Having Problems?** and **HopStop**[EBJ].

Right-Left-Triple!

The **Right-Left-Triple** is a combination of three **Syncopations** thrown one after the other in a **Passing Pattern**. The juggler throws two diagonal **Double** passes and finishes the move off with a high tramline **Triple** pass.

With only slight modifications this trick can be thrown in the **Four Count**, the **Two Count** and even the **One Count**. In each case the move starts on the *pass* beat.

Before attempting the **Right-Left-Triple** you'll need to be able to throw reasonable **Late Doubles**, **Early Doubles** and **Early Triples** —these are the throws that make up the trick.

•In the **Four Count** you throw a **Late Double** on the *pass* beat, followed two beats later by an **Early Double**, and then two beats after that you throw the **Early Triple**. The count goes:

Double[RTR]*-two-three-***Double**[LTL]*-Gap - two-***Triple!**...

You then get a two beat **Gap** before the pattern settles back to normal —enough time to turn a pirouette if you want to!

Concentrate on getting good throw heights, well-aimed passes and, of course, the right amount of spin on each club. It may seem difficult at *your* end of the pattern but your partner actually has to *catch* all of this stuff!

Continued overleaf...

•As with all of the other **Doubles, Triples** and so on, the actual number of spins is not critical, it's the airtime that matters. You can make all three throws as **Flats** if you like, or throw the '**Doubles**' as **Singles** and so on.

•It's perfectly possible to throw the **Right-Left-Triple** combination with each throw made from behind your back, in the style of **Back Crosses**. Possible, but not *easy!*

•Throwing a **Right-Left-Triple** in a **Two Count** is simplicity itself, you lead into the move on the *pass* beat and make the three throws consecutively:

Double^RTR^ - **Double**^LTL^ - **Triple**^RTL^

You end up with your right hand completely empty for a couple of beats after you throw that **Triple.**

•In a three-person, nine-club **Feed** where the feeder is working a **Two Count** against the fed jugglers' **Four Counts**, *anyone* can throw a **Right-Left-Triple** whenever they like. This can get quite frantic but it will work perfectly well as long as everybody keeps to the rhythm of the pattern.

*A **Causal Diagram** of the **Right-Left-Triple!** being thrown in a **Four Count.***

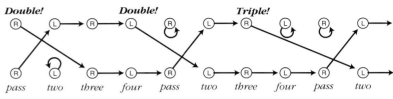

*When a **Right-Left-Triple** is thrown in a **Two Count** your right hand is completely empty for a beat.*

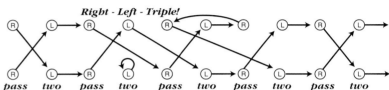

*In a **One Count** the trick is thrown exactly as in a **Two Count**.*

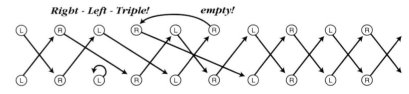

•The **Right-Left-Triple** combination does not fit into the scheme of the **Three Count** for reasons of basic mathematics, though you can still have a lot of fun mixing **Double** and **Triple** passes into this pattern.

•In the **One Count** it does work though —just throw the combination exactly as you would in a **Two Count**. Start with a **Late Double**, immediately follow this with an

Early Double and then follow that with the **Early Triple**. You get an empty hand after the **Triple** and your partner gets a **Gap** in the left hand for a beat.

Because the **One Count** is ambidextrous you can throw the mirror image of the trick —the result is a *Left-Right-Triple!*

•The **Right-Left-Triple** combination can be extended by the addition of a **Quad**, this is a diagonal pass. In a right-handed **Four Count** the extended combination now runs as follows (starting on a *pass* beat):

Double^RTR-two-three-Double^LTL-Gap - two-Triple-Gap-Gap-Quad^LTL...

You get a huge **Gap** after this and a round of applause.

•To throw the **Right-Left-Triple** plus **Quad** combination in a **Two Count** you make all four throws consecutively in one clear blast. Height, accuracy and control of spin are absolutely vital here.

•In a **One Count** the **Quad** can also be added. To avoid crashing the pattern you'll need to juggle a *self* after the **Quad** —your juggler's instinct will guide you here!

•The idea of the **Right-Left-Triple** can also be applied to the seven-club pattern **Staggered Doubles**.

Since the whole pattern runs 'one notch higher' than the six-club **Two Count** (the normal throws are **Doubles** rather than **Triples**) the three throws of the **Right-Left Triple** need to be one notch higher too, so you throw two **Triples** and a **Quad** —that's

a right to right **Triple** immediately followed by a left to left **Triple** and then a right to left **Quad**.

•Yes, you can tack a **Quin** onto the end of that sequence if you wish too.

•A classic **Finish** to a two person club-passing routine is for both jugglers to throw **Right-Left-Triple** combinations at each other simultaneously. Both jugglers make a full pirouette under the last **Triple**. Catch those last two clubs as close the ground as possible!

Robin Hood

Fans of the **Four Count** love to put visual puns into their juggling. Here's an impersonation of the famous rogue of Sherwood Forest to add to your repertoire.

•Toss an **Early Double** to buy a little time at your end of the show. Arrange two clubs in your right hand into the shape of a bow, holding by the knobs so that they point in opposite directions.

Catch your partner's next pass in your left hand and use it as an arrow, drawing it back gradually and then lobbing it as a **Flat** on the next pass beat. If your partner is really hot they might be able to catch the 'arrow' under their arm, fall over and feign an Oscar-winning death. Buskers can use the opportunity for some gags about stealing from the rich (the audience) to give to the poor (your merrie olde selves).

Runarounds

These are **Passing Patterns** in which the jugglers, as well as the clubs they are juggling, move around and change positions.

• A two-person **Runaround** consists of a **Three Club Cascade** that is shared between two jugglers who constantly **Steal** the pattern off each other. It's a naturally comical piece of juggling, especially if the jugglers add a bit of chat and banter as they work the trick.

This is exactly the same as the **Runaround**[EBJ] listed in the ENCYCLOPÆDIA OF BALL JUGGLING except that it is juggled with clubs. You can learn the pattern in slow motion, doing just one throw at a time and then slowly build up to full speed as you become familiar with the sequence.

Grab your partner, take three clubs and name yourselves **A** (The Guy in the Hat) and **B** (the Guy with the shades). Costume is optional.

A starts with two clubs, one in each hand. **B** starts with one club in the right hand and stands *behind* **A**.

1. **B** *throws under A's right arm and...*

2. ...swoops around behind **A** *to catch the club in the left hand.*

3. **A** *throws more or less straight up from the left hand and moves back to make way for* **B** *who...*

4. ...catches the throw in their right hand. (You have now swapped places, **B** *is in front.)*

5. **A** *throws under B's right arm and...*

6. ...swoops around behind **B** *to catch the club in the left hand.*

7. **B** *throws more or less straight up from the left hand and moves back to make way for* **A** *who...*

8. ...catches the throw in their right hand. You are now back at the beginning.

Repeat this sequence, slowly at first, and then build up speed until you find a **Three Club Cascade** floating mysteriously in the air while two mad fools run around each other in circles juggling it.

•A three-person, six-club **Runaround** is quite different but just as much fun..

Arrange yourselves **A**, **B** and **C** as if for a **Feed**. **B** is the feeder, facing **A** on the left and **C** on the right. **A** and **B** start with three clubs each and **C** gets *none*.

A and **B** get the pattern running and set the tempo by juggling a **Two Count** for a few throws while **C** waits.

Suddenly (no warning is required) **B**'s passes 'swing' from **A** to **C** and the **Runaround** has started. **A** is now running out of clubs and **C** is gaining them. When **A** passes their last club they walk (or run) forwards and turn to face **C** who starts to pass clubs to them —suddenly *they* have become the feeder.

The next person to run out of clubs is **B** who, on passing the last club to **C** walks forwards and turns to receive passes from **A** and so it goes around. Everybody passes clubs to the person opposite them on the right, and on running out of clubs dashes over to the *right* of their last pass and turns to receive more clubs. Timing is everything.

•If anyone should **Drop** then the person walking across the pattern should be able to bend down and pick up on their way to their new position.

•You can gain a little extra time for your walk by *not passing the last club* and carrying it with you instead. Acrobatically inclined jugglers can use this extra time to turn a cartwheel as they change position.

•Extending the trick with the addition of a seventh club is quite possible, in this case *everybody* carries the last club on the walk.

Should you want to add an eighth club you'd all better start passing on **Doubles**.

•The **Runaround** can be extended to work with four jugglers, using a **Star** formation with a 'hole' in it. Some call this pattern the **Wandering Star**, others the *Shooting Star*.

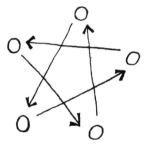

You'd do well to locate a fifth juggler first and practise juggling a fifteen club (three each) **Star** on a **Two Count**. Everybody passes to the person opposite them and to the right and somehow the clubs miss each other in the middle. The point of this exercise is to reinforce in all your minds the importance of keeping a tidy **Star** arrangement and staying in time. That done you can persuade the extra juggler that what you are about to attempt is dangerous, stupid and not-to-be-trifled with. Thanks, goodbye and take your clubs with you!

Runarounds...

Back to business. There are now four of you left and there is a *hole* in the **Star**. Whoever *would* have been passing to the *hole* is to dispose of their clubs —if that's you then you are juggler **X**. The juggler on your immediate *left* is juggler **Y**, everybody else is anonymous and there are just nine clubs in the pattern. You are ready to start.

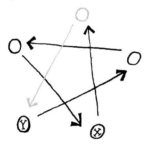

Up-Down-Go! Everybody with clubs starts to pass on a **Two Count** (to the person opposite and to their right).

Juggler **X** (yes you!) is now gaining clubs and juggler **Y** is losing them (because **Y** isn't getting passes from anyone). After three passes **X** (you again) is about to start throwing clubs at the *hole* and meanwhile **Y** has run out of clubs.

Y steps into the middle of the **Star** right after their last pass, narrowly avoiding a club flying from left to right.

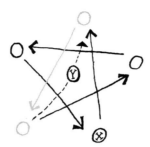

Y then looks to the right to judge the moment of **X**'s first pass into the hole and manages to arrive at the hole position in time to catch it *and* avoid being hit by another club that is flying from right to left.

Y is a very brave person.

The hole has now moved to where **Y** used to be and the whole thing repeats itself two clicks around the **Star** and three passes later. If you manage to get through fifteen passes (everybody has walked once by then) then you are all utter, utter hero-types and I want to be your friend.

Never, ever, forget the **Golden Rules of Club Passing,** especially when juggling patterns as dangerous as this one!

For more strolling stuff see also **Speed Weave** and **W-Feed**.

Scissor Catch

What an elegant finish! The juggler tosses a club high and then catches it by the knob 'scissored' between two other clubs. Thus all three clubs end up in one hand.

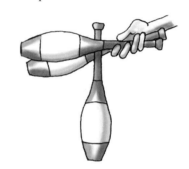

•For a basic right hand **Scissor Catch** you will be forming the 'scissors' with two clubs held in the right hand in a **Circus Grip**. The third club is thrown from the left hand on a **Double** spin and scissored.

Juggle a **Three Club Cascade** and collect two clubs in the right hand in a **Circus Grip**. Now, without breaking the rhythm, you throw the left **Double** and go for the **Scissor Catch**. You should be concentrating on the *knob* of the club as it turns over and it's going to take you quite a bit of practice before you learn to 'clench' the scissors at precisely the right moment.

A good **Scissor Catch** leaves the club gripped by the handle slightly below the knob, rather than hanging on by the skin of its teeth.

•Note that the critical first stage of this move is the formation of a good pair of 'scissors' in the right hand. I have advocated a direct stop into a **Circus Grip** but many jugglers prefer to *place* the second half of the scissors into the right hand. If this is you then the lead into the move is slightly different.

Begin the move by throwing a right self **Double** then immediately **Feed** the club from your left hand into the right, forming the **Circus Grip**. Now make the **Scissor Catch**.

This is not as elegant as the previous method but if you feel safer with it, then make it your choice!

•As your confidence grows you'll be catching **Triples** and maybe even **Quads** with the **Scissor Catch**. You should also work on catching **Back Crosses** this way, and how about executing **Scissor Catches** from an **Under the Leg** position?

•After a **Scissor Catch** you can restart your pattern by throwing the club up from the scissor grip as a **Double** spin and then tossing up the 'scissors' as a two club **Multiplex**.

•Alternatively, swing the scissored club up through one hundred and eighty degrees into a **Balance**, toss it up from there as a **Flat** and then start juggling again.

•A **Scissor Catch** can be used to trap a **Reverse Spin** club as well. For this the trap is made with the 'scissors' pointing backwards. One way of doing this is to make a **Triple** or **Double** throw **Over the Shoulder** (these throws have **Reverse Spin**) and bring the two clubs up as if bidding at an auction. The trapped club ends up hanging over your shoulder in a fit of utter nonchalance.

Continued overleaf...

Scissor Catch...

• Another way of ending up with the 'scissored' club draped over your shoulder is to use a **One Eighty** to bring you, the 'scissors' and the trapped club into position.

Juggle a **Three Club Cascade** and get two clubs in the right hand into a **Circus Grip** as for the standard **Scissor Catch**.

Now throw a left **Double** (or **Triple**) straight up and turn a **One Eighty** to the right (elegant) or left (easier but lower marks for style). After an about-face you are in exactly the same position as you were for the **Over the Shoulder** catch. Snik! —and you have the club draped once more over your shoulder.

• In a **Passing Pattern** it's possible to catch **Double** and **Triple** passes in reverse scissor style, (normal spin passes from your partner arrive as **Reverse Spins**). Having trapped the club it can be thrown back as a **Tomahawk**, from the scissor grip.

• The best time of all to make a **Scissor Catch** simply *has* to be in a game of **VolleyClub** —think about it!

Scoop Pickup

The **Scoop Pickup** is an elegant way of recovering from a **Drop** in a **Passing Pattern**. For the purposes of the description I'll assume that you are passing **Every Others** (**Four Count**) with your partner. A club has been dropped and you are both **Holding Through the Gap**.

• Arrange matters so that the dropped club is on the ground a couple of feet in front of you at ninety degrees to the line of your passes.

Now make a pass and *immediately* flip your two remaining clubs half a turn so that you have them by the fat ends. Bend forwards and stroke the floored club backwards with your two clubs and then roll it onto the two outstretched handles. You must make sure that the dropped club's centre of balance is between the handles. Once you have the club in this position you flick it over to your partner (on the *pass* beat of course) and resume the full six club pattern.

You'll need to be completely happy with handling clubs at the **Wrong End** to master this one since you restart your pattern with two reversed clubs.

See also **Khyber Pass**, **Toe Kick** and **Pickup**.

Seven Club Cascade

To reach the level of skill required to juggle a **Seven Club Cascade** you will need to be a true athlete. This is an achievement to be compared with that of running a four minute mile *without* using the drugs that sporting types are so fond of these days.

I asked an old Zen Master of the Art of Juggling to tell me the secret of the **Seven Club Cascade**.

'It's quite impossible,' he replied. 'Human beings can do, at most, *two* things at once.'

That's Zen Mastery for you. I can't help feeling that he had a point —if only I could work out what is was!

- Every throw in a **Seven Club Cascade** is a **Quin** or **7**, usually thrown with **Triple** spin. You need to devote a great deal of attention to every aspect of your juggling if you wish to succeed, starting with your choice of clubs, which are likely to be narrower and lighter than the ones that you use for three and four club work.

- The **Seven Club Cascade** is the hardest trick listed in the COMPENDIUM OF CLUB JUGGLING and it is highly unlikely that more than one or two readers will ever have

the actual experience of driving this pattern. You might, however, wish to have a go at juggling *half* of it!

Juggle the four club pattern, **Triple-Singles** and practise throwing **7**'s out of the pattern. The normal **Triple-Singles** pattern reads in **SiteSwap Notation** as:

5 3 5 3 5 3 5 3..

Throwing a **7** (use four or five spins for this) allows you to make a couple of throws of a **Three Club Cascade** underneath the high one before resuming regular **Triple-Singles**.

5 3 5 3 5 3 **7 3 3 3** 5 3 5 3..

When that's solid you can try juggling a five club **Half Shower** in which your right hand throws constant **Quins** or **7**'s while the left hand throws **Singles** or **3**'s.

7 3 7 3 7 3 7 3...

If you can do that then you are juggling half of a seven club pattern in your right hand, and half of a three club pattern in your left hand!

Two things at once —hmmm!

Seven Club Cascade

Seven Club One Count

This is a very unusual **Passing Pattern**—one of the very few in the COMPENDIUM OF CLUB JUGGLING that uses *half* beats. Since this is a **One Count** *every throw* is a pass. The pattern can be juggled with either **Double** or **Single** spin.

•Stand facing your partner, you have four clubs (two in each hand) and they have three, unusually it's two in the *left* and one in the right.

On every throw you make a *diagonal* pass to your partner while they throw *tramlines* back. Many jugglers work this pattern on **Single** spins for the sake of simplicity (less spins means that there is less going on, hence less to go wrong!) but **Double** spins, if you can manage them, create a more relaxed pattern.

You lead the juggling with a right to right pass and then keep throwing diagonal passes from alternate hands.

Your partner leads with a left to right tramline pass *half a beat* after your first pass and then continues throwing tramline passes from alternate hands at normal juggling speed.

Half a beat is a tricky thing to pin down, a good rule of thumb is that their pass should be made exactly halfway between your first and second throws.

•The curious half-beat phasing can be avoided if one of you passes **Doubles** against the other's **Singles**.

Start as before, you get four clubs, your partner has three, two in the *left* hand as before.

You start first, throwing diagonal **Double** passes from alternate hands, starting with the right. Your partner starts one beat later, throwing tramline **Single** passes from alternate hands, starting with the *left*.

•This pattern also works with your partner throwing tramline **Doubles** to your diagonal **Singles**. The start is a little different.

You get four clubs, as before, your partner has three; once again two in the *left* and one in the right. This time you both start simultaneously, you lead with a diagonal **Single** from the right hand and then continue. Your partner leads with a tramline **Double** from the left hand.

If you enjoy these mad seven club patterns then you should see also **Popcorn** and **Pass-Pass-Self**.

The **Seven Club One Count** is the big brother of the very easy **Five Club One Count** and together with the **Nine Club One Count** they form a series of increasing amazingness.

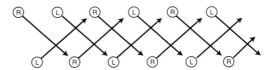

*A **Causal Diagram** of the **Seven Club One Count**. Notice how the two jugglers are working half a beat out of phase. Each throw is a **3.5**.*

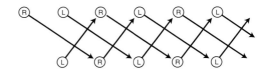

*If you throw **Doubles** against your partner's **Singles** the half beat phasing is avoided. The throws are now **4**'s against **3**'s.*

Seven Club Passing

Seven clubs can be passed between two jugglers using a number of different patterns. Adding that extra club over the usual three-clubs-per-juggler scheme is not as difficult as you might think, certainly a lot easier than juggling four clubs solo.

Here are some pointers to other entries in the COMPENDIUM that will interest the three and a half club juggler.

Staggered Doubles is the usual beginner's pattern. After that comes **Triple-Self (seven clubs)** which is simple enough though you need to be able to pass reliable **Triples** to succeed with it.

When you have mastered **Seven Club Passing** you can also team up with more jugglers for patterns like the **Ten Club Feed** and the **Random Feed**, both of which use the same techniques as **Staggered Doubles**.

Lovers of exotic and interwoven rhythms will adore **Popcorn**, the **Seven Club One Count** and the **Pass-Pass-Self** patterns for seven clubs.

The three-person, six-club **Runaround** can also be upgraded to seven clubs.

Seven Club Pickup

A well-known and widely imitated comic juggling duo have been juggling a routine based on the **Seven Club Pickup** for more years than either would care to admit to. I'll protect their identities by means of subtle anagrams, calling them '*Read any Cliché*' and '*He's Magic Gold*'.

Every last atom of comic possibility was sucked out of this routine years ago. It remains, however, a good test of your juggling skills and it's great fun too. Have a go and you'll see what I mean.

You and your partner need to be fluent with seven clubs on **Staggered Doubles** if you hope to get to the end of the routine.

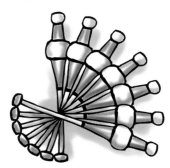

*The stack of clubs at the start of the **Seven Club Pickup**.*

• *Read any Cliché* (that's *you*) arranges seven clubs in a stack, the first club is laid on the ground with its nose facing *He's Magic Gold* (your partner) and each successive club is laid to the right of the last with its knob resting on the handle below. You'll see that this is an ideal arrangement because your right hand is now perfectly placed to grab each club in turn and lob it across to *HMG* —let battle commence.

In the pure, skill-based **Seven Club Pickup** you pick up each club in turn and throw it to *HMG* as a **Double** so that by the time you get to the last club you are both juggling seven clubs on **Staggered Doubles**. Fat chance!

• In the real-life version you **Shower** out three clubs on **Singles** and then explore the comic potential of trying to grab the fourth before *HMG* passes club number one back to you. This **Three Around** situation has natural comic potential because of its timing and establishes the basic gag (viz: you aren't nearly as amazing as you are cracked up to be). Then you pick up number four and indulge in further hilarious antics as you try and grab the fifth —and so on.

Continued overleaf...

•Picking up the sixth club is just like recovering from a **Drop** in a six-club **Two Count** and once this club enters the pattern there are no longer any **Gaps** left to play with.

•You now push the pattern 'up a level' by starting to pass **Doubles**, your partner responds in kind and you have a seven club **Staggered Doubles** pattern with a **Gap** in it. You should know what to do now (if not see **Picking Up** for advice on grabbing that last club).

When seven clubs are running you can choose your own finish; a couple of high throws are good and so is getting *HMG* to catch all seven.

•Jugglers who suffer from **Numbers Juggling** will of course wish to come up with the totally 'original' idea of the *Eight Club Pickup*. The best eight club pattern to use is the **Two Count** juggled on **Triples**.

*The last club in the **Seven Club Pickup**. You have to grab it blind, having noted its position a beat or two earlier while the **Gap** was running through your left hand.*

To get there you push the pattern up 'one more level' by starting to throw **Triples** to each other —now you have an eight club pattern with a **Gap**.

Bending down to pick up the eighth club is possible but *very difficult* so you are going to have to use a **Kickup** which is also very difficult. One easy cheat, that still impresses audiences, is to use a **Foot Lift**. This is a very easy and reliable technique which is good because you don't want to fall at the last fence in a routine like this.

•There is a much easier, but unfortunately not very impressive, method of getting the eighth club into the air.

Instead of pushing the pattern up from seven into an eight club **Gap** pattern go into the **Triple Self, (seven clubs)** pattern. This is a **Four Count** so you have plenty of time between passes, to stop your end of the pattern for a moment, pick up the eighth club, and restart in eight-club mode.

The reason it doesn't impress so much is that there is nothing desperate or skillful (to an audience's eyes anyway) in what you are doing. They need to see you do something *clever* to get that last club into the air.

Shower

Shower, **Cascade**, **Fountain**; the three fundamental types of solo juggling pattern. Have you noticed the *water* link here? The fourth fundamental is the **Drop**.

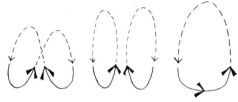

Cascade   Fountain   Shower

A **Shower** is a pattern in which all of the objects being juggled follow each other around in a loop. If you are juggling solo then a **Shower** usually means a pattern in which one hand throws to the other while the other **Feeds** back.

The word **Shower** is also used to describe **Two Count** two-person **Passing Patterns**. Once again, the objects in the pattern follow each other around in a loop, passing through each of the four hands in the pattern in turn.

Solo Shower Patterns

The thing about **Shower** patterns is that they are very easy to understand —I'll bet that the very first juggling pattern you ever came across was the **Two Ball Shower**[EBJ]. It's even easy to see how extra objects can be added to the pattern, just lob those rights higher!

Unfortunately, as more objects are added, the throws required soon become uncontrollably high and **Shower** patterns turn out to be far from the easiest method of juggling a given number of objects.

•A *One Club* **Shower** is simply the action of passing a club back and forth between two hands. Nervous performers are often seen doing this at dead points in their shows —I suppose it must be a deeply ingrained instinct.

•A *Two Club* **Shower** has your right hand throwing **3**'s to the left while the left **Feeds** back. **3**'s are usually **Single** spin throws though this pattern feels a mite less awkward if you throw **Flats** instead. Somehow this pattern just doesn't quite look, feel or taste that good.

•The *Three Club* **Shower** does work though. The right throws **5**'s and the left **Feeds** back. Most jugglers will use **Triple**

spins for the **5**'s though **Doubles** and **Quads** (if you can control them) work equally well.

•Mixing **Under the Hand** throws with ordinary throws in a three club **Shower** produces a wild pattern. While you are at it you can try making the rights as **Back Crosses** for extra thrill points.

•You can also try throwing those **Triples** with different planes of spin, using **Dips**, **Over the Tops** and **Tomahawk** throws.

•If you do decide to devote a significant portion of your juggling career to mastering the three club **Shower** just promise me one thing —you will learn to **Shower** from your *left* hand as well won't you?

•The *Four Club* **Shower** is where the whole system starts to fall apart due to serious difficulty. The pattern is even harder to juggle than **Three in One Hand**!

Your right hand throws **7's** while the left hand **Feeds** back. Take your pick of **Triples** or **Quads**. Start with three clubs in your right hand and lead off as you would for **Three Clubs in One Hand** only a little higher and more up-tempo. Good luck — you'll need it.

•The *Five Club* **Shower** is almost unheard of, the right throws **9**'s and the left **Feeds**. A *Six Club* **Shower** would use **11**'s, a *Seven Club* **Shower**, **13**'s, and so on.

We have moved into the realms of impossibility.

See also **Half Shower**.

Shower Passing Patterns

As I mentioned earlier, the term **Shower** also refers to **Two Count** passing patterns and it is a very popular pastime among the **Numbers Jugglers** to see just how many clubs an adroit partnership can **Shower** between them.

•Leaving aside such obscure patterns as the four and five-club **Shower** passing patterns we start with the six-club **Shower**. Two jugglers stand face to face and juggle in time, every right is a pass and every left is a self and the clubs follow each other around in a circle taking twelve **Beats** to make a complete circuit.

There are a million variations on the basic pattern and quite a few are listed under **Two Count**.

•Adding an extra club to the pattern is simply (hah!) a matter of making a bit of extra room in the circular path that the clubs take. There is a rule about the **Capacity**ᴱᴮᴶ of a pattern that says that when all of the objects in a juggling pattern follow a simple circuit (as they do in all **Shower** patterns) the number of **Beats** that they take to go around is *double the number of objects that the pattern can support*. Each object must be separated from the next by *two* beats of time.

Therefore, to add a seventh club to the **Two Count** you need to make the circuit take *two beats longer*. There are many different ways of doing this. One way is for both jugglers to throw **4**'s as passes instead of **3**'s which results in the well-known seven club passing pattern **Staggered Doubles**.

Another way is for one juggler to throw **5**'s and the other to throw **3**'s. In this variant we see one juggler showering **Triples** while the other showers **Singles** back.

Alternatively you *could* alter the weights of the self throws instead. One juggler could throw **Triple** *selfs* while every other throw remains a **Single** and you would have room for seven clubs once again. A really bizarre seven-club **Shower** pattern would have both jugglers throwing **Double** selfs while passing **Singles**. A side-effect of this is that both jugglers would be making *simultaneous* throws with right and left hands. I have never seen this one done!

There are a large number of possibilities and it's up to you to work them out. You can use the *Circuit Diagrams* that I described in the Encyclopædia of Ball Juggling (see **Capacity**ᴱᴮᴶ) or just work them out by numbers, it's up to you.

•For an eight club **Shower Pattern** we need a circuit of sixteen beats. Jugglers commonly use **3**'s as selfs (**Singles**) and **5**'s as passes (thrown either as **Doubles** or **Triples**).

A popular alternative is to juggle eight clubs using **Singles**. Actually, every throw is a **4** thrown with a **Single** spin. This can be pretty horrendous to juggle since *all four hands throw together*.

•When you move on to nine clubs you are entering serious **Numbers Juggling** territory. It's not so much a matter of finding out how many ways you can do the trick, as finding out whether you can do it *at all!* On this basis it turns out that, while there are myriads of possibilities for the arrangement of throws in a nine club **Shower,** it is easiest to get the *right* hands to concentrate on the throws while the *lefts* do the catching. Therefore you are well advised to fill the eighteen beat circuit with the throws **3**, **6**, **3**, **6**. The **3**'s are ordinary left to right **Singles** and the **6**'s are high and lazy **Triple** passes.

• Ten clubs are usually showered using the throws **3**, **7**, **3**, **7** though my old pal *'He's Magic Gold'* also recommends the simultaneous throw pattern **4**, **6**, **4**, **6**.

In theory, two very talented five club jugglers ought to be able to manage ten clubs as **5**, **5**, **5**, **5** —all juggled on **Double** spins.

They don't call this **Numbers Juggling** for nothing! If you want to go further then you can work it out for yourself!

*A **Single** pass actually turns one and a half times in the air.*

Single

A **Single** is a throw of a club that turns once in the air before the catch. This is, of course, the throw used in the very first pattern that a new club juggler learns, the **Three Club Cascade**.

This pattern can, if you wish, be juggled using any amount of **Spin** that you can handle. This includes no spins at all (**Flats**) and **Reverse Spin**.

Generally, when a club juggler talks about throwing a **Single**, they are talking about throwing what **SiteSwap Notation** calls a **3**.

It is not generally appreciated that when a juggler first learns the **Three Club Cascade** what they are *really* learning is the **Single** spin. After all, they can invariably already juggle a **Three Ball Cascade**[EBJ] and it's simply the **Spin** that messes them up and causes all those fumbles, drops and collisions.

When a pass is made as a **Single** spin the club actually makes nearly one and a half turns because it starts pointing downward and ends up pointing upwards.

See also **Double**, **Triple**, **Quad**, **Quin** and **Spin**.

Single Double Triple

H ere's a warmup exercise for three clubs that might *sound* simple but until you get the rhythm it's infuriatingly awkward. Learn to love that feeling —it means you are *learning* something!

• Juggle three clubs in a **Cascade** pattern so that you are throwing the sequence:

Single - Double - Triple - Single - Double - Triple ...

It takes six throws for the pattern to complete a cycle and until you find the rhythm your throws will be all over the place!

Simple exercises like this one are a good way of loosening yourself up before you start to work on the *serious* stuff!

• The four club juggling pattern **Five-Three-Four** also combines **Singles**, **Doubles** and **Triples** in a single pattern.

• Likewise the passing pattern **Popcorn** for seven clubs and two jugglers is a great exercise in controlling and matching these three throws.

SiteSwap Notation

This increasingly well-known and often controversial system of transmuting juggling patterns into rows of numbers was discussed at some length in the ENCYCLOPÆDIA OF BALL JUGGLING (see **SiteSwap Notation**[EBJ]) and was also responsible for several pages of solid numbers in the APPENDIX OF BALL JUGGLING that claimed to be juggling patterns.

SiteSwap is part notation and part mathematical theory, inhabiting that wild frontier on the edge of science along with *Chaos Theory* and other exotic beasts. The dual role of **SiteSwap** is what causes the controversy. It can be applied as a useful form of notation but the lovers of theory, the technically minded mathematical types, can see it as a game in its own right and play with the numbers and diagrams of the system with a carefree lack of regard for reality that infuriates those who feel that they operate in the *real* world.

How it works

In **SiteSwap Notation** each throw in a pattern is given a number and rather conveniently, the number is equal to the number of objects you would be juggling if you just kept making that sort of throw.

Thus every throw in a **Three Club Cascade** is a **3**, every throw in a **Four Club Fountain** is a **4** and so on. Actually, it makes no difference *what* you are juggling with, a **3** is a **3** whether you are juggling balls, clubs, rings or your accounts.

Cascade three objects and **SiteSwap Notation** would record:

3 3 3 3 3 3 3 3 3...

Fountain four objects and you get:

4 4 4 4 4 4 4 4 4...

Juggle **Triple-Singles**, where one hand juggles half of a five object pattern to the other's three object pattern, and you get:

5 3 5 3 5 3 5 3 5 3...

SiteSwap is not interested in catches, hold times, twiddly bits, body moves, **Spin** or what brand of juggling club you are using —it simply records throws.

As a practical **Notation** for the juggler, **SiteSwap** is limited to patterns in which the hands take it in turns to throw (*asynchronous* patterns). The pattern **Five-Three-Four** appears as:

5 3 4 5 3 4 5 3 4...

Clearly if the hands are taking it in turns

and the *right* hand threw the first **5** then it must be the *left* hand that threw the following **3** and so on. It's also possible to tell *where* each throw is headed because in an asynchronous pattern every *odd* number denotes a *crossing throw* while every *even* number denotes a *self throw*. Thus in our example pattern (**5 3 4 ...**) the **5**'s and **3**'s cross, while the **4**'s are selfs.

What the numbers really mean

3's, **4**'s, **5**'s and **6**'s translate into normal clubspeak as **Singles**, **Doubles**, **Triples**, and **Quads** respectively. The actual amount of spin is not important here, it's the *weight* of the throw, its actual *airtime*, that matters.

The precise meaning of a number **3** in **SiteSwap Notation** is that the object being thrown will be ready to be thrown again precisely *three beats later*. Armed with this knowledge it only takes a little bit of thought to decode a sequence of throws like this one:

4 4 4 4 5 3 5 3 5 3 5 3 4 4 4 4 ...

—juggle four throws of a **Four Club Fountain**, then four 'rounds' of **Triple-Singles** and then drop back down to the **Fountain**.

The numbers **0**, **1** and **2** are less intuitively obvious in their meaning but they fit, nevertheless, into an entirely logical pattern.

0's are **Gaps**. An empty hand does nothing.

1's are **Feeds**. One hand places an object directly into the other.

2's are not quite so simple. They *can* mean a **Hopstop**[EBJ] to the same hand with just one beat of airtime or they *can* mean **Holding through the Gap**. This may seem inconsistent until you realise that in either case a **2** amounts to an action between hand and object that leaves the hand ready to throw the *same* object exactly *two beats* later.

Most juggling patterns are a repeating sequence of throws. In **SiteSwap** you can reduce these sequences to one 'repeat', so the **Cascade** becomes just plain '**3**' and **Five-Three-Four** becomes '**534**'.

There are a number of mathematical rules that you can use to check that a given series of numbers is, in fact, a juggling pattern, and the same rules allow you to invent new patterns which, skill permitting, are guaranteed to be juggleable.

RULE 1: In any sequence of throws written in **SiteSwap Notation** you can always tell how many objects are being juggled by calculating the *average number* of the sequence. Thus **5 3 1**... (repeated as a pattern) is a *three object pattern* because the average of **5** and **3** and **1** is three.

RULE 2: With any repeating sequence you can add the *length of the sequence* to any number in it to create a new, juggleable pattern for one more object. Thus **5 3 1** can be converted to **5 3 4** (I've added *three* to the **1**) converting a *three* object pattern into a *four* object pattern.

Alternatively, by writing the pattern as two 'repeats', **5 3 1 5 3 1**, we can derive the new pattern **5 3 1 5 3 7**, by adding six to the last '**1**'.

RULE 3: Similarly, you can *subtract* the length of the sequence from any number in it to create a pattern for one less object provided that your number doesn't go below zero —for that would imply an object travelling backwards in time (spooky stuff!). Using these two rules you can create multitudes of new patterns from old ones.

RULE 4: Even numbers are *self* throws, odd numbers are *crossing* throws.

RULE 5: Not every sequence of numbers is a juggleable pattern. To understand why, we need a little more theory —the theory of *Landing Schedules*.

Think of the objects in a juggling pattern as a set of planes stacked up and waiting to land at an airport. As each plane comes in to land the juggler sends it off again on another flight. Since your hands are throwing alternately, they are also catching alternately and so it's a rule that only one 'plane' can be landing at any given moment.

A juggling pattern therefore consists of a number of objects 'stacked up' in a queue waiting to land. The normal state of a **Cascade** of three is a queue of three objects which can be written as:

A B C

The juggler catches object A (scheduled to land first) and sends it to the back of the queue, *three spaces to the right*, hence they have thrown a **3**. Then the queue moves down a space:

B C A

Continued overleaf...

SiteSwap Notation...

The action of moving A from one position to another in the queue is what gives **SiteSwap** its name —the object is *swapping sites* in the landing schedule.

As the pattern progresses each object 'lands' and gets dispatched to the back of the queue. The **Cascade** continues as a continuous series of **3**'s, each of which sends an object three spaces to the right.

The **Cascades** and **Fountains** both work on this very simple principle, but things can, and do, get considerably more complicated. Here's a normal landing schedule for a **Cascade** of three again.

A B C

Let's suppose we throw object A as a **5** (just to be flash).

B C - - A

Two holes in the queue appear because we sent object A two spaces further than we actually needed to. In fact, we could have thrown object A with anything from a **3** upwards —there's an unlimited amount of sky up there!

Now it's time to deal with object B which *must* be thrown to a space in the queue. A **1** is out, because that would clash

with C, so is a **4** because that would clash with B. Let's go for a **5** again, just to be flash.

C - - A B

Object C is next to land and we can throw anything except a **3** or a **4**. I'll go for a **5** yet again and now we have

- - A B C

There are now no 'planes' due to land for two 'beats' of the pattern. When this happens you 'throw' a **0**. In other words, do nothing, your hand is empty.

- A B C

Again, there is a nothing landing so we 'throw' a **0** again.

A B C

We're back to normal. Our flashy sequence of throws, inserted into a regular **Three Club Cascade** turns out to be a three club **Flash**, in **SiteSwap** the whole sequence reads as:

3 3 3 3 **5 5 5 0 0** 3 3 3...

We know that this is a juggleable sequence for two reasons, firstly it obeys all the rules of landing schedules —no two 'planes' land at once. Secondly it's a trick

that you have almost certainly heard of before!

To work out your own sequences you can start by writing a 'plain vanilla' Landing Schedule for the number of objects in your pattern; here's the starting point for four objects.

A	B	C	D					
?								

The question mark is where you write down your choice of what throw to give object A, anything from a **4** upwards is fine because that's where the spaces start. We'll write a **6** in and then copy object A into the landing schedule six spaces to the right.

A	B	C	D	B		A		
6	?							

Now you have to decide what to do with B, and so you carry on. Here's how your composition might look after you've composed a few more throws.

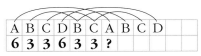

A	B	C	D	B	C	A	B	C	D		
6	3	3	6	3	3	?					

We've just composed a short sequence of the four object pattern **Six-Three-Three**

The linking lines are a clue to the simplest method of checking whether a given sequence of numbers is actually juggleable. Just write down your series of numbers and connect each number (call it *x*) with a line that hops *x* spaces to the right. When you've finished there should be exactly one line into and one line out of each number in the sequence. It gets fiddly at the ends of course —you have 'wrap around' back to the beginning.

• **SiteSwap Notation** is not, at least in the form I have described it, capable of handling patterns in which more than one hand is throwing at a time (for example **Four Club Synch Doubles** and nearly all **Passing Patterns**) —the queueing situation becomes too complicated to be handled by a single row of numbers. Various extensions to the system have been devised to cope with this, but usually at the expense of any kind of readability.

If this sort of technical approach appeals to you then you will find more information about **SiteSwap Notation** and other areas of mathematical juggling theory at the **Juggling Information Service** on the Internet.

See also **SiteSwap Notation**[EBJ].

Six Club Fountain

Few jugglers reach such dizzy heights as the **Six Club Fountain**. To juggle it you must be able to juggle **Three in One Hand** in both hands at the same time.

• As with the **Four Club Fountain** the clubs do not cross so you can juggle the pattern either with alternate throws (a pure **Fountain**) or with simultaneous throws, like **Four Club Synch Doubles**. Every throw in the pattern is a **6** or **Quad**, though it is almost universally juggled using **Triple** spins. Seven club jugglers have claimed that the **Six Club Fountain** is a harder pattern to juggle than the **Seven Club Cascade** because of collision problems. It seems unlikely to me that juggling *more* can be easier than juggling *less*, but who am I to argue?

Six Club Pickup

The trick of starting a two person, six club **Two Count** (or **Shower**) with all the clubs resting on the floor.

See **Seven Club Pickup** and read only paragraphs three, six and seven, substituting the word 'six' for 'seven' as appropriate.

Six-Three-Three

Here's a rarely seen pattern for four clubs. It's very high, with tremendous visual power and it's also very difficult. It's a good pattern to switch into for a few beats when juggling four clubs to add some variety and pizzazz to your performance.

This pattern is listed in the ENCYCLOPÆDIA OF BALL JUGGLING under the same name and you would be well advised to learn it with balls before attempting it with clubs.

The name is of course, based on the throwing sequence expressed in **SiteSwap Notation**.

6 3 3 6 3 3 6 3 3 6 3 3 6 3 3...

The **6**'s are **Quads** or **Three in One Hand** throws though you are at liberty to throw them with **Triple** spins if you prefer. These throws return to the same hand and they are *very* high.

The **3**'s are ordinary **Singles** or **Cascade** throws and they cross the pattern as usual.

Continued overleaf...

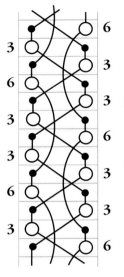

A chart of the Six-Three-Three. Note that two of the clubs are always thrown as 6's while the other two stay on 3's.

• It is, in my opinion, easiest to start this pattern from a running **Four Club Fountain** and to learn it by trying very short bursts of **Six-Three-Three** and slowly building up the time you spend in the high pattern. Try throwing this sequence:

4 4 4 4 4 4 **6 3 3** 4 4 4 4...

In plain English; juggle a **Four Club Fountain** and then throw a right* self **Quad**, juggle two throws of a **Three Club**

*It could equally well be a *left* self **Quad** if you prefer, **SiteSwap Notation** is directionally dyslexic.

Cascade underneath it and then resume the **Fountain**. When you are having some success with this you can extend the move to:

4 4 4 4 4 4 **6 3 3 6 3 3** 4 4 4 4...

Translating again, for those who feel sick whenever they see more than two numbers next to each other; you juggle a **Four Club Fountain**, then throw a right self **Quad** followed by two throws of a **Cascade**, then a left self **Quad** and two more throws of **Cascade** before dropping back down into the **Fountain**.

• It *is* a difficult move and you may need to warm up your **Quad** throwing skills with the following simpler exercise.

3 3 3 **6 3 3 0** 3 3 3 3

Juggle a **Three Club Cascade** and then launch a right self **Quad** out of the pattern. While the high throw is in the air you continue the **Cascade** underneath it with the remaining two clubs for two throws. A knacksome move indeed but tremendously satisfying when it works. Practise thoroughly on both sides and your chances with the **Six-Three-Three** vastly improved.

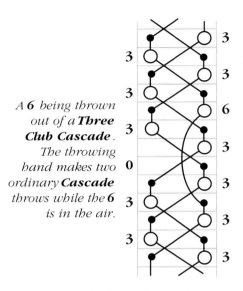

A 6 being thrown out of a Three Club Cascade. The throwing hand makes two ordinary Cascade throws while the 6 is in the air.

• One round of **Six-Three-Three** can be thrown in a two-person, six-club **Four Count** as an exotic **Syncopation**. You lead into the move on the *Pass* beat, throwing:

6 3 3 6

That's a right self **Quad** (instead of the regular pass), then a left self **Quad** two beats later. Effectively you have gone into four club juggling for a few throws. Your partner is left holding two clubs until you resume the regular pattern on the next *pass* beat.

166

Slap Kick

Juggling clubs are expensive items, well-balanced, well-finished and resistant to the constant dropping that they have to endure. I mention this because the **Slap Kick** tests the construction of your clubs to the limit.

It's considerably harder to master than a normal **Kickup** and each different design of club behaves differently —some just break. If you want to upset a juggler just start practising your **Slap Kicks** on *their* clubs instead of using your own.

•Place a club on the ground in front of you, the knob pointing away from you. Now strike the nose of the club with a firm stepping action and (with luck) the club will flip into the air to an easy catch after one and a half spins.

It's one thing to do this cold with a single club, but it's quite another to **Slap Kick** a club into a running pattern.

HERE!

To get the club to rise into the air the ***Slap Kick*** *is applied to the nose of the club, forward of the point at which the body touches the ground.*

It's rather like the **Bounce**, if the club flies gracefully and elegantly into the air then no damage has been done. The time to start worrying is when your foot smashes down onto the club and it doesn't go anywhere —that means that the force of the **Slap Kick** has been absorbed by the *structure* of the club, which may not be able to cope!

•A more gentle version of the **Slap Kick** simply lifts the handle into your waiting hand. You don't have to go for spin or height here, just flip the handle into your hand by tapping the nose of the club with your toes.

•Skilled **Slap Kickers** can lift a club that's lying on the floor behind them. Point the nose of the club forwards and walk casually over it, striking the nose with your heel as you do so. You'll have to practise a lot to pull this off with the nonchalance that it deserves.

•It's a funny thing, but once you start to write a COMPENDIUM OF CLUB JUGGLING you get all sorts of people making suggestions for tricks and patterns to include. I'm very grateful to all of those contributors —all of them that is, except for two dastardly villains of the juggling world who just 'phoned me up and tried to *sell* me a trick.

Slap Kick...

It sounded like there was a bit of a party going on at the other end of the line and I can only assume that Haggis and Jules were horribly drunk and thought their new invention was the best thing *ever*. I refused to pay. However, human nature being what it is —they couldn't resist telling me anyway!

The idea is that you **Slap Kick** *three* clubs into your hand simultaneously.

Lay the first club on the floor, as for a normal **Slap Kick**, and then lay two more, one on each side, so that their handles rest on top of the first in an elegant 'fan' shape with their bodies touching.

Slap Kick the middle club *gently* and all three clubs should flip into your waiting hand.

Good isn't it?

Slapover

A **Slapover** is a **Reverse Spin** pass, very like an **Over the Shoulder** throw except that it is thrown more over the back of the hand than over the shoulder itself.

Lead into a **Slapover** as you would an **Over the Shoulder** throw, but propel the club forward as a pass, rather than upward as you would for a self throw. You lean forwards a little when making this throw and the power comes from the wrist rather than the arm.

•A **Slapover** adds a brilliant finishing touch to a **Flourish**. This works very well because the club, at the end of the **Flourish**, has exactly the right position and momentum to lead straight into the **Slapover**.

FLOURISH!

In a right-handed **Two Count** you buy enough time for a right hand **Flourish** by first throwing an **Early Double**. Then you make the **Reverse Catch** and **Flourish** in the right hand —now tack on the **Slapover** and the crowd will go wild.

This sequence can be juggled continuously so that your partner is catching **Early Doubles** and **Slapovers** alternately and your end of the pattern becomes a sea of elaborate curlicues!

Slow Cascade

Slow Cascade is a **Cascade** juggled to a slower rhythm as a result of using throws of greater weights than normal. For the three club juggler this means using **4**'s, **5**'s or more instead of the usual **3**'s (**Singles**). This is a *rhythm* thing!

• If you juggle a **Three Club Cascade** using **Doubles** you'll find that there are two distinct styles you can 'lock into'. In one style you simply juggle the **Cascade** with extra spin, keeping the **Doubles** low and tight. In the other you loft the clubs higher and find yourself *waiting* between throws. This slower pattern is the **Slow Cascade.**

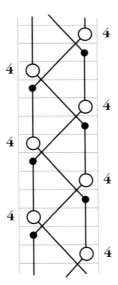

A chart of a **Slow Cascade** *juggled on* **4**'s *(***Doubles***). The pattern is very different to the regular* **Cascade**. *Beginners tend to lock into this rhythm because only one hand is actually juggling at a time.*

The throws are **4**'s, instead of the normal **3**'s and you are now making one throw every *two* beats, instead of on *every* beat.

Only one hand is working at a time, first the right catches and throws, then it's the left hand's turn. In the regular **Cascade** the action of the two hands overlaps.

Beginners often try to lock into the **Slow Cascade** rhythm when juggling clubs for the first time (just like ball jugglers) because only one hand is doing anything at any given moment. This accounts for the

enormous difference between the beginner's up-and-down pattern and the more experienced club-juggler's smooth figure of eight. Each hand gets to hold its club for three beats before throwing it again. This is long enough to allow the juggler to execute a **Flourish** before every single throw—you'll need to make every catch a **Reverse Catch** to do that.

• The **Slow Cascade** rhythm is the basis for an interesting **Syncopation** in a six-club, two-person **Two Count** passing pattern. I'll assume you are passing right-handed.

Begin by throwing constant **Early Doubles** to your partner, that is, left to left diagonal passes on the *two* beat. Your right hand is entirely idle while you do this. Now let your hands take it in turns to throw the **Early Double** and you'll find yourself juggling a **Slow Cascade** rhythm to their regular rhythm, making passes and catches in alternate hands in the style of a **One Count**. It's a lot easier than it sounds!

Because of the long holds you could, in theory, **Flourish** every single club in this pattern.

Continued overleaf...

•Moving up a level and returning to solo work, we come to the **Slow Cascade** juggled on **5**'s (**Triples**). On checking out the pattern in **Ladder Notation** it turns out that there are two distinct ways of juggling this pattern.

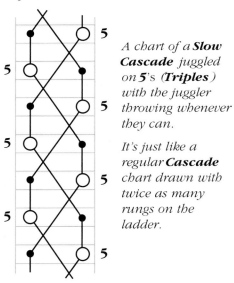

*A chart of a **Slow Cascade** juggled on **5**'s (**Triples**) with the juggler throwing whenever they can.*

*It's just like a regular **Cascade** chart drawn with twice as many rungs on the ladder.*

The first method, throwing whenever you *can*, results in a chart that looks identical to the ordinary **Cascade** on **3**'s except that there are twice as many 'rungs' on the ladder as usual. This is just a 'bigger' **Three Club Cascade** and accounts for the fact that three clubs, juggled well on

Triples has all the smoothness and elegance of the classic **Three Club Cascade**. Traditional circus jugglers have always been fond of this high-powered pattern.

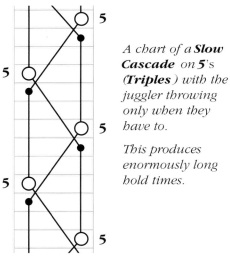

*A chart of a **Slow Cascade** on **5**'s (**Triples**) with the juggler throwing only when they have to.*

This produces enormously long hold times.

The second method, throwing only when you *have to*, results in utterly enormous hold times of *five beats*. This feels completely different and is a great way of practising **Triples** because you have so long to think about what you are doing. When jugglers are learning **Triple Back Crosses** this is the tempo that they usually work to. It's slow and easy —apart from the **Back Crosses** of course!

•Note that in this pattern there is a throw made every *three* beats, so it i perfectly possible (with a little imagination to juggle to this tempo in a **Three Coun** passing pattern, lobbing your partne continuous **Triple** passes from alternate hands. I leave the workings out as a exercise for the reader.

•Moving up a level we come to the **Slow Cascade** juggled on **6**'s, or **Quads** There are three possible rhythms for thi and it's a great exercise in control to see i you can 'lock into' each one of them.

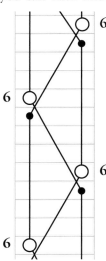

*The first way of juggling a **Slow Cascade** on **6**'s is to throw 'only when you have to'. This results in very long hold time and a throw every four beats. You could use this rhythm as a **Syncopation** in a **Four Count**; passing constant **Quads** to your partner from alternate hands.*

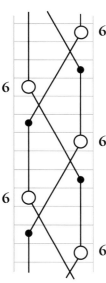

A slightly more up-tempo pattern results if you throw 'earlier than you have to'. Now there is a throw every three beats.

This is quite a hard rhythm to lock into but you'll know when you've got it.

When you hit the rhythm of the *'earlier than you have to'* pattern you'll feel the pulse of the pattern as:

Catch-throw-pause-catch-throw-pause...

There's something very musical about the combination of one throw every three beats, four beats of hold time and five beats of airtime.

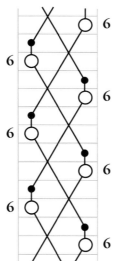

*The most exciting **Slow Cascade** on **6**'s feels anything but slow.*

*The juggler throws 'whenever they can' and the result is dramatic. The pattern can be thought of as **Three in One Hand** with the hands taking it in turns to juggle the pattern.*

The last option, *throwing whenever you can* is the most exciting of the three, this is **Hot Potato**, the art of keeping three clubs out of your hands and in the air as much as you possibly can. It's a very satisfying rhythm when you get it. **Triple** spins are probably the best choice and once again, it's a favourite with high-speed traditional circus stars. Examining the **Ladder Notation** for the pattern you should be able to see that this pattern is identical to **Three in One Hand** except that your hands take it in turn to make the throws.

Slow Start

A **Slow Start** is a method of starting a **Passing Pattern** in which each juggler makes a few throws to themselves, to synchronise the pattern, before making the first pass. The alternative is a **Fast Start** in which the *very first throw* is a pass.

• The **Slow Start** is the preferred method for beginners. To start a two person six-club **Four Count** (**Every Others** to most of the world) you both do an **Up-Down-Go!** and then start to juggle from the right hand, counting:

*One - and - two - and - **Pass!***

The *'ands'* are left hand throws.

The **Slow Start** is part of the international language of juggling, so if a foreign juggler signs to you that you are to juggle a couple of selfs before starting to pass then you should use a **Slow Start** and you won't go far wrong.

Slow Start

Solids

Passing clubs with a partner on a **Two Count** is known by some as **Solids**. It's also called **Showers** and probably more besides.

Let's face it, sometimes the great risk of juggling is not so much that of a **Drop** as the threat of drowning in a sea of terminology.

In the **Two Count**, alias **Solids** or **Showers**, every second throw is a pass, the usual arrangement being that every right hand throw is a pass while every left is a self.

For the full story see **Two Count**.

Speed Weave

Here's a **Passing Pattern** for four jugglers and twelve clubs. The main feature of this pattern is that three of the jugglers juggle *themselves* as they walk around each other in a **Cascade** pattern. It's quite likely that this pattern was originally called the *'Feed Weave'*. The name has probably been corrupted because of all the running around involved in it.

• This pattern is a **Feed**. The feeder stands still, passing to three stationary points *(right-middle-left-middle-right)* while the three fed jugglers move around in a figure-of-eight passing *Six Counts* as they pass through the three points.

*The **Speed Weave**, the feeder juggles a **Two Count** while the 'fed' walk a figure-of-eight juggling Six Counts.*

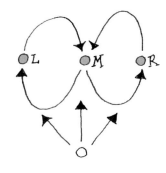

The imaginary figure-of-eight is laid ove the three imaginary points that the feede passes to, so that the *middle* pass arrives a the 'Grand Central Junction'. The fe jugglers move so that they are walkin *forwards* when they are in the *middl* position and *backwards* at the *right* and *le* points. It's important to move forward quickly when it's your turn at Gran Central.

Note that as the feeder is swinging from a *middle* pass to a *right* pass, the 'fed juggler in the *middle* is walking to the *le* point.

The **Speed Weave** is quite an exercise i organisation but once everybody know their part it runs like clockwork.

Spin

Ball jugglers don't have to worry too much about **Spin** —a ball is the same whichever way up it is and it looks and feels pretty much the same whether it is turning or not.

For the club juggler it's a different story. **Spin** is what club juggling is all about. You should make it your business to explore all of the possibilities that **Spin** has to offer.

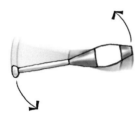

•To begin with, the novice club juggler needs only to learn to handle a **Single** spin. This is all it takes to juggle a **Three Club Cascade** and a host of other tricks. They can even pass clubs without ever using the more revolved and involved throws, although some practice at recovering from **Wrong End** catches, using *one and a half* or *half* spins is very useful. You can practise this technique solo, and once mastered it will enable you to recover from the most dreadful passes without missing a beat.

•To progress further, every juggler should aim to master **Doubles** and **Triples** at least. Here's a useful exercise.

Take one juggling club in your best hand and start with a **Single** spin toss back to the same hand and then increase this to a **Double**, then a **Triple** and so on. Keep going until you are out of your depth. Every juggler quickly hits their limit with this exercise. Beginners may find even the **Double** beyond their scope.

It can be very difficult to follow the turns of a club with your eye —all you see is a wheeling blur.

A useful trick is to *watch the knob*, rather than the whole club. You'll find that you can count the **Spin** on a club and catch it far more easily this way.

•Jugglers also need to master the technique of catching viciously spinning clubs *without* knowing how many turns they have made. A throw with *really* wild spin is called a **Buzz Saw**. Throw a club into the air and *really* crack some spin onto it. You can make a club literally *hum* if you spin it hard enough!

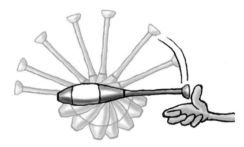

When a club is spinning this fast you can catch it by inserting your hand a couple of inches *into the blur* —the handle will slap hard, right into your hand. This works because the centre of gravity of a club is high, so the handle 'sticks out' further than the rest of the club. Some clubs have higher centres of gravity than others, especially the 'circus' style clubs, and so they work better for this.

Continued overleaf...

Spin...

• The true **Volleyclub** and club-passing expert should be able to chuck a club up with any old **Spin** and make a good catch.

To practise this (and I know this sounds silly) juggle three clubs and, on every fifth throw, chuck a high throw that is *complete rubbish*, any old spin, any old angle. Make them really nasty. You can use **Dips**, **Over the Tops**, **Tomahawks** or just plain violent **Buzz Saws**.

• Four club jugglers can make the game a little more intense by using **Triple-Singles** as the base pattern and throwing *really awful* **Triples** to themselves, and I do mean *really awful* —if the thing actually turns three times in the right direction then you are being far too nice to yourself!

These exercises are amazingly good practice for club passing and regular work on them is guaranteed to make you one of the best catchers around.

• Moving back to slightly more tame, sober and sensible juggling; here's an excellent warmup exercise based on **Spin**.

Juggle three clubs on **Single** spins until your muscles start to loosen a little and the pattern feels smooth. Now take the pattern up to **Doubles**, keeping the whole exercise as relaxed and un-frantic as possible. Now keep going up to the comfortable limits of your capability, this may be **Triples** or it may be beyond.

Because this is a warmup exercise you should not be trying to break new ground. Instead you should aim to juggle the smoothest, most relaxed and solid patterns that you can manage. I guarantee that in five minutes you will be loosened up and ready to do some serious work. Finish the exercise *before* you drop with your most elegant **Finish**. If there are any bystanders around you may even get a round of applause!

When working on your **Spin** skills it's worth considering (and practising) all of the possibilities:

Reverse Spin

Start by tossing the occasional **Reverse Spin** into a **Three Club Cascade** and then work your way through all of the combinations; every right, every left, same club every time and, the hardest of all, *every throw* made with **Reverse Spin**.

You can throw **Doubles** and **Triples** with **Reverse Spin** as well. The throwing action is less natural than for ordinary throws but catching a **Reverse Spin** is just like catching a club from your partner when passing clubs. This is obvious really, since when you stand face to face with another juggler your patterns rotate in opposite directions.

Tomahawks and **Slapovers** (which can be used in solo patterns as well as club passing) put **Reverse Spin** on a club too.

Side Spin

Throughout the COMPENDIUM I've used the terms **Dip** and **Over the Top** to denote the two possible directions of *Side Spin*.

Some call these two alternatives *inside* and *outside* spin, but I find that rather

OVER

DIP

confusing and prefer to name them after the basic tricks instead. **Dip** throws send clubs from the right hand clockwise while **Over the Top** throws send them anti-clockwise. Either way, the clubs turn like forward facing propellers.

Flat Spin

This is **Helicopter** style spin. A *Flat Spin* from the right hand will almost invariably be made so as to spin *clockwise* as seen from above (the same direction that a **Thumb Twirl** rotates). It's not that the opposite spin is impossible, just that a weakness in the design of the human hand makes the anti-clockwise spin very difficult to apply.

Fractional Spin

By this I mean amounts of **Spin** that do not add up to whole numbers. This is the realm of *half spin, one and a half spin, two and a half spin* and so on. Club jugglers must develop skills in this area to be able to recover from bad throws without dropping.

For a really interesting exercise in *Fractional Spin* you should practise juggling a **Three Club Cascade** with three plain sticks instead of juggling clubs.

With **Single Spins** the trick is not too difficult, but try *half spins* —another thing altogether. You may need to mark the sticks with white tape to keep track of what's going on.

Remember, if a trick sounds like it ought to be easy and then ties your brain into a complex celtic knot (as this one will) then it means that you are *learning* something!

•In club juggling it's very common to refer to certain *weights* of throw as **Singles**, **Doubles**, **Triples** and so on. These names refer to the *usual* amount of **Spin** for the throw. It's important to realise that the actual amount of **Spin** on a throw is arbitrary and completely at the discretion of the juggler. It would be more accurate, and quite probably save a lot of confusion, to refer to different weights of throws by their **SiteSwap** values instead —**Singles** are **3**'s, **Doubles** are **4**'s, **Triple**s are **5**'s and so on.

However jugglers are not like that, being lovers of complication and confusion they seem to positively enjoy the mishmash of terminology that goes with their art and I have to say that I love it too.

See also **Single, Double, Triple, Quad, Dip, Over the Top, Helicopter, Tomahawk** and **Having Problems?**

Spreads

Non-jugglers find this elegant four club pattern almost as impressive as the **Five Club Cascade**. This is good news, because **Spreads** is a very difficult pattern to learn and it makes all that practice worthwhile.

•**Spreads** is **Four Club Synch Doubles** juggled in a different shape, instead of making each paired throw up through the middle of the pattern you throw one pair always to the right and the other always to the left so that you end up working in four columns.

As you throw to the *left* you need to be looking to the *right*, the same technique is used when juggling **Back Crosses**.

You'll have a lot of problems with collisions and find that it's very hard to throw perfectly matched pairs of **Doubles** while working from side to side. Take your time, don't expect to perfect the pattern in a short period of time and you *will* get there.

One very useful tip is to throw 'from your stomach' —get your centre of gravity right underneath each pair of **Doubles** as you throw them and don't be shy of swinging extravagantly from side to side as you juggle.

•Experts at **Spreads** take the pattern up to **Triple** and **Quadruple** spins and add flashy touches like pirouettes —many world class routines have been based on this pattern.

The paired throws seem really *big* in the air and the overall pattern is very simple to watch making it easy for a non-juggling audience to see exactly what's going on. Believe me, when they *understand* what's happening they like it even more!

Staggered Doubles

This pattern is the most common method for passing seven clubs between two jugglers. It's a **Two Count** in which you and your partner throw **Doubles** to each other in a staggered timing —first you throw a pass, then they do. It has a great rhythm.

The pattern is similar to the six-club **Two Count** or **Shower** pattern, the 'space' for the extra club is made by upping the weights of the passes from **3**'s to **4**'s (from **Singles** to **Doubles**. This has the side effect of causing the staggered timing.

•Stand facing your partner, you start with four clubs and they start with three.

You lead straight into a **Two Count**, making every right hand throw a tramline **Double** to your partner's left hand. They wait for *one beat* and then start passing **Doubles** back to you and the pattern is running. You both need to concentrate on throwing nice smooth catchable **Doubles** for the pattern to work. Remember that if your partner's passes seem to be too *high* it's probably because your passes are too *low.* There is a natural instinct to adjust your own throws to compensate for your partner's mistakes. Step on that habit!

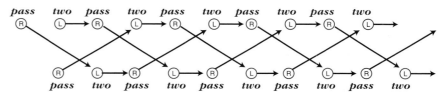

*The **Causal Diagram** for **Staggered Doubles** has a spooky similarity to the **Ladder Notation** for a **Cascade** of three. Note that the two jugglers count off their beats in opposite time.*

•Sometimes jugglers that are new to this pattern find the timing of the start a little tricky so here's an alternative that is becoming very fashionable.

You start with four clubs as before, two in each hand. Your partner starts with two in the *left* hand and one in the right. You both do an **Up-Down-Go!** Your first throw is a right hand pass as before but your partner's first throw is a left hand *self*. This usually does the trick and gets you both in perfect synch from the start.

•After you have the basic pattern solid you can try some **Syncopations**. As a general rule of thumb, any **Syncopated** pass that's possible in a six club **Two Count**

is also possible in **Staggered Doubles** (which is after all still a **Two Count**) except that all the throws need to be taken *up a level*. So an **Early Double**, for example, becomes a **Triple**.

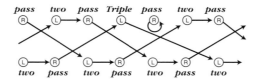

•The **Early Triple** pass is thrown diagonally from left to left on the *two* beat. This gives you a brief **Gap** in your pattern —the exact equivalent of the **Early Double** in the six-club **Two Count**.

•A **Late Triple** pass can be thrown on the *pass* beat. It goes diagonally from right to right and your partner gets the **Gap** — this is just like the **Late Double** of the six-club **Two Count**.

•A right to left **Quad** pass (a **6**) can be thrown on the *pass* beat but you must 'set up' the move by throwing an **Early Triple** (left to left) immediately beforehand. The count goes:

*pass - two - pass -**Triple**[LTL] -**Quad**[RTL]*

You end up with an empty right hand for a moment.

Continued overleaf...

Staggered Doubles...

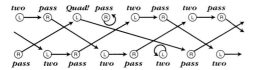

two pass *Quad!* pass two pass two pass

pass two pass two pass two pass two

•A left to right **Quad** pass is a far simpler beast. You throw it on the *two* beat and miss your next pass, both you and your partner get a **Gap**. This is a '*Late Quad*' and equates to the **Late Triple** in a six-club **Two Count**.

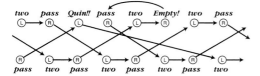

two pass *Quin!!* pass two *Empty!* two pass

pass two pass two pass two pass two

•A left to left **Quin** (a **7**!) can be thrown on the *and* beat but you must follow it immediately with a normal pass. You get an empty hand a couple of beats later on (I'll never get used to that backwards arrow!)

In case you hadn't guessed we are getting into the realm of the considerably exotic here, a **Quin** is a *high* throw! I particularly like this trick because you send off one pass, and then follow it with another one that gets there *first*. Well, it's all fine in *theory* anyway —it would be nice to see it done in *reality*.

•A commonly juggled variation on **Staggered Doubles** is to juggle the pattern on **Singles**. The passes are still **4**'s but the whole pattern is juggled lower and faster. Many jugglers find this very difficult because they make the mistake of trying to throw the **Single** passes as low as the **Single** selfs, this doesn't work —those passes need to be 'floated' otherwise the pattern speeds up horribly and ends up chasing its own tail into oblivion.

Obviously, if you are juggling seven clubs on **Singles** your **Syncopations** will come down one level spinwise too. If you think in terms of a six-club **Two Count** you won't go far wrong.

•Making the change from **Single** spins to **Doubles** and back again in a running pattern is a great exercise in control, teamwork and coordination. When dropping down from **Doubles**, the first **Single** should be a real 'floater' —virtually the same height as the **Doubles**. Changing up again is far easier.

See also **Shower**, **Seven Club Pickup**, **Ten Club Feed**, **Triple-Self (seven clubs)**, **Popcorn** and **Seven Club One Count**.

Star

When five jugglers get together to pass clubs they can use the elegant and interesting **Star** formation.

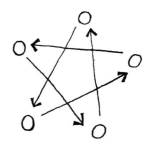

•The passes usually follow the diagonals of the star, in the style of the mystic *pentangle*.

Arrange yourself and four others in a **Star** layout, it's usual to space yourselves out by holding your clubs at arm's length to form an even circle. Each juggler gets three clubs and you all agree to pass a **Four Count** (just to get warmed up). Everybody passes to the juggler two spaces to their right while receiving from the juggler two spaces to the left. Anybody else who is hanging around looking bored can be invited to lie on the ground, head in the middle of the star, and look up for the show of the century (crash helmet optional but advisable!).

• Now increase the tempo and get everybody to juggle a **Three Count**, passing first to the right and then to the left. Any hapless volunteers lying in the middle will probably make their excuses and leave at this point!

• You can up the tempo still further and try juggling **Two Counts**, **One Counts**, **Pass-pass-self** and so on —all tremendously good fun but pretty useless from the performance point of view because the only people who can really see what is going on are the jugglers themselves and any idiots still hanging around in the middle!

For other variations on the **Star** theme see **Runarounds** and **Boston Circle**.

Steals and Takeouts

These are tricks in which you **Steal** one club, or a complete running pattern, from another juggler.

• Stealing just *one* club is often called a **Takeout**.

Stand to the right of a juggler who is working a **Three Club Cascade** and intercept a club that they are about to catch in their right hand with *your* right hand. Now swing this club *underneath* their right arm and toss it back into the pattern.

• Repeating the **Takeout** on alternate sides with the same club leaves your partner with just two clubs (in a **Gap** pattern) while you juggle the third one for them.

• To add comedy to the move your partner can raise their leg to allow you to make your throws **Under the Leg**.

• By similar mad logic, **Back Crosses** are a doddle, you just carry the stolen club around behind their back. It may be kids' stuff but what's wrong with that?

• A **Takeout** from a passing pattern works very well. Get two jugglers to pass a six-club **Four Count** and stand to the left of juggler A. Stick your hand out and intercept the pass that they are about to catch and then walk *diagonally* through the pattern and toss the club nonchalantly back into B's left hand *exactly two beats later*.

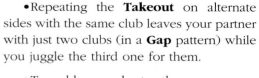

An elegant variation is to steal the incoming pass and then turn a one-handed cartwheel diagonally through the middle of the pattern, tossing the stolen club to the juggler at the opposite end as you complete your acrobatic turn.

Continued overleaf...

Steals and Takeouts...

•An assisted **Takeout** in a **Four Count** works very well. By 'assisted' I mean that the two passing jugglers actively cooperate in the move.

Stand facing the audience, right in the middle of a six club **Four Count** pattern so that the passes are flying both in front of you and behind you.

To assist the **Takeout** the juggler on your right makes a normal pass and then follows it (on the *three* beat) with a **Flat** that you intercept, hold for a beat and then send on its way to your left. This is clever, comical and cool and when combined with suitable banter and improvisation, makes a great three-person routine.

•To **Steal** an entire **Three Club Cascade** you need to move positively and decisively as the slightest hesitation or false start is likely to cause your partner to drop in anticipation.

The standard method is the *Side Steal*. The jugglers stand side by side (facing the audience) and one grabs a running **Three Club Cascade** from the other. There are two basic methods of doing this, depending on whether you take the first club from the near side or the far side of the pattern. We'll start with the 'far side'.

*A 'far side' **Steal**, the numbers indicate the order in which you purloin the pattern.*

Stand to the left of your three club juggler and get your head running in time with their **Cascade**. Now reach across the pattern with your right hand and make the first catch —intercepting a club on its way to *their* right hand. You are now utterly committed and you should walk right into their juggling space, almost pushing them out of the way as you make the immediately following left hand catch. The third catch (right hand again) should not be a problem as long as your partner remembers to throw it —often they forget!

•Many jugglers prefer to make the first catch on the near side instead. Your left hand makes a catch on the left side of your partner's pattern *then* you reach over to make catch number two on the right.

*A 'near side' **Steal**.*

•When your pattern has been stolen, you can **Steal** it right back again, and both you and your partner should practise **Steals** from both sides in the continuing pursuit of ambidexterity. Get a rhythm going; let your partner make three throws of **Cascade** before you steal, and have them **Steal** back after *you* have made three throws. Now, reduce that to *two* throws!

If you take this to the limit (a new **Steal** commencing on *every* throw) you'll find yourselves juggling the hilarious **Runaround**.

•When your **Stealing** skills start to get solid you can attempt to **Steal** one end of a **Passing Pattern**. Get two jugglers to juggle a **Four Count** with six clubs and stand to the right of one of them. Get your head ticking to that **Four Count** rhythm and prepare to make your move!

Since there are four beats to the **Four Count** there are four distinct moments at which you could make your move. Different jugglers have different ideas about which is the easiest moment. I prefer to take the club that the 'victim of crime' *would* have caught in their right hand *immediately after their pass*.

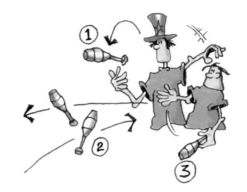

This is a near side catch with your right hand. Immediately afterwards you grab their *incoming pass* with your left hand. The third catch should follow naturally as you bump the 'victim' out of the way.

*The **Stevie Spangle Shuffle** —tasteless costume optional.*

*The hardest part is catching the last club in a **Neck Grip**.*

Stevie Spangle Shuffle

Here's a ludicrous trick that you can attempt while **Showering** six clubs with a partner, it's a comic combination of a number of different tricks.

•Juggle a **Two Count** and instruct your partner to keep passing no matter what happens, just don't blame them when you get a club in the mush later on!

Your job is to dispose of each club as it comes in *without* passing any back.

Begin the move by placing the club you are about to pass into a **Khyber Pass** grip (i.e. jam it between your legs), that's *one down*. As your partner's pass comes in catch it and jam it into a right **Armpit Grip**, that's *two*. Now slam the club in your right hand into a left **Armpit Grip**, that's *three*. Catch your partner's next pass and toss it to your right hand, that's *four*. Another pass comes in and you hang on to it in your left hand, that's *five*. There's one more club to go and no hands left to catch it so trap it with a **Neck Grip** and that's *all six!*

Execute a couple of nifty **Thumb Twirls** with the two clubs in your hands and deliver all six clubs back into the pattern in the reverse order —brilliant!

Summertime Kickup

O nly during those lazy hazy crazy days of summer will you be making this throw, for the **Summertime Kickup** absolutely requires that you are wearing neither shoes nor socks.

It's a shame that the human race has so little time for its feet, for here you have two whole extra sets of fingers —slightly stumpy and sleepy from spending their whole lives hidden in socks, but fingers nevertheless.

•Juggle all shoeless and unashamed and wait until a club hits the floor. Grasp it between your big toe and the first little

piggy and toss it back into the air. You'll find that the spin is perfectly easy to control and that this is a very useful **Pickup**.

You'll find that the **Summertime Kickup** can be thrown as a pass just as easily as a solo throw.

•An alternative **Summertime Kickup** is made from behind the back. Stand over the dropped club so that its knob points backwards and grasp it, once again, between your big toe and index toe. Hoist it into the air as a **Double** spin, directed **Over the Shoulder,** and resume your pattern.

Synchronised Routines

S ynchronised Routines are multi-person juggling routines *withou* passing. Two, three or more jugglers stand side by side, facing their audience and juggle exactly the same moves in perfec time with each other.

This is much easier, and more reliable than designing a multi-person passing pattern and the visual effect is dramatic Juggling tricks that normally just befuddle the minds of the spectator suddenly appea to have symmetry and logic instead of looking like a random collection of throws and catches.

•The whole idea of a **Synchronised Routine** is to get each juggler working in perfect time and you should therefore avoid

Syncopation

pushing the limits of anyone's skills. Keep to the simple stuff! A team of jugglers can build up a very impressive routine in a couple of hours of practice.

Begin with a **Slow Start** and then agree on the first trick that you will throw. You all count off the routine out loud as you juggle —the 'script' might go:

*One - Two -***Leg!**

...meaning that you will all throw an **Under the Leg** with the third right hand throw. Then you just keep tacking on more moves:

*One - Two -***Leg** *- One - Two -***Dip** *- One - Two -***Double** *...*

...and so on.

This might sound too simple for words, especially if your team are all hot and keen club-passers, but the impact on an audience is always dramatic. Also, unlike a **Passing Pattern**, you are looking straight out at the crowd and as every performer should know, *eye contact* is what showbiz is all about.

T his is one of those annoying words that you *think* you understand, letting it sail by unchallenged in conversation feeling that it has something or other to do with that old fashioned cream-tea style of jazzy music that your grandmother used to rave to. The years go by and now you are too old to get away with owning up to your total illiteracy. Fear not! The COMPENDIUM OF CLUB JUGGLING comes riding to the rescue! You are about to *learn* something.

Syncopation means stressing a normally unaccented beat.

In musical terms this equates to getting funky with the rhythm.

In juggling terms I use the word to describe all those **Doubles** and **Triples** that you can chuck into **Passing Patterns** to spice things up. The great thing about these

throws is that they can all be thrown without prior rehearsal. The first thing your partner knows about a **Right-Left-Triple** combination is that it is falling out the air in front of them. Since these throws are made within the basic rhythmical structure of the juggling, they are catchable even when completely unexpected.

Throughout the COMPENDIUM you'll find details of all kinds of different **Syncopations** that you can throw in different passing patterns —and there is an almost infinite range of possibilities out there for you to learn and discover. What's really surprising is that all these different tricks can be boiled down to just a few basic techniques, and if you understand the basics, all that complexity will start to make perfect sense.

Continued overleaf...

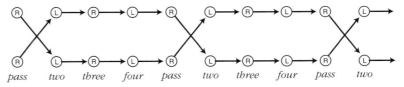

*A **Causal Diagram** is an excellent tool for recording and inventing **Syncopations**. This diagram shows the standard scheme of a **Four Count** in which you and your partner agree to make every fourth throw a pass.*

Syncopation...

•When you juggle (for example) a six-club **Four Count**, you and your partner are working to a very simple agreed 'routine'. You both juggle **Cascades** in time with each other and make every *fourth* throw a pass.

I'll use the **Four Count** as an example to show some of the basic types of **Syncopation**, but do remember, what follows is not a set of *rules*, it's more a set of guidelines.

Early throws

An early pass works on the principle that, as long as a pass arrives 'on time' it doesn't matter when it was thrown. Thus instead of throwing a regular **Single** pass you can throw an **Early Double** pass that leaves your hand a beat early but nevertheless arrives on time.

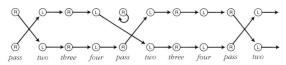

In the **Four Count** this means that we throw the pass on the *three* beat, from the left hand and send it *diagonally* across the pattern. By extending this idea we get to the **Early Triple**, **Quad** and even further if we

wish. Most jugglers quickly develop a natural instinct for the *early* **Syncopations**, and if even you can't work these tricks out in your head you can always sketch a quick **Causal Diagram** to help you.

Late throws

Rather surprisingly, you don't *have* to limit yourself to passes that always arrive in the correct hand at the correct time. Somebody, way back in the mists of time, made the amazing discovery that, in most **Passing Patterns**, you can send a pass to your partner that arrives one beat *late* and in the *wrong hand*. This opens the way for **Syncopated** passes like the **Late Double**, **Late Triple** and so on.

Here's how a **Late Double** fits into a **Four Count**.

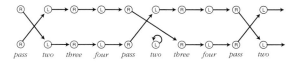

At first glance this seems unlikely to work, and indeed, the very first time you are thrown one you will, most likely, drop in confusion. However, the skill of catching late passes is easily acquired and once learned is never forgotten.

Self Throws

Another method of **Syncopating** a pattern is to mess around with *your* end of the pattern. You can do whatever you like as long as you keep delivering passes that arrive on time (or one beat late in the wrong hand).

Here's a juggler throwing a couple of **Doubles** to themselves while juggling a **Four Count**. Their partner's pattern is completely unaffected.

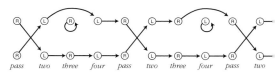

Mixing it all up

You can add so many **Syncopated** throws to a **Passing Pattern** that the original rhythm of the pattern seems to have entirely disappeared. It may *look* to an audience as though you are just making the routine up in a fit of wild improvisation but you are actually still juggling to the underlying **Four Count** rhythm.

The possible **Syncopations** for a passing pattern resemble the notes in musical scale, and provided that these notes re played carefully you should never hit the juggler's equivalent of a 'bum note' where two clubs arrive in the same place at the same time.

If this does happen then it means that one of the jugglers has made an 'illegal' throw.

All **Early**, **Late** and **Self Throw Syncopations** as so far described are 'legal' *provided* that everybody in the pattern **Holds though the Gap** whenever one occurs. In other words, as long as every hand in the pattern *only throws when a club is approaching*.

You can throw one round of a **Four-Four-One** as a **Self Throw Syncopation** while passing a **Four Count**.

Here's the **Causal Diagram**.

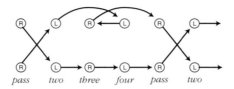

The arrow pointing backwards is the **Feed**, or **1**. No matter how many times I see this it bothers me, but I've learned to accept it as a quirk of **Causal Diagrams**, anyway, I'm getting off the point.

Let's suppose you have psyched yourself up to do this trick but your partner throws you a **Late Double** just before your flashy bit:

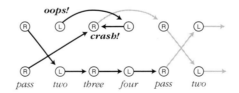

The **Causal Diagram** shows the resulting disaster. At the point marked *'oops!'* I have started my **Four-Four-One** move. Alas I have *ignored* the incoming **Late Double** and I end up with two clubs heading simultaneously for my right hand.. The fundamental *cause* of the clash is that I

threw a club from my left hand when nothing was approaching it. In other words I failed to **Hold Through the Gap**. This is very clear from the **Causal Diagram** if you know what to look for —*there's no incoming arrow at the point marked 'oops'*.

Expert club passers develop special techniques for dealing with these timing accidents such as 'wrong-handing' clubs or even catching under the arm so as to leave the hand free to deal with the other club.

Really Mad Stuff

When you tire of 'legal' tricks you can always go completely berserk instead and see just what it is possible to get away with; things like juggling a **Three Count** at *your* end of the pattern while your partner juggles a **Four Count** at theirs. This means that you are juggling at a slightly slower speed than your partner while passing and receiving in alternate hands.

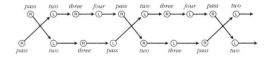

Continued overleaf...

Syncopation...

Forced Passes

A recent discovery made by Martin Frost (who may well know more about **Passing Patterns** than anybody else on the planet) is the **Forced Pass**. Until Martin described them in his JUGGLER'S WORKSHOP column in JUGGLER'S WORLD* nobody had ever heard of such a thing.

Martin pointed out that when a juggler receives a **Late** pass (like a **Late Double**) they make a *forced response*. They have to modify their pattern (by **Holding through the Gap**) in order to catch the **Late** pass successfully.

A **Forced Pass** is a more complex response. A juggler, in answer to a **Syncopation**, is *forced* to make an extra pass. Typically a **Forced Pass** is made in response to an 'illegal' throw that would otherwise cause two clubs to arrive in the same hand at the same time. Martin gave, as an example, the situation in a right-handed **Two Count** where one juggler throws a **Late Double** followed by an **Early Double**.

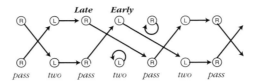

A common mistake is to throw these two **Doubles** in the *wrong order*, which is an 'illegal' combination:

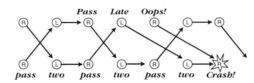

If you are the juggler on the receiving end of this illegal move you are in trouble, but an extra pass, made on the *two* beat just before the crash will save the day —nearly!

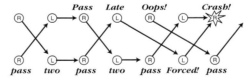

Making this extra pass (which is a learnable skill like the *forced response* to a **Late Double**) saves *your* end of the pattern and passes the problem back to your partner (who made the illegal throw in the first place). The pattern still crashes but if

we make one more modification to th[e] sequence the pattern will rock on quit[e] happily.

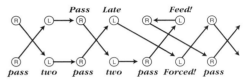

Now we have a workable trick. Th[e] juggler *leading* the move throws a **Lat[e] Double** immediately followed by an **Earl[y] Double** and then follows that with a left t[o] right **Feed**. The juggler *responding* to th[e] move simply throws one extra **Forced Pass**

The first time you try this out the juggle[r] *following* will almost certainly drop, just a[s] we all did the first time we were thrown [a] **Late Double**, but after a bit of practice th[e] **Forced Pass** will start to feel natural an[d] you'll have a new club-passing skill to pla[y] around with.

The **Forced Pass** is, at the time o[f] writing, still largely unexplored territory. [I] have a gut feeling that any jugglers wh[o] work in this area are likely to discover som[e] very enjoyable and rewarding ne[w] techniques.

---

*Summer 1994 issue. This was also the article in which another of his original ideas appeared —**Causal Diagrams**. I'm very grateful to Martin Frost for allowing me to make use of this material in the COMPENDIUM.

Ten Club Feed

This **Passing Pattern** is sheer elegance in the air. You need three jugglers (at least one of whom is solid with seven club passing on **Staggered Doubles**) and of course, ten clubs.

• Arrange yourselves in vee formation and if this is your first attempt at the pattern, put the strongest juggler in the feeding position.

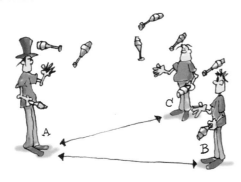

The feeder (A) starts with four clubs and the fed (B & C) with three clubs each.

When the pattern is running A is juggling a **Two Count**, passing right to left **Doubles** alternately to B and C —just like juggling seven clubs on **Staggered Doubles** except that the passes are shared between two jugglers.

B and C will both be juggling a **Four Count**, just like **Every Others**, except that every pass they make will be a **Double** instead of a **Single**.

To start the pattern A leads off with a **Fast Start** passing first to the right and then to the left.

B waits until A's first pass is *halfway over* before replying with a **Double** pass and then continuing with a **Four Count**.

C has to wait another couple of beats for A's first pass and then replies exactly as B did.

Until you all become familiar with the pattern you'll find that it can be a little collision-prone —outgoing passes from A to C can clash with incoming passes from B to A if they are not aimed right. Once you solve that problem you'll be able to enjoy the clocklike magic of the **Ten Club Feed**.

• For **Syncopations** the feeder (A) can throw any tricks that would work in seven club **Staggered Doubles** as long as they end up with the right person. For example, a received pass may be immediately returned to the passer as an **Early Triple** pass. Also, instead of making a normal right to left **Double** pass, you may make a **Late Triple** pass.

The fed jugglers (B and C) can throw tricks that would work in **Every Others** but moved *up a level,* so to speak. Hence the diagonally thrown **Late Double** becomes a **Triple** and the **Right-Left-Triple** combination transmutes from two **Doubles** and a **Triple** to two **Triples** and a **Quad**! Wonderful stuff indeed!

See also **Random Feed, Staggered Doubles, Double Returns, Eleven Club Feed**.

*A **Causal Diagram** of the **Ten Club Feed** showing the delayed action start in which B waits, and C waits still longer, to begin passing.*

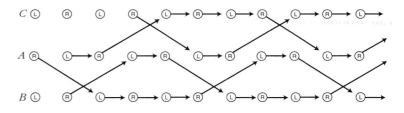

Tennis

Ball jugglers know the trick **Tennis**[EBJ] as the three ball trick in which one (or two) balls bob up and down pretending to be the net while the third flies back and forth in an imitation of a tennis ball.

Club jugglers can juggle the equivalent trick (as we shall see in a moment) but they are more likely to see **Tennis** possibilities based on using juggling clubs as improvised tennis rackets.

First the old ball juggling trick translated into clubs:

•Juggle the three club pattern, **One-Up Two-Up,** throwing the *One-Ups* as **Over the Top** throws which fly back and forth over the *Two-Up* throws.

This looks nothing like real tennis at all, not even vaguely, but it's a handsome trick in its own right.

In theory the *One-Ups* represent the 'tennis' ball and the *Two-Ups* represent the net. In practice it's just very pretty to watch, especially if you are fire juggling in the dark.

*The ball juggler's trick **Tennis**[EBJ] looks nothing like real tennis at all when juggled with clubs, but it's still a pretty trick.*

*When club jugglers talk **Tennis** they are more likely to be thinking about batting clubs across the pattern*

•The classic **Tennis** trick for the club juggler is that of smashing a club across a **Passing Pattern** with an improvised tennis racket.

In a **Four Count** you achieve this by gathering two clubs in your right hand immediately after the *pass*. Use these two clubs as a racket to slam the third club across to your partner on the next *pass* beat. This is a gentle, *forehand* serve; for good control you should aim to send the 'tennis ball' across as a **Flat**. *Don't* just whack it as hard as you can and hope that your partner will be able to sort it out at their end —you may find that they don't want to juggle with you any more.

•When, and only when, you are completely solid with the last trick can you try the *backhand return*.

This is a very tricky move indeed, some considerable experience with **Hits** will come in handy here.

In the **Four Count** you pass as normal and then, as your partner's pass comes in you strike it exactly at the moment you would normally have caught it, with the club held in your right hand (hence *backhand*).

INCOMING
PASS

The point of impact should be more or less exactly level with the club's centre of gravity and should propel the club upwards and diagonally back across the pattern to your partner like an **Early Double**. It needs to be a little higher than a normal **Double** though because there is no *hold* time before the throw. The actual amount of **Spin** on the 'throw' is anybody's guess.

There are many ways that this can go wrong but it's great when you pull it off.

•A more subtle, elegant, and horrendously difficult **Tennis** like pass is also just possible. (I've seen it done anyway).

Juggle a **Four Count** and make the throw on the *four* beat (the left hand throw just before you pass) a really floaty single. Now, in your imagination, freeze the pattern at the precise moment that this club is lying horizontally in the air with its knob pointing towards your partner.

PUSH!

At this instant the club in your right hand, held vertically (like a hammer you are using to drive a nail into a wall) half taps and half *pushes* the floating club over to your partner.

The great skill of a juggler who can manage this pass is that, even at full juggling speed, it *looks as if time has stood still for a moment*.

Three Around

If you are learning to pass clubs then **Three Around** is a good exercise. All you need is three clubs and a partner and you'll be passing by teatime. The pattern is a reduced version of the six-club **Two Count** passing pattern.

•Beginners can start by working with just one club between you. Stand facing your partner, two or three paces apart and hold the club in your left hand.

Toss the club from your left hand to your right, with a **Single** spin. Then pass it to your partner's left hand with a **Single** spin pass.

Where to aim.

Aim just to the right of their left shoulder, a good pass is caught comfortably in a vertical orientation.

Continued overleaf...

Three Around...

Your partner then tosses the club from their left hand to their right, just as you did. Next they pass back to you. That's one complete circuit. Now send that club around about twenty times or until it starts to feel easy and natural. Note that there are only two different throws; a *left* and a *pass*.

•Now it's time to add the second club.

Start with one club in each hand (your partner's hands are empty). The first throw you make is from your *left* hand —not the right!

You throw *left-pass* and the two clubs have moved one space around the pattern. Pause for thought.

Now you throw *pass* and then your partner throws *left*. Pause again. Your partner now has both clubs.

Your partner throws *left-pass*, and now you have one each, finally your partner throws *pass* and you throw *left* and the clubs are back to the beginning.

You should be getting the idea now, the clubs circulate anti-clockwise, and the first club to be thrown is always the last one in the queue. It's not so much *follow-my-leader* as *pushing from the back*. Play this game of two-around for a few rounds until you've got all the lumps out of it.

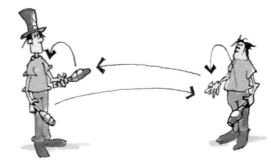

•Now you can add the third club. Start holding one in each hand with the third in your partner's left hand.

Once again, it's shoving from the back of the queue that keeps the pattern running. You throw *left-pass* and your partner throws *left*. Pause for thought.

Now you throw *pass* and your partner throws *left-pass* and so it goes around.

Start slowly, allowing pauses between one move and the next and then let your natural enthusiasm build the speed up until the pattern flows smoothly.

•Having got the basic **Three Around** running you can start to play games with it. One obvious route to take is that of adding an extra club and doing a 'Four Around' pattern. Keep going in that direction for a couple more clubs and you will be juggling a six club **Two Count** by teatime tomorrow!

•Alternatively, you'll find that you can receive the three clubs from your partner and juggle them as a **Three Club Cascade** for a few throws before sending them around again. This skill, once learned, enables you to pass a running **Cascade** to your partner any time you like (perhaps while you go off for a tea break).

•**Three Around** is not just beginner's stuff. It's used by very skilled and experienced club-passers as a way of practising tricky throws like **Tomahawks** and **Slapovers**. You juggle **Three Around** and use the *last* club in the chain as the practice club.

It's easy to concentrate on this club as here are no more following it. It's also a ery useful pattern for comic double-acts ecause the focus of the juggling is onstantly changing ends while the udience's eyes follow the action like a ennis ball at Wimbledon. Try combining it ith some suitable argumentative banter long the lines of:

TELEPHONE RINGS OFFSTAGE.

"That'll be the 'phone. You hold these for minute and I'll answer it..."

"No, you have them, it's probably for me."

"No, no. I'm definitely expecting a call, nd it's private."

"Then I'm definitely answering it, hold hese a moment."

—and so on. This sort of theme has been sed by many acts to good effect (including he anagrammatically named juggling artnership, *Hairgag and Chisel*).

See also **Shower**, **Two Count**, **Runaround**, **Six Club Pickup** and **Seven Club Pickup**.

Three Club Cascade

Beginners start here! The **Three Club Cascade** is the most basic club juggling pattern, and it's the same as the **Three Ball Cascade**[EBJ] with the exciting addition of end-over-end **Spin**.

I've listed quite a few simple exercises below for the novice club juggler and they are all worth doing, but be warned that it may take you a little while to get through them all.

Have patience. If you try to rush into this skill you'll only end up disappointing yourself.

You need three juggling clubs (pop out and get somebody to buy you some) and optionally, two beanbags or juggling balls and one juggling ring.

Now read on.

The Grip

Begin by getting your hands used to the first principles of holding and throwing juggling clubs. You need just one juggling club for the first exercises. Put the other two down!

The club should be held comfortably about halfway down the handle, as you might hold a hammer. Many beginners seem to grab a club by the very end of the handle, but you don't get such good control that way.

Getting the feel of a club

• Practise tossing the club into the air with one full spin before the catch. You can't practise this too much, so toss at least a hundred throws experimenting with *self throws* (one hand throws to itself) and *crossing throws* (one hand throws to the other). Try little low throws, for which you need a quick flick-like spin, and great, slow, high, lazy throws, which need to be 'floated' into the air.

Continued overleaf...

Three Club Cascade...

Hot tip

While a club spins through the air you should concentrate on watching the knob (rather than the whole club) as it curves through the air back to your catching hand. The catch is easier this way.

Mixed objects

• Before moving on to the two and three club exercises you might like to try juggling with two beanbags and one club. In this way you get to mix your new **Single** spin skills with your old three-ball skills.

• You can develop your **Mixed Object Juggling** skills still further and learn to juggle with one ball, one ring and one club at the same time. This is a brilliant exercise in coordination since all three objects use different throwing and catching techniques.

• If you enjoy this you might like to try the ultimate ball, ring and club trick.

Bat the ball *through* the ring with the club while juggling!

The starting position

• There are two types of grip used for this, the **Circus Grip** and the **Normal Grip** which are mirror images of each other.

It is probably best for beginners to use a **Normal Grip** unless you have *true circus*

blood in which case the famou[s] disadvantage of the **Circus Grip** i[s] reckoned to be good for you —the firs[t] throw tends to smack you in the teeth!

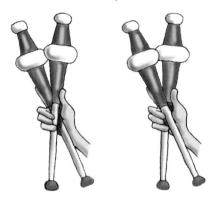

Circus Grip and *Normal Grip*, eithe[r] way, the first club to get thrown is the one pointing to the left.

To form a **Normal Grip** in the righ[t] hand grasp club number one by the middl[e] of its handle and place the second club o[n] top of it with its body to the left. For a left handed **Normal Grip** just translate thes[e] instructions mirrorwise.

• It's club number two, the topmost club that gets thrown first from the **Norma[l] Grip**. You will need a little practice her[e] because the extra inertia of the two hel[d] clubs tends to affect your throw, particularly with regard to the amount of **Spin** you put on the club.

The finishing position

•After a few attempts you'll find that you are developing control and you are ready for stage two. Having thrown one club across, throw the second so that you end up with two in your *left* hand —*clack!* Thus you are practising the **Finish** of a three club juggle.

Make sure that you make this catch with the already held club on the *outside*, otherwise you'll find your two caught clubs are in a **Circus Grip**, which could cause you some problems.

•Happy with that? Now repeat the exercise the other way around. In no time at all you'll be moving those clubs from hand to hand with the grace and elan of a *truly great juggler*. Note that I am encouraging you to a develop truly ambidextrous familiarity with your clubs. You should be equally comfortable with these moves whichever way around they are juggled.

The exchange

•This is the secret of all **Toss Juggling**[EBJ], as an object falls towards a full hand, that hand throws the object it is holding so as to clear itself for the catch.

Start with a club in each hand.

Lead with a right hand throw, when the club is halfway across make a left hand throw so that the second club passes *under* the first.

It's just like learning the **Three Ball Cascade**[EBJ] all over again!

This is quite a tricky move, there's the **Spin** to contend with as well as collisions, general timing and the unfamiliarity of your new props. Here's a useful tip that might help to get the exchange to fall into place. You'll note that before you throw a juggling club *up* your hand naturally swings it *down*

to develop the momentum for the throw. As you are throwing the first club *up* you should be swinging the second club *down*.

•When you have managed a few *right-left* exchanges you should balance the work with some *left-rights* as well. Work on every possible combination of start, finish and exchange. You cannot practise these moves enough.

If you get them really solid *before* turning the page you are virtually guaranteed instant success when you go for the full **Three Club Cascade**.

Continued overleaf...

Three clubs

•Hold two clubs in a **Normal Grip** in your right hand and the third club in your left. Make sure that your grip is halfway down the handle of each club.

Make just three throws and aim for a clean **Finish** —*right-left-right!*

Keep trying!

Upon success...

•As soon as you have made three throws to a clean finish you are a fully qualified (if rather inexperienced) real live and 100% genuine *Club Juggler*. Congratulations!

It wasn't so hard was it?

You have moved on from mere *Ball Juggling* to a higher plane of existence and can now look forward to the previously intangible mysteries of **Combat Juggling**, **Passing Patterns**, **Fire Juggling** and much, much more.

Improving

•It takes quite a while to get a solid **Three Club Cascade** of the smooth, natural and easy variety. Gradually the rather 'up and downy' beginner's pattern drops down low into the smooth and easy cascade of the experienced juggler. The key to this change is to work on juggling with *minimum effort* and *dropped shoulders*.

The perfect **Three Club Cascade** is as natural and easy as walking.

Pain and suffering

•By the way, I'm sorry about your sore thumbs. Every new club juggler has this problem. It's amazing just how painful the repeated impact of a club handle on the outstretched end of your thumb can be. If you start to develop severe bruising you should apply a couple of layers of elastoplast *before* you start a practice session.

What to learn next

•Learn to pass clubs as soon as possible see **Passing Patterns** and **Three Around** for advice on getting started. Club passing is just about the most fantastic fun you can have without the risk of getting arrested.

•Learn to handle **Wrong End** catches (this requires some expertise with *one and a half spin* throws). After that you can move on to **Doubles** and **Triples** and maybe even **Quads** —controlling **Spin** is what club juggling is all about.

•You'll find that **Under the Leg** is pretty easy to master once your **Cascade** is solid, **Back Crosses** and **Chops** are greater challenges.

•Finally, don't make the mistake of thinking that you should learn every trick in this book. The author admits freely that he can't juggle all of them himself and has no intention of trying to. The COMPENDIUM OF CLUB JUGGLING is not a definitive guide to club juggling, it's a source of ideas that will, I hope, inspire you to create some wild new tricks and a style of your very own.

Mind you, the very next entry is a pretty good one.

Three Club Start

There is more than one way to skin a cat (check out the *Concise Cat-Skinner's Guide* if you want actual details on the methods used) and there is also more than one way to make a flying start to a three club routine.

The **Three Club Start** is an old favourite. You chuck everything into the air dramatically, catch the lot and then move on to the *really* flashy stuff.

•The **Three Club Start** is a **Multiplex** throw. You set the move up by arranging the clubs carefully in your hand. The first two clubs are held in a **Circus Grip** with the hand a little further up the handles than normal.

Place the third club underneath and between the first two so that its knob touches the base of your ring finger and then try and hold the whole arrangement together.

•Now for the throw itself. The two **Circus Gripped** clubs are going to make **Single** spins while the extra club makes a **Double**. Swing the whole arrangement up as a unit and, using more wrist than arm, toss the trio into the air. Concentrate mainly on getting the **Singles** to go where you want —they should fall to an easy catch, one in each hand.

You'll find that it's the *wrist* which controls the spin on the clubs and the *arm* which controls the direction and height of the third club. In no time at all you'll get the feel for the right balance of these two components and you'll be able to send the third club up to just the right height to allow it to drop back down into the pattern after a perfect **Double** spin.

•The **Single-Double** variant of the **Three Club Start** is certainly the easiest, but most jugglers prefer the more flashy **Double-Triple** version. The secret is exactly as before. Get the grip right, concentrate mainly on the **Double** spin pair, and get the balance of wrist and arm right.

•You hardly need telling, I'm sure, that the **Three Club Start** can be thrown **Under the Leg**, as **Back Crosses** or **Under the Arm**. A really flashy trick is to throw it as a **Flash Pirouette** —what a way to start a show!

Continued overleaf...

Three Club Start...

•The **Three Club Start** can be thrown as a **Multiplex** in the *middle* of a juggling routine but you will need to exercise some good showmanship to cover the setup time if you want to avoid an unrhythmic pregnant pause. One answer is to form the **Circus Grip** on the fly (simply catch two clubs in your right hand —see **Circus Grip** for more tips on this) and then catch the third club in your opposite hand and execute a nifty pirouette while you tuck it into position. Now throw the **Three Club Start** before catching and continuing your routine.

•Truly legendary characters throw a **Three Club Start**, pirouette once under the low pair and then turn *once more* under the high one. You might need to use a **Triple-Quin** combination for a move like that!

See also **Circus Grip**, **Kickup** and **Multiplex**.

Three Count

A **Passing Pattern** in which every *third* throw is a pass is known as a **Three Count**, or more affectionately as **Waltzing**. As this is an odd-number count you make passes from *both* hands.

True believers in ambidexterity shun the **Four Count** for its right-handedness and hail the **Three Count** as one of the most elegant of all passing rhythms.

•Find six clubs and a partner, stand face to face and juggle a **Three Count**. If you are not used to making left hand passes you'll find the **Three Count** is an excellent practice pattern. Each juggler counts:

Pass - *two* - *three* - **Pass** - *two* - *three...*

Every pass is a tramline **Single**. You'll notice, once you start juggling, that it's the *same two clubs* being passed back and forth across the pattern.

•Should you **Drop** (well, you shouldn't but you *will*) you can recover, just as you can in a **Four Count**.

You'll find that **Holding Through the Gap** results in the **Gap** staying on one side of the pattern. You'll still be passing on the *left* but nothing much is happening on the *right* (or vice versa of course). You need to manœuvre yourself so that the dropped club is on the *same side* as the **Gap** before you make a **Pickup**. Once you are in position you'll be able to pick up the club and launch it straight out to your partner as a pass.

The **Three Count**, like any other passing rhythm, can be **Syncopated** to bits. The boring old **Four Counters** may think that the pattern is more limited but that's just because their left hands don't work properly! Since the pattern is symmetrical, anything that can be thrown on one side can also be thrown on the other.

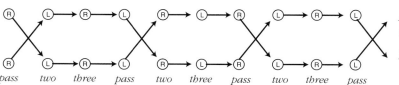

*A **Causal Diagram** of a si club **Three Count**.*

Every third throw is a pass.

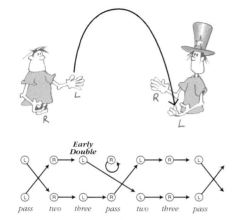

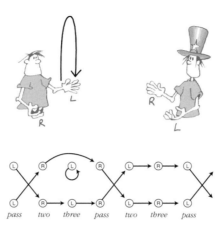

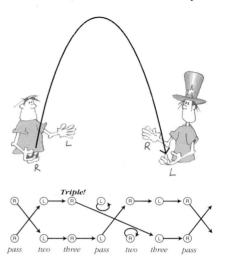

• An **Early Double** can be thrown on the *three* beat. Think of it as a '*pass - and - Double!* '

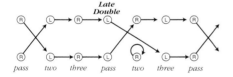

• A **Late Double** can be thrown on the *pass* beat. This is easier to master, just throw a diagonal **Double** on the *pass* beat. Your partner gets the **Gap**.

• A self **Double** can be thrown on the *two* beat, this has no effect on your partner's pattern and you get a **Gap**.

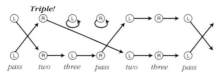

• An **Early Triple** pass (tramline) can be made on any *two* beat, you get the **Gap**, your partner's pattern does not alter (assuming they can catch your **Triple**).

• A **Late Triple** pass can be made on the *three* beat. You get a **Gap** and must miss your next scheduled pass (otherwise your partner ends up with too many clubs).

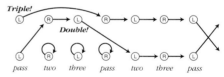

• A crossing *self* **Triple** can be thrown on the *pass* beat if you patch up the pattern with an **Early Double** on the next *three* beat. Effectively you are going into four club juggling for a couple of throws.

Continued overleaf...

Three Count...

Three in One Hand

Juggling three clubs in one hand is half of a **Six Club Fountain**. Every throw is a **6** or a **Quad**, though club jugglers usually use **Triple** spins for this trick.

In theory there are five distinct shapes possible for this pattern. Here are the first three.

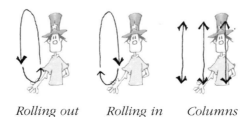

Rolling out   *Rolling in*   *Columns*

Now, these are by no means *all* of the **Syncopations** that are possible but you will find, as you work your way through them, that other ideas may just 'click'. In any count there is usually at least one way of throwing any weight of throw (**Double**, **Triple**, **Quad** etc.) on *each* beat of the pattern. You could make it your mission to work all of these tricks out.

•Adding **Tomahawks**, **Slapovers** and similar tricks is perfectly possible and is much better practice than using them in a **Four Count** because you get to work on each move with *both* hands.

•The **Triangle** is an obvious formation for three jugglers to use with the **Three Count** rhythm —threes going with threes. I'm encouraging you to be inventive here!

•You can juggle a **Feed** with three jugglers in which the fed jugglers work **Three Counts** to the feeder's **Pass-Pass-Self** rhythm.

•The **Three Count** is not limited to patterns of the three-clubs-per-juggler variety.

See also **Seven Club Passing** for some interesting **Three Count** patterns.

The 'normal' shape is *rolling out*, where throws are made on the inside and catches on the outside, just like **Two in One Hand** only higher and harder.

Rolling in, that is throws on the outside and catches on the inside, is rarely used by club jugglers because it's just too difficult.

Columns are quite popular. The clubs rise and fall in three vertical columns while the throwing hand works its way up and down the line, typewriter style.

Normal and Reverse Cascade, obviously a real **Three in One Hand** *pattern is juggled much higher than this!*

The two remaining possibilities are the **Cascade** shapes, either normal or reverse. The **Reverse Cascade** shape can be pretty much discounted for clubs. As with *rolling in,* the human frame simply doesn't agree with it very well. The normal **Cascade** shape is quite realistic though, it's **Hot Potato** juggled with one hand only!

•Most beginners will use the *rolling out* shape. Start with three clubs in the right hand and launch straight into the pattern. **Quads** will work fine, but controlling that much spin can cause you to come unstuck, so you may wish to use lazier **Triples**.

•It's good practice to try throwing **Flashes** of **Three in One Hand**. Start with the three clubs in a **Normal Grip** and throw each one just once, catching them back in the throwing hand.

Throw - Throw - Throw - Catch - Clack - Clack!

The '*clacks*' are the sound of clubs being gathered back into the **Normal Grip**.

•You may find the start very difficult, so instead of starting from cold you can begin by juggling a **Three Club Cascade** and then going into **Two in One Hand** in the right hand (while holding number three in the left hand). Now start throwing **Quads** (or lazy **Triples**) and **Feed** the third club into your right hand when the **Gap** appears.

•Juggling **Three in One Hand** requires you to become tuned to the 'note' of a **Quad** (or **6**) so it can be useful to work on easier patterns that use this weight of throw as practice for **Three in One Hand**.

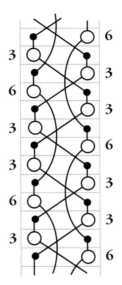

The four club pattern **Six-Three-Three** (that is, **Quad - Single - Single**) is perfect for this.

•**Hot Potato** is another good practice pattern. You juggle a **Slow Cascade** of three clubs using **Quads** and throwing *as often as you can*, so as to keep the clubs out of your hands as much as possible. **Hot Potato** can be thought of as **Three in One Hand** juggled with your hands taking it in turns to make the throws.

If you juggle a solid **Hot Potato** you can let one hand take over the whole pattern

and you'll be juggling **Three in One Hand** with the clubs moving in a **Cascade** shape.

•A sneaky way of practising your **Three in One Hand** skills (i.e. your **Quads**) is to work within a **Passing Pattern**, you get to make the throws, your partner has the awful job of making the *catches*.

Juggle a six club **Two Count** with a partner and start throwing continuous **Early Quad** passes. You end up juggling your end of the pattern with *one hand only*, in **Three in One Hand** style.

You can't go straight into the move, instead you have to build up by throwing an **Early Double** and an **Early Triple** first:

*Pass -**Double** - **Triple** -**Quad** -**Quad***...

This is a good way to practise throwing **Quads** because it's your *partner* who has to actually catch the damn things!

See also **Two Count**, **Quad** and **Six Club Fountain**.

Three in One Hand

Three Three Ten

The **Three Three Ten** is the classic exercise in right-handed club passing for the beginner. It's a short routine with a beginning, a middle, and an end.

•To juggle a **Three Three Ten** you stand opposite your partner, with three clubs each and juggle a **Slow Start** followed by three passes of a **Six Count**, three passes of a **Four Count** and finish off with ten passes of a **Two Count** and a high self **Triple** for good measure. The count goes:

*(and) One - and - two - and -****Pass!***
*And - one - and - two - and -****Pass!***
*And - one - and - two - and -****Pass!***
*And - one - and -****Pass!***
*And - one - and -****Pass!***
*And - one - and -****Pass!****
*And -****Pass!***
*And -****Pass!***
*And -****Pass!***
*And -****Pass!***
*And -****Pass!***
*And -****Pass!***
*And -****Pass!***
*And -****Pass!***
*And -****Pass!***
*And -****Triple!!!***

Take a bow, enjoy the applause, buy some beer and giggle.

This is a fairly simple routine as routines go but it should not be sniffed at. Instead of juggling 'till you drop' which is the normal style, you actually have some chance of reaching the end of a **Three Three Ten** *without* a drop, thus finishing on a note of success rather than failure. This is good psychology because it makes you feel good about what you are doing, and hence more likely to improve.

The only bad thing to say about the **Three Three Ten** is that is uses only *even* counts, and hence is almost always juggled *right-handed*.

For a useful passing routine that uses *both* hands, and is therefore less 'directionally prejudiced' see **Four Four Eight**.

---

* Many jugglers make the mistake of counting this pass as the first of the 'Ten'. This converts the pattern into a *'Three Two Nine'* and it's wrong! Well, not actually wrong since there are no absolute rules in juggling (apart from the friendly advice in the **Golden Rules of Club Passing**) —it just helps enormously if you and your partner are trying to juggle the same routine!

Thumb Twirl

Here's something you can do with a single club in your idle moments or perhaps while your other hand is occupied with some more serious juggling.

•Hold a club in your right hand, in normal grip and turn your palm upward. With a deft flick of your thumb, open your fingers and give the club a twitch that causes it to rotate clockwise, like a record on a turntable. Let it make one full turn and return to the starting position.

Tricky isn't it?

Keep trying until you can rotate the club
nce reliably and without dropping it. Now
l you have to do is to let it keep turning!
n each spin the thumb gives it a little
udge. Experts can keep a **Thumb Twirl**
oing all day.

•When you start to have some success
ou can try juggling **Two in One Hand**
hile keeping a **Thumb Twirl** going in the
her hand.

•Don't forget to practise with both
ands. The best way to learn the trick is to
rry a club with you twenty four hours a
ay and just keep trying. It may annoy your
iends and family but skill like this doesn't
me cheap!

See also **Flourish**.

hunder Shower

More wild terminology here I'm
afraid. A **Thunder Shower** is
another name for the **One Count**,
Passing Pattern in which *every single*
brow is a pass, it's also called **Ultimates** by
me and why not?

See **One Count**.

Toe Kick

Here's an excellent **Drop** recovery
for a **Passing Pattern**. The **Toe
Kick** is easier and more reliable
than a normal **Kick Up** and it has a certain
carefree flair about it that I just love.

•Juggle a six-club **Four Count** with
your partner and drop a club 'accidentally
on purpose'.

Using the **Gap** you should arrange the
club so that it lies in front of your right foot,
pointing left to right.

At the next opportunity for a pass you
tuck the toes of your right foot under the
club, bang on its centre of gravity and kick
it (gently) to your partner as a **Flat** pass.

For extra control, some jugglers start the
move with their foot on top of the floored
club and set it rolling backwards just before
the kick so that it 'climbs' onto their foot for
the **Toe Kick**.

•There's a great visual joke you can do
with the **Toe Kick** —instead of kicking the
club across you kick your *shoe* across.
You'll need to have a loose fitting shoe to
do this.

•The **Toe Kick** is such a neat trick that
it's worth putting in a deliberate **Drop** just
to give you the chance to show it off.

•You can also juggle **Toe Kicks**
continuously. As one club gets kicked
across you drop another, trapping it in
position with your right foot so as to have it
perfectly lined up for the next kick.

See also **Kick Up**, **Slap Kick** and
Summertime Pass.

Tomahawk

Knife throwers and native Americans throw their weapons overhand, rather than using the underhand throw of normal juggling. Hence a **Tomahawk** throw is an *overhand* throw made with a juggling club. It has **Reverse Spin**.

Tomahawk throws feel very awkward to the the beginner and yet once learned they look incredibly smooth and flashy. Some juggling tricks are like this, the harder they feel on the first attempt, the smoother they look when perfected. **Chops** are much the same in this respect.

•**Tomahawks** are often used in passing patterns to spice things up. Practise throwing them in a six club **Four Count** until you get the knack and then try continuous **Tomahawks** in a **Two Count**.

Thrown correctly* a **Tomahawk** pass is made from the *inside* of your pattern —not the outside. There is a bit of a knack to

Inside versus outside, and throwing from high to low.

avoiding a collision between the **Tomahawk** and the rising club on the same side of the pattern. You should aim a **Tomahawk** pass so that your partner can catch it *low*, at the same level as their self throws.

•**Tomahawks** can be thrown as **Doubles** and **Triples** if you wish. Try a **Triple Tomahawk** pass in a **Four Count**. You throw it on the *three* beat.

•You can throw **Multiplex** passes as **Tomahawks** too. As with a normal **Multiplex** throw, you need to arrange your clubs into a **Circus Grip** to avoid problems.

---

*Actually there are no rules in juggling! Throw them however you like. This way just happens to work best. Incidentally, I throw them the *wrong* way.

Trebla

This is quite possibly the ugliest name for a juggling trick ever invented. A **Trebla** is a type of **Under the Leg** throw. As the name suggests, it's the reverse of an **Albert**, named after *Albert Lucas,* a famous **Numbers Juggler** who didn't actually invent the trick, though he does it very well.

•For a **Trebla** a club is thrown from behind, passing between your legs and rising on a **Single** spin, in front of you. Sounds like **Under the Leg**? Sorry, I forgot to say that *you don't take your feet off the floor!*

See **Albert** and **Under the Leg**.

Triangle

The **Triangle** is an obvious formation for a three-person **Passing Pattern**. There are many patterns that can be juggled in a **Triangle**, including the infamous **Hovey's Nightmare**.

•Patterns for the **Triangle** are normally worked out in terms of 'ins', 'outs' and 'selfs'. 'Outs' are passes that run around the outside of the **Triangle** (e.g. a right to left pass to the juggler on your right). 'Ins' go through the middle of the **Triangle** (e.g. a right to left pass to the juggler on your *left*).

A **Four Count**, where all the jugglers pass alternate ins and outs in time with each other can therefore be abbreviated to the simple script:

O S S S I S S S

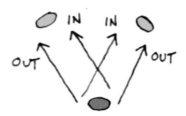

The ins and outs of the **Triangle**.

•It's a simple matter to fit patterns like a **Two Count** or a **Three Three Ten** into the **Triangle** so the COMPENDIUM recommends that you put this book down and get straight to work!

•The **Triangle** is well suited to the ambidextrous **Three Count** and **Pass-Pass-Self** rhythms. Here's a sample script for three jugglers in which two are working **Pass-Pass-Self** while the third juggles a **Three Count**. Name yourselves A, B and C clockwise around the **Triangle** and juggle this repeating sequence of six throws:

A: O O O S I I S... (**Pass-Pass-Self**)
B: O I S I O S... (**Pass-Pass-Self**)
C: O S S I S S... (**Three Count**)

The first pass is *triangular*, involving all three jugglers, the second is an exchange of clubs between two while the other selfs. There are a million more possibilities for the

three-clubs-per-juggler **Triangle** just waiting to be worked out!

•If we want to add a tenth club then an even more complex arrangement is required. Here's one way of doing it.

Each juggler works a **Three Count**, throwing diagonal (that is *right to right* and *left to left*) **Doubles** to the juggler on their left, while receiving from their right. Since the passes are *diagonal* they don't fit into the regular scheme of *ins* and *outs*. The pattern uses a three-way staggered timing. No two passes are being made at the same moment. Arrange yourselves A, B and C clockwise around the **Triangle**. A gets four clubs, B and C get three each. You all do an **Up Down Go!** and begin juggling (from the right hand) simultaneously.

A leads with a right to right pass to B, while B and C self.

On the next beat B makes a left to left pass to C while A and C self.

Then C makes a right to right pass to A while A and B self.

You all keep going on your **Three Counts** making diagonal passes to the juggler on your left. It *does* work —honest!

Triple

A **Triple** is the throw that **SiteSwap Notation** calls a **5**. This follows neatly from the **Single** (a **3**) and a **Double** (a **4**).

There is no hard and fast rule that says that a **5** *has* to be thrown with **Triple** spin, sometimes it is, and sometimes it isn't. The classic example of this is the **Five Club Cascade** in which every throw in the pattern is a **5** though most jugglers prefer to work the pattern on **Double** spins.

If you think of the **'Doubles'** of the **Five Club Cascade** as lazily thrown **Triples** then hopefully all this chaos will start to make a little more sense.

A more accurate way to talk about throw weights would be to forget all about **Spin** and refer to throws by **SiteSwap** numbers instead, but the majority of jugglers wouldn't feel happy with this and I, for one, don't blame them.

Another reason for sticking to the **Single**, **Double**, **Triple** scheme is that these names make perfect sense when you are working with **Causal Diagrams** —a **Triple**, for example, produces an arrow that moves *three beats* along the chart.

Proficient club jugglers reach a level at which they have excellent control and precision with their **Triple** spins and this skill comes only with long practice with patterns like the **Three Club Cascade** juggled on **Triple** spins (a **Slow Cascade**), **Triple-Singles**, and the three club **Shower**.

In **Passing Patterns** you can use **Triples** to throw **Syncopations** like the **Early Triple**, the **Late Triple** and **Right-Left-Triple!**

Since the word 'Triple' really describes the *airtime* of the throw more than its actual amount of **Spin** —you can throw an **Early Triple** as a **Flat** if you wish (no spin at all). What's important is that it arrives *on time*. So the real measure of a **Triple** is that it corresponds airtimewise, and hence heightwise, with your **Doubles**, **Singles** and **Quads**. You know when it has because it lands 'on time' without disrupting the regular rhythm of the pattern.

See also **Single**, **Double**, **Quad** and **Spin**.

Triple-Singles

In the ENCYCLOPÆDIA OF BALL JUGGLING the equivalent pattern is listed under **Five-Three**[EBJ]. This is a four club pattern in which one hand (usually the right) throws continuous **Triples** and the other throws **Singles**. To put this in terms of **SiteSwap Notation** one hand throws **5**'s while the other throws **3**'s —think of it as a very lopsided **Cascade**.

Many club jugglers get their first taste of juggling four clubs with this pattern.

*In **Triple-Singles** one hand is working half of a **Five Club Cascade** while the other is working half of a **Three Club Cascade**, the average of five and three is four and that's how many clubs you end up juggling.*

The advantage of **Triple-Singles** over the more symmetrical **Four Club Fountain** is that your strongest hand (usually the right) gets to do all the hard work. It is a useful shortcut to **Four Club Juggling** but I cannot over-stress the importance of balancing the skills of both hands. Once you can juggle this pattern right-handed, you should make the effort to learn the left-handed version as well.

•A good warmup for **Triple-Singles** is to juggle a few hundred throws of a three club **Shower** to get your right hand warmed up to throwing constant **Triples**. The only difference between the two patterns is that in the **Shower** your left hand is **Feeding**, while in **Triple-Singles** it is throwing ordinary **Singles** (and there's the small matter of that extra club as well!)

•After your warmup, take four clubs, two in each hand and lead off with a **Triple** from the right, then a **Single** from the left and keep going. You'll find that because you are looking *up* at the **Triples** you don't get a very good view of the **Singles**, perhaps only a glimpse of the handle as each one turns over. The most common mistake is that of throwing the **Singles** too high —this wrecks the rhythm of the pattern. Instead of a smooth throwing tempo:

left—right—left—right—left—right...

You end up juggling:

leftright—leftright—leftright...

It does take quite a lot of practice to get a solid **Triple-Singles** pattern so be patient and proceed in easy stages, always ending your practice (if you can) with a clean **Finish**.

•If you can already juggle a **Four Club Fountain** then you can work on switching between the two patterns while you juggle. The throwing sequence of **Triple-Singles** is:

5 3 5 3 5 3 5 3 5 3...

A **Four Club Fountain** is:

4 4 4 4 4 4 4 4 4 4...

The **5**'s, **4**'s and **3**'s equate to **Triples**, **Doubles** and **Singles** respectively.

To change from a running **Four Club Fountain** to **Triple-Singles** you just lead from the right hand with a **Triple**:

4 4 4 4 4 4 **5 3 5 3** ...

To change back again you also lead from the right, by throwing the first **Double** from the right hand:

5 3 5 3 5 3 **4 4 4 4**...

You can throw *just one round* of **Triple-Singles** in a **Four Club Fountain**:

4 4 4 **5 3** 4 4 4 4 4...

In other words, juggle a **Four Club Fountain** and then throw a **Triple** from the right, *immediately* followed by a **Single** from the left and then resume the **Fountain**. This should happen with no perceptible change in the rhythm of the clubs slapping into your hands —it's all about getting the throw heights right. Two clubs swap sides across the pattern which is great fun if you are working with four differently coloured clubs —you can play games trying to rearrange them in the air.

•Don't forget to learn to throw in both *right-handed* and *left-handed* rounds of **Triple-Singles**.

Continued overleaf...

Triple-Singles...

Triple Self (seven clubs)

• Continuing on the same theme, a good ambidextrous sequence to juggle is:

4 4 4 **5 3** 4 4 4 **5 3** 4 4 4 **5 3** 4 4 4...

In this sequence single 'rounds' of **Triple-Singles** are thrown, from alternate sides, in a **Four Club Fountain**. The **Triple** is thrown with the *same club every time*. This is the same as the ball juggling pattern **Four Ball Tennis**[EBJ]. Substitute a football for that high-spinning club and you have a very impressive trick:

"Hey look! I'm juggling three clubs and playing catch with myself at the same time!"

• Going back to the pure **Triple-Singles** pattern, there are other games you can play apart from juggling the numbers. Try throwing the **Triples** as **Back Crosses**, **Tomahawks**, **Dips**, **Over the Top** throws and **Flats**, or throw every **Single** as a **Back Cross** throw.

• A really nice trick to throw from **Triple-Singles** is a *wild high one*.

In this trick you throw a **Quin**, or **7**, which is a *really* high throw instead of a **Triple**. This gives you time to juggle three throws of a **Three Club Cascade** underneath it before resuming your regular **Triple-Single** pattern. The throwing

sequence is:

5 3 5 3 **7 3 3 3** 5 3 5 3...

The number of spins on the **Quin** is up to you, in a **Seven Club Cascade** a juggler would usually use three spins but to match the tempo and style of **Triple-Singles** four or five spins would be more appropriate. This is a very satisfying trick when you get it.

• If you get *very* good at throwing *wild high ones* you might like to try juggling five clubs using **7**'s from the right and **3**'s from the left (**Quins** and **Singles**).

• A lower version of **Triple-Singles** can be juggled using **Doubles** and **Singles**. The scheme of the pattern is the same, it's simply juggled in a smaller airspace, and the timing becomes a little 'lumpy'.

Many jugglers find this easier than full-blown **Triple-Singles** and while it lacks some of the elegance of the high pattern it is impressive for the way that it packs four clubs into just a few cubic feet of air.

See also **Five-Three-Four**, **Six-Three-Three**, **Eight Club Passing** and **Five Club Gap**.

Not to be confused with **Triple-Singles** (a four club solo pattern) **Triple-Self** is a **Four Count** passing pattern for two jugglers and seven clubs.

Triple-Self is an 'upgraded' version of the six-club **Four Count** in which extra space for a seventh club is made by increasing the weights of the passes from **3**'s to **5**'s (from **Singles** to **Triples**). A side effect of this change is that the two jugglers pass *alternately* which looks quite spectacular.

• Find a partner and seven clubs and stand face to face. You start with four clubs and they get three. All passes are made as right to left (tramline) **Triples**.

You both do an **Up-Down-Go!** You make your first pass immediately, and they make theirs two selfs later.

YOU: ***Pass***-*two-three-four...*
PARTNER: *three-four-**Pass**-two...*

Now you both keep juggling your **Four Counts** two beats out of phase. The secret of the pattern is to throw each other reliable and accurate **Triples**.

• Most partnerships that juggle this pattern will already be able to juggle seven lubs on **Staggered Doubles** and it's useful o know how to change from one pattern to ne other 'on the fly' —there's a secret to his.

To change 'up' from **Staggered Doubles** ne juggler breaks the rhythm by throwing vo consecutive **Triple** passes (instead of oubles) and then continues in **Triple Self** node. The other juggler responds to this ignal by pausing for a moment (which gets ne hands into the new synchronisation) nd then starting their **Triple Self** pattern. Vith practice you should be able to make his change without needing to 'call out the ick' to your partner.

•Changing 'down a gear' is more wkward but a good team should be able to naster it without too much trouble. You'll lmost certainly need to 'call the trick'.

As you juggle **Triple Self** shout '*doubles!*' as you make a pass and on your *next* scheduled pass launch a really 'floaty' **Double** pass and then continue in **Staggered Doubles** mode. Your partner responds in kind and, skill permitting, the miracle has been achieved.

•**Triple Self** is the pattern juggled by the 'fed' jugglers in an **Eleven Club Feed** while the feeder throws **Triples** on a **Two Count**.

•Throwing **Syncopations** in the **Triple Self** pattern can be hectic because the passes are *already* **Triples** and most **Syncopations** involve making higher-than-usual throws.

You can throw any *self throw* **Syncopations** that would work in a six-club **Four Count** with no problems; a left

self **Double** on the *two* beat or a right self **Double** on the *three* beat for example.

•**Syncopated** *passes* are more difficult because they start at the level of a **Quad**. A diagonal left to left **Early Quad** pass on the *four* beat is the equivalent of the more familiar **Early Double** from the six-club pattern. Likewise a **Late Double** becomes a **Late Quad**, thrown diagonally right to right on the *pass* beat.

•A **Drop** in the **Triple-Self** pattern should present no serious problems since the **Four Count** rhythm gives you plenty of time to take a quick break and grab the club. There is a messy moment when you need to be looking *up* for your partner's approaching pass and *down* for the **Pickup**.

See also **Staggered Doubles**, **Eleven Club Feed** and **Popcorn**.

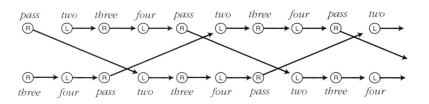

The **Triple Self** *pattern for two jugglers and seven clubs. The two jugglers are working* **Four Counts** *which are two beats out of phase with each other.*

In the other popular seven club pattern, **Staggered Doubles,** *the jugglers work* **Two Counts** *that are one beat out of phase, this makes changing from one pattern to the other a little tricky!*

Triple Self (seven clubs)

Two Count

The **Two Count** is also known as **Showers** or **Solids**. Every second throw (usually every *right* hand throw) is a pass. The **Two Count** is probably the second most popular way of passing six clubs between two jugglers (after the **Four Count**) and is the style favoured by **Numbers Juggling** duos. It's a great pattern with the single glaring fault that it is not ambidextrous.

•To juggle a six-club two-person **Two Count** stand facing your partner, three clubs each and juggle in time making every right hand throw a 'tramline' pass to your partner's left hand. Every throw in the plain vanilla pattern is a **Single** (or a **3** if you want to talk **SiteSwap**).

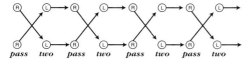

The count (in your head or out loud) runs:

Pass-two-Pass-two-Pass-two-Pass-two...

If you find this difficult (everybody does at first) then start by playing **Three Around** and gradually add clubs until you are working with a full set of six.

You can add **Syncopations** without causing the pattern to disintegrate. Here are some of the methods for throwing **Doubles**, **Triples** and **Quads**.

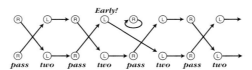

•An **Early Double** pass can be thrown on the *two* beat. It travels diagonally from your left hand to your partner's left and gives you a brief **Gap** in your pattern. The pass should drop into their hand *exactly* on time and is commonly used to buy you enough time to execute a **Flourish** in the right hand or perform some other trick. It's also a 'setup' move for the **Early Triple** which we'll come to in a moment.

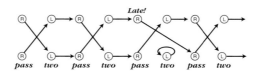

•A **Late Double** pass can be thrown on the *pass* beat. Your partner gets the **Gap** this time. This is used for the sole purpose of being flash. Your partner is unlikely to be able to make use of the **Gap** since they won't know it's coming until it's in the air.

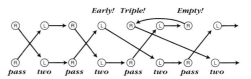

•Here's the **Early Triple** pass. It's a tramline pass made on the *pass* beat but you must 'set up' the move by throwing an **Early Double** immediately beforehand. Your right hand ends up completely empty a couple of beats later which produces that bizarre backward-pointing arrow in the **Causal Diagram**.

The **Early Triple** looks flash and it buys you easily enough time to turn a pirouette *and* execute a **Flourish** should you wish.

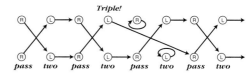

•A **Late Triple** pass can be thrown on the *two* beat. It's a tramline pass from your left hand. You miss your next pass and both jugglers get a **Gap**.

The **Doubles** and **Triples** so far described form the normal repertoire of a reasonably skilled six-club **Two Count** partnership. Now we'll move on to the *difficult stuff*.

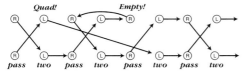

●A diagonal left to left **Quad** (an **Early Quad**) can be thrown on the *two* beat but you must follow it immediately with a normal pass. Your right hand becomes empty a few beats later on —looks weird on paper, feels *great* to throw!

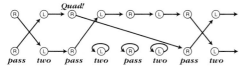

●A right to right **Quad** can be thrown on the *pass* beat, you must miss your next regular pass by throwing a *self* instead. This throw doesn't come into the usual classification of **Early** and **Late** throws, it's more a complete interruption of the pattern that forces it into a **Four Count** rhythm for a few beats.

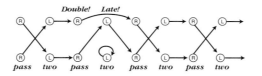

●Here's the infamous **Late Single** which is thrown on the *two* beat. This move has to be 'set up' by missing a pass immediately beforehand. The usual method is to throw a *right self* **Double** on the *pass* beat —then follow this with the **Late Single**.

Most of these **Syncopations** can be combined pretty much however you like and as you become more experienced you will develop an instinctive *feel* for what is possible. Having said that, there are one or two special moves that deserve a mention.

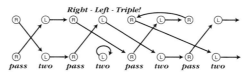

●The **Right-Left-Triple!** combination is an exciting move because it's executed on three consecutive throws. Starting on a *pass* beat you throw a **Late Double** followed straight away by an **Early Double**, followed by an **Early Triple**.

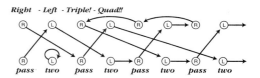

●If you are feeling really ambitious it's possible to tack a **Quad** onto the end of a **Right-Left-Triple!** This is a diagonal left to left throw right after the **Triple**. Your right hand becomes empty for quite a while after this move (most of the clubs are somewhere near the ceiling!)

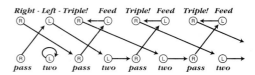

●After a **Right-Left-Triple!** you can just keep throwing **Triples** to your partner, you'll need to catch each incoming pass and **Feed** it into your right hand. Effectively you are juggling a three club **Shower** to your partner's **Three Club Cascade**.

Note that the **Feeds** produce disconcerting backward-pointing arrows in the **Causal Diagram**.

Continued overleaf...

Two Count...

•A similar move is to throw the **Right-Left-Triple - Quad!** combination and then just keep throwing those *left to left* **Quads** to your partner. You'll find that you are now using your left hand only to keep your end of the pattern going. Your right hand is *completely empty!* Effectively you are juggling **Three in One Hand** to their **Cascade**. This is very advanced juggling.

•Here's a much simpler trick. You end up juggling a slow **One Count** to your partner's **Two Count**.

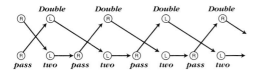

Start by throwing a normal **Early Double** on the *two* beat. Miss the following pass. Throw a *right to left* **Double** on the next *two* beat and catch your partner's pass with your *right hand*. Now keep repeating the sequence. You are throwing **Doubles** from alternate hands —each aimed for your partner's left hand while catching the incoming passes in alternate hands.

This trick is using the **Slow Cascade** rhythm, every throw is a **4** and you make a throw only every *two beats*. This results in

tremendously long hold times —*three beats* instead of the normal *one*. In the **Causal Diagram** you can see how the speed of your hand rhythm has halved against that of your partner.

•Flashy so-and-so's throw every **Double** as a **Tomahawk**.

•Really flashy jugglers **Flourish** every club (making use of that long hold time) before throwing it.

•Really incredibly fantastically flashy jugglers **Flourish** every club *and* throw it as a **Tomahawk** when juggling a **One Count** against their partner's **Two Count**.

•Humungeously brilliant jugglers of the third kind can flip into a **Five Club Cascade** from a six-club **Two Count**.

Warn your partner to keep passing until they have *just one club left*. Their passes are going to be very consistent because you'll be catching the last one completely blind as you gaze up into the underbelly of your five club pattern.

Your **Five Club Cascade** must be juggled on **Triples** to match the tempo of the **Two Count**.

Start by missing a pass, throwing a club straight up as a right self **Double** instead. Now lead into a **Five Club Cascade** (juggled on **Triples**) from your *left* hand.

The rest is up to you.

*A **Causal Diagram** of a juggler going into a **Five Club Cascade** from a six-club **Two Count**. You can see the three causal lines of the **Five Club Cascade** on the top row. The other juggler is left holding one club in the left hand while the right hand is empty. It looks elegant doesn't it?*

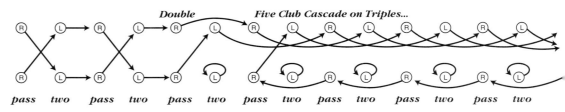

So far we've looked exclusively at the six-club **Two Count** but the rhythm can be used for other numbers of clubs. **Numbers Jugglers** often use the **Two Count** when they are trying to get just one more club into the air. Space for each additional club is made by increasing the weights of the passes from **3**'s to **4**'s to **5**'s and so on.

Every time the weight of the passes is increased by one another object can be fitted into the pattern.

•Increasing the passes to tramline **Doubles** (**4**'s) allows seven clubs to be juggled. The jugglers work out of phase in this pattern —as one passes the other selfs. This pattern is known as **Staggered Doubles** and has its own entry in the COMPENDIUM.

•If both jugglers pass **Triples** (**5**'s) in a **Two Count** you can fit *eight* clubs into the pattern and the jugglers are working in phase again —see **Eight Club Passing**.

•Increasing the throws to tramline **Quads** (**6**'s) will allow *nine* clubs to be juggled. Most jugglers use lazy **Triple** spins for this, just as the five club juggler tends to use lazy **Double** spins instead of **Triples.** The timing is out of phase as it is with seven clubs.

•Very few partnerships get as far as the nine-club **Two Count** and even fewer get to *ten* clubs where you need to be passing **Quins** or **7**'s (these will be thrown as either lazy **Quads** or **Triples**).

See also **Three Count** and **Seven Club Pickup**.

Two in One Hand

Juggling two clubs in one hand is something that every new club juggler should aim to master just as soon as they can. It opens the door to a million new tricks.

•The pattern is usually juggled with **Double** spins in the *rolling out* style —the throws made on the inside and catches on the outside (just as you do in a **Cascade**). Alternatively, you can juggle **Two in One Hand** in *columns*.

Rolling out   *Columns*

There is also a third possibility, *rolling in*, where throws are made on the outside and catches on the inside. This feels unnatural and is rarely seen.

Continued overleaf...

Two in One Hand...

•A good way of learning **Two in One Hand** is to practise throwing *self* **Doubles** out of a **Three Club Cascade**.

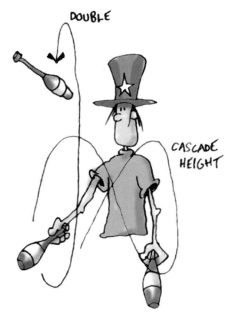

DOUBLE

CASCADE HEIGHT

Juggle three clubs and break the regular pattern by throwing a club straight up, as a **Double**. The pattern pauses for a moment until the club drops back down and you resume the **Cascade**.

The **Double** should rise to about twice the height of the regular pattern.

Practise this on both sides and then try throwing *two* self **Doubles** before going back to the **Cascade**. By building up from this move you'll soon be juggling **Two in One Hand** with the best of them. The inside throws and outside catches lead naturally to the *rolling out* style which most jugglers find easiest.

•Once your pattern is solid in either hand you can start work on the **Four Club Fountain** which is **Two in One Hand** juggled in *both hands* at the same time.

•Really advanced **Two in One Hand** jugglers can do a **Flourish** while juggling **Two in One Hand**.

QUAD!

*Juggle **Two in One Hand** as normal and then throw one club high as a **Quad**.*

*You now have time to **Reverse Catch** and **Flourish** the second club before the **Quad** drops back into the pattern.*

- The skill of juggling **Two in One Hand** is often used to buy some time for a trick. By breaking the rhythm of a **Cascade** with a self **Double** (think of this as just one throw of the **Two in One Hand** pattern) the opposite hand gets a free moment or two to do something with the club it is holding.

Mopping your Brow is one such trick, **flourishing** a club is another.

- The same principle is used in **Passing Patterns**, where a juggler may throw themselves, or their partner, a **Double** to create some free time in which to do a trick.

See also **Double**, **Four Club Juggling**, **One-up Two-up**, **Tennis** and **Four-Four-One**.

PING!

Typewriter Feed

This is a multi-person **Feed** arrangement that you can try out at a juggling convention or a workshop. It comes in both simple and complex varieties.

- In the simple **Typewriter Feed** (as you have probably guessed) the feeder makes passes on a **Two Count** to a row of jugglers (from left to right of course). On reaching the end of the line the passes swing straight back to the beginning.

The second juggler from the end can optionally say 'ping' when it's their turn.

- Deadlier versions of the **Typewriter Feed** use passes from both hands.

Imagine a feeder passing a **One Count** to two other jugglers so that *each of their hands* will be passed to in turn. The 'fed' end up using a rhythm hitherto unknown to juggling science. The one to the feeder's left juggles *pass-pass-self-self* while the juggler to the right juggles *self-self-pass-pass*.

Don't forget the 'ping!'

- **Three Count** and **Pass-Pass-Self** rhythms can also be used for **Typewriter Feeds**. I leave the workings out to the reader.

Ultimates

Passing clubs so that *every single throw* is a pass (a **One Count**) is often called **Ultimates**. It's also sometimes known as a **Thunder Shower**.

The other passing rhythms also have flowery names; the **Four Count** is often called *every others* or *seconds*, the **Three Count** has been called *alternates* or *waltzing* and the **Two Count** is commonly known as *showers* or *solids*. I'm sure there are many other names besides.

Ultimates is a good name for the **One Count** because it quite correctly, implies that you couldn't pass any more if you tried!

- You can juggle a three-person **Feed** so that the feeder juggles **Ultimates** while the 'fed' jugglers **Shower** back, one right handed and one left handed (a **One Count** against two **Two Counts**).

Making *every* throw a pass might sound very difficult but if you have a go at the **Five Club One Count** you'll be pleasantly surprised by the simplicity of this beginner's pattern.

See **One Count**.

Under the Arm

Think of an **Under the Arm** throw as a **Back Cross** that passes in *front* of your body. The club is swung in the sideways plane and rises with **Dip** spin.

*Like a **Back Cross**, as you throw to the right you look to the left.*

• Practise **Under the Arm** throws in a **Three Club Cascade**, making each throw as gibbon-like as possible, really *swing* that club low. Learning to juggle really good **Under the Arm** throws takes as much work as it does to develop really smooth **Chops**. The continuous pattern (where *every* throw is made **Under the Arm**) has a very smooth and surreal look to it. You can use **Single** or **Double** spin.

• The throw really is very closely related to the **Back Cross** —the main difference between the two being the placement of your body rather than the style of the throws.

To go from continuous **Under the Arm** to continuous **Back Crosses** you simply step forwards, while the juggling pattern stays in the same place.

• If you juggle a mixture of **Double** spin **Under the Arm**, **Back Crosses**, **Over the Tops** and **Dips** on *every* throw you are creating a wonderful display of sideways **Spin** control.

Under the Leg

Beginners (as soon as they have managed to crack the **Three Club Cascade**) immediately start to work on **Under the Leg** as if driven by some deep and basic instinct —nobody knows why this is.

• Everybody makes the same mistake at first. They try to wrap the juggling pattern around their leg. This doesn't work.

Instead you bring your leg *into the juggling pattern*. The easiest **Under the Leg** throw is a right hand throw under the right leg (or a left hand throw under the left leg if you are left-handed of course). Before attempting the throw have a look at the shape of the pattern and you'll see where your leg has to go.

It is, of course, very much easier to juggle **Under the Leg** once your pattern has settled down from the high and uptight beginner's style to the relaxed, shoulders-dropped style of the more experienced club juggler.

•Either hand can throw under *either* leg in a **Three Club Cascade** and you should work on all of the combinations you can think of including *every club under the same leg.*

•The ultimate trick is to throw *every single club* **Under the Leg**. To do this you end up jumping around as if your feet are burning on hot coals!

•Next there are **Trebla** throws —**Under the Leg** throws made *without taking your feet off the floor.* Then there are **Alberts** which are the same thing *the other way around!* —see **Albert** and **Trebla**, or should that be **Albert** and **ɟɹǝqlA**?

•Neither the Guy in the Hat nor the author are great fans of **Under the Leg** work —but that's just our opinion. The best use I have found for **Under the Leg** is as a terrific warmup on cold and frosty English winter mornings. Juggle a **Three Club Cascade** and make every *third* throw (same club every time) an **Under the Leg** throw.

I guarantee that you'll be warm enough to take your coat, hat and gloves off within five minutes.

•Mind you, the **Under the Leg** *catch* gets my vote as a great **Finish**.

Juggle a **Three Club Cascade** and launch a **Double** from the right hand while dropping onto your left knee. Gather the two other clubs into your right hand and catch the **Double** with your left hand from *under* your right leg.

Under the Leg

Up Down Go!

Synchronisation in **Passing Patterns** is often achieved using an **Up-Down-Go!** The jugglers, armed and ready to do battle, all raise their clubs into the air (*up*), swing them down together (*down*) and then start to juggle (*go*). This ritual display is vital for large multi-person patterns where the start can be a hiccup of gargantuan proportions.

Have got in synch the jugglers may use a **Fast Start** (the very first throw is a pass) or a **Slow Start** (two right hand throws are made *before* the first pass.)

Having learned how to *start* it's a good idea to learn how to *stop* and what to do when things start to go badly wrong. See **Hup!** and the **Golden Rules of Club Passing**.

Valley of the Shadow of the Low-flying Juggling Club

See **W-Feed**.

Vamp

It sounds like a Transylvanian horror and to some mathematically-minded jugglers that is exactly what it is; for this is the throw that **SiteSwap Notation** abhors as a nightmarish abomination* and yet *it simply will not die.*

A **Vamp** is a *crossing* **2**.

CUE CLAPS OF THUNDER OFFSTAGE AND LONG PIERCING SCREAM OF A CLUB FALLING FROM GREAT HEIGHT AND BOUNCING HORRIBLY ON A HARD FLOOR - THEN DOOMED SILENCE.

A **2** normally signifies either **Holding Through the Gap** or a very quick toss that lands right back in the throwing hand (like a natty little **Reverse Spin**). Either way, the club ends up back in the throwing hand *one beat* later. The **Vamp** on the other hand manages to mysteriously travel from one hand to the other in this short space of time. It takes one beat less to do this than a **Single** (a **3**) and one beat *more* than a **Feed** (a **1**)

The **Vamp** is needed in situations where both hands are throwing together (like the three club **Half Shower** and the **Box**). It's also used when a juggler is desperate to 'gain' a beat of time out of a pattern to help them achieve some wildly impossible feat.

• Usually a **Vamp** is thrown as a **Flat** since there is so little airtime that it's difficult to get even a **Single** spin onto this throw.

The best practice pattern for the **Vamp** is the **Box**.

The **Vamp** *is a very unnatural-feeling throw and is usually thrown as a* **Flat**.

• Passing eight clubs on 'singles' uses **Vamps** with **Single** spin —see **Eight Club Passing**.

---

*This is not because **SiteSwap Notation** was invented by a catholic priest (it wasn't). It's because **SiteSwap** can't cope in a readable manner with simultaneous throws in a pattern and disintegrates in a puff of logic when confronted with patterns that switch from alternate to simultaneous rhythms while running. These are the sort of things that are going on in your pattern if you use **Vamps**.

Volleyclub

Of the two truly tremendous games for the club juggler the game of **Volleyclub** is the one in which the highest level of pure skill is required. The other great game is of course **Gladiators**. Neither of them should be taken *too* seriously.

•Mark out a court twelve metres by six and divide it into two halves by a rope or net, running two metres from the ground. **Volleyclub** is played by two teams of up to six players each, (three a side is best). Each player has two clubs and there is one extra club, the **Volleyclub**, which should be clearly different to the rest so that it doesn't get muddled up.

The game is played and scored in the general style of Volleyball. One player serves, starting with their two clubs and the **Volleyclub** which they launch over the net to start play. It's a convention that the serve should be *moderately* catchable.

After the **Volleyclub** crosses the net the receiving player can touch it just *three times* before returning the **Volleyclub** over the net or passing it to a team member. Up to three team members can handle the **Volleyclub** while it is on their side of the

The 'Slam': some referees frown on such tactics, others simply laugh and the vicious team gain a point.

net. In some games the allowed number of 'touches' may be reduced as a handicap for very skilled players.

Play continues until the **Volleyclub** fails to cross the net, somebody drops or until a play results in the **Volleyclub** being 'out'. If the serving team messed up then the serve goes to the other team and no points are scored. If the other team are at fault then the serving team win a point and serve again.

The first team to get eleven points are the winners. Time for another game!

Volleyclub tests the throwing and catching skills of the players to the limit and makes a very entertaining show for an audience.

•One trick, which may be outlawed in some games, is the *Slam*. One player floats a **Flat** up to a point a foot or so above the net while a team mate leaps up and smashes it downward with their clubs as hard as they can. A good *Slam* is practically uncatchable.

•**Tomahawks**, especially when thrown close to the net, are almost impossible to catch. **Buzzsaw** throws are very good technique as well. The best *catch* is a **Scissor Catch** because it *freezes* the game completely.

•The experienced club-passer will find that it is psychologically very difficult to make life *really* hard for their opponents. Hundreds of hours of practice with **Passing Patterns** reinforce the habit of making things as easy as possible for one's opposite number. The subconscious mind doesn't *want* to see a drop.

Step on that habit and you'll go far!

W-Feed

Here's a passing pattern that any number of jugglers greater than three can join in with. It's called a **W-Feed** because, with five jugglers playing, you stand in the shape of a letter W. If there are more than five then the W becomes a zigzag.

• You get three clubs each and form two lines facing each other (the zigs face the zags).

You all do an **Up-Down-Go!** followed by a **Slow Start** and then start passing. You are all **Feeding** (on a **Two Count**) except for the two jugglers at the end of the zigzag who are juggling **Four Counts**. It's a convention that the first pass is always to the *right*. If you are at the end with nobody on your right then you wait until it's time to pass to the left two beats later.

The **W-Feed** is tremendous fun at workshops because you can all join in.

• **Drops** are a fact of life in juggling, especially in big patterns like the **W-Feed**. You'll find that the pattern is a great way of learning all about **Holding Through the Gap**.

When a **Drop** occurs you should all keep juggling whenever you have three clubs, and pause when you have only two. The **Gap** will move rapidly up and down the pattern until, with luck, it will arrive in the hands of the juggler best placed to pick up the missing club and restore the full pattern.

A confident **W-Feed** team should be able to keep going even with two or three clubs missing from the pattern.

• A good game is for one of the jugglers on the end of the line to shout 'break!' to their opposite number, who stops passing to them while they move to the other end of the **W-Feed** and rejoin it there. Having reached the new position they call 'in!' as a signal to start passing again.

• For more mad antics you should try the deadly **W-Feed Runaround** —also known as,

The Valley of the Shadow of the Low-flying Juggling Club

And lo, the multitude did hurl their missiles from one unto the other beset apart in lines and they saw that it was good. And one who stood at the end of all things spake saying, 'as I say "break!" thou shalt hurl thine missiles unto me no more,' and it was so and the one who had spoken then stood apart and gazed into the **Valley of the Shadow of the Low-flying Juggling Club** and saw that it was set all about with perils and dangers.

Fearing with great fear, the one who had spoken walked alone through the valley from one end unto the other counting quietly as they went and passed out of the valley and stood trembling and yet unharmed. They spake once more to the throng saying, 'and when I say "in" thou

'HALT HURL THINE MISSILES TO ME ONCE MORE.'
AND THEY DID AND IT WAS GOOD.

AND SO ANOTHER, SEEKING TO PASS THE SAME WAY, SPAKE LIKEWISE "BREAK!" AND HASTENED TO PASS THROUGH THE VALLEY. FEARING WITH GREAT AND MIGHTY FEAR THEY WENT FORTH IN HASTE AND DID NOT COUNT AND RECEIVED MANY BLOWS ABOUT THE HEAD AND DEADLY WOUNDS AND EVEN AS THEY LAY THE VALLEY COLLAPSED ALL ABOUT THEM AND WAS NO MORE.

Wandering Star

The **Wandering Star** is a four person, nine club **Runaround** pattern with plenty of possibilities for serious head injuries. Much like the **Valley** in fact. Fun? You bet!

See **Runaround**.

Wrong End

Since juggling clubs only have a handle at one end it's a good idea to practise getting into and out of a **Wrong End** catch situation. This skill is very useful in **Passing Patterns** where you never have the slightest control over the rubbish that gets thrown to you from the other end of the pattern.

• Juggle a **Three Club Cascade** and turn one club into a **Wrong End** catch deliberately. The easiest way to do this is with a *one and a half* spin throw, though some jugglers prefer to use a *half* spin.

Keep the pattern going with two clubs the right way around and one reversed so as to get the feel of it. This feels very odd which is good because it means you are *learning* something!

• Once you are happy with this pattern you should practise getting out of the situation by tossing the **Wrong Ended** club with a further *one and a half* spin. I'll lay money that on your first attempt you'll flip the wrong club! Practise going into and out of **Wrong End** situations from both hands. Fun isn't it?

• Chances are that you will have stumbled on the next exercise while trying to do the last one. Try flipping *two* clubs the wrong way and juggling that! This is horribly confusing. The pattern is almost, but not quite completely, wrong and takes some getting used to. The recovery is even more confusing.

• The next stage is altogether easier. Juggle the cascade and flip *all three* to the **Wrong End** (on three consecutive throws), juggle the pattern for a few beats and then flip all three back.

• The hardest exercise of all is to flip each club on *every single throw*. This is a **Cascade** juggled entirely on one and a half spin throws.

When you are juggling with fire clubs the whole issue of a **Wrong End** catch becomes far more serious. No matter how careful you are, sooner or later you will find yourself shaking hands with the business end of a flaming brand of fire.

I have to be responsible here (to avoid getting sued by my readers for negligence) so I must remind you that before you attempt any tricks with fire torches you should look up **Fire Juggling** and read the notes on safety there.

Continued overleaf...

Wrong end...

Make sure, before practising **Wrong End** catches with fire, that there is a bucket of cold water handy. If you burn your hand, even slightly, you can minimise the injury by *immediately* plunging your hand into cold water and keeping it there.

• Now, working with unlit (and preferably brand new —hence *clean*) fire clubs you should run through the **Wrong End** catch exercises as already described for ordinary clubs but with one slight modification. Instead of catching the torch by the *end* (i.e. the wick) you should handle it by grasping the body instead.

This is awkward and difficult to master but as you develop the skill you'll notice that the contortion required from your hand to manage this catch has the welcome side-effect of keeping your forearm well away from the wick which reduces the chances of a burn to zero.

This body-handling technique is the right way to handle a fire torch when it's the wrong way around and ideally it's the *only* technique that you should ever use.

• Body-handling only works if you notice that the torch is the wrong way

You have one third of a second to deal with this —I'd drop it if I were you!

around *before* you catch it. In the real world things don't always work out like that and the day will come, sooner or later, when you find yourself with a handful of fire. Your natural instinct will be to drop it immediately —a good plan.

Some brave jugglers have learned that, with the right torches, a gentle grip, and a very quick response (under a third of a second) you can get away with making a **Wrong End** catch and a *one and a half spin* recovery. The safety of this move depends on many factors. How long have the clubs been lit? Those are *aluminium* shafts aren't they? That is a new and fluffy wick isn't it?

Contact with any hot metal other than aluminium (and this includes the screws and washers that hold the wick on) will burn flesh. If you think you can get away with it then good luck to you.

The big problem with this technique is that once you have managed to get away with it a few times your natural instinct to drop will becomes unlearnt and *that's* when you get burned!

Learn body-handling!

Zenith and the Art of Pattern Maintenance

THERE WAS ONCE a young man called Zenith who became a juggler. His name was appropriate because 'zenith' means 'the point directly overhead'. This is just a few inches behind the point that devoted jugglers spend much of their time looking at with great concentration. Zenith was also intending to spend a lot of time watching that space, for his ambition was to master the Five Club Cascade.

This was a lesser goal than that of another juggler whom Zenith had read about in a story which told of a young man who had been consumed by the wish to become 'the greatest juggler that there ever had been, or ever would be, in all the world'.

According to the story this had been an absurd and impossible ambition although the young man had eventually managed to juggle with fifteen balls (which seemed improbable to Zenith) and learned something of the nature of 'Perfect Juggling' from the last living Zen Master of the Art of Juggling who lived in a cave in faraway mountains, as people in that kind of story tend to do.

Zenith had spotted a terrible flaw in the story — how could anyone spend their whole life learning to juggle fifteen balls and never get around to juggling with clubs? It was quite ridiculous.

"I can't be bothered with silly stories, I want to juggle five clubs by this time last week and that's all there is to it." Impressive words for a complete beginner.

Zenith went to the juggling shop, bought six clubs (one as a spare) and started work. After an hour of fruitless practice he came to the conclusion that it would be a really good idea to learn to juggle with balls first so he returned to the juggling shop and bought a set of juggling balls. He was convinced that once he had learned to juggle a Five Ball Cascade he would be able to translate his skill to clubs by simply adding spin to the pattern.

Three balls was easy, four balls a little harder and five balls took ages. Nevertheless, after a few months Zenith's Five Ball Cascade started to gain a him a reputation and he won prizes at juggling conventions for its enduring qualities. Zenith then began to work seriously with clubs. The Three Club Cascade, as he had suspected, was just a matter of adding spin to the Three Ball Cascade. The same logic seemed to apply to the Four Club Fountain though it took a considerably longer than Zenith had expected to put his theory into practice.

The Five Club Cascade was another matter entirely.

Somehow it just didn't seem learnable. Everything about it was just that little bit too difficult. Zenith's attitude had slowly transformed from bold enthusiasm to dogged determination and finally to a special sort of self-induced misery as ever-increasing efforts produced smaller and smaller rewards. The frustration of knowing exactly what he was trying to do and yet being so utterly incapable of doing it ate into him and filled him with a deep sense of failure. He had started on this road convinced that continuous effort would eventually take him to his goal but he was beginning to suspect that he was fundamentally incapable of juggling five clubs and that it had all been a huge waste of time.

One day, after a particularly gruesome and fruitless session, he climbed into bed feeling exhausted, useless and miserable.

"I wonder what it really feels like to hold five clubs in the air?"

Tired eyes closed and Zenith began to dream.

* * *

Zenith saw a vast wintry sky above a circling horizon of snow-capped mountains. One mountain stood out, taller than the rest and some way below the peak Zenith saw a wide rocky ledge set into a vertical cliff. In this cliff was an old wooden door with curious symbols carved deeply into its ancient cracked timber. In the centre of the door was a knocker.

Zenith knocked and the door was opened, just a crack, by a white haired old man who was, of course, the last living Zen Master of the Art of Juggling.

"What do you want?" Snapped the old man, his impatience making it quite clear that guests were not welcome at his cave.

"I want to juggle five clubs," said Zenith, "and I have heard of another juggler who came to you. Through your teaching, they learned to juggle with fifteen balls. Since my ambition is more modest I feel sure that you can help me to achieve it."

"There are so many errors in what you have just said that I hardly know where to begin," said the Master frostily, "So I'll go straight to the end. Goodbye!"

Zenith and the Art of Pattern Maintenance...

The door was slammed in his face.

Zenith decided to make camp at the doorstep and wait for the Master to change his mind —however long that might take. He started to pitch his tent right in front of the door but at the sound of the first peg being hammered into the stony ground the door opened again.

"Aha!" thought Zenith, "He has realised that I shall wait forever if necessary and has decided to start my teaching right away."

"If you are refusing to leave then I must insist that you go and camp with the others," snapped the Master.

"The others?"

Zenith was unceremoniously directed around the corner where he was amazed to find a large encampment. Tents of all sizes were pitched everywhere, campfires burned and the sound of musical instruments tweeted and twanged through the air which had a familiar canvassy, woodsmokey, dinnerish, rainy smell —it was a festival!

Or to be more precise, judging from that large big top in the centre of the camp and the familiar battered buses of Captain Bob's Circus—

A Juggling Convention!

* * *

"That's *ridiculous*," thought Zenith who had woken up in disgust thinking the dream hardly worth sleeping for. It was still the middle of the night and the stars shone brightly outside.

"I'm sure I can dream better than that!"

He rolled over and went back to sleep and immediately fell into an even more curious dream.

* * *

There was once a young beanbag who wanted more than anything else in the world to be a juggling club. He loved juggling but was not satisfied to be an object of such little worth that was intended more for dropping than staying in the air. Juggling clubs seemed to curve through the air with a grace and elegance that he could not match with his small lumpy form.

His brothers and sisters couldn't understand his ambition and teased him for wanting to be such a snobby juggler's prop.

"Trust you to want to be *difficult*," they giggled and fell about on the floor in hysterical laughter in their usual style.

The Beanbag couldn't stand it and went to hide under the sofa as beanbags often do when they don't want to play any more.

It was dark and dusty under there and as his eyes

became accustomed to the gloom he saw that he was not alone, for many other strange shapes sulked in this hidden place. There was a set of car keys, a large selection of unmatched (and unwashed) socks, a television remote control, some things that had been chased in by the cat, paper clips, an assortment of pens, the seven of hearts, and something that had at one time been quite delicious but which now quietly oozed and stuck to the floor.

"What are all of you doing here?" asked the Beanbag.

"We like to feel wanted, or at least missed," said the seven of Hearts.

"But you're getting all dirty and horrible."

"We don't care," said the Car Keys. "It's better than being taken for granted. I'm planning to stay here forever."

"You get used to it after a while," said one of the Socks wrinkling up its nose, "It's a lot better than the life I had out there —you can't imagine the hell I used to go through with all those horrible feet and washing machines."

"Well I can see that *you* might have a point," said the Beanbag, "but I don't want to give up, I want to *improve* myself."

"You won't get any help here," said Something that had Once been Delicious.

The Beanbag realised this was probably true but having no wish to go back outside and get teased again he set off deeper into the darkness to see what else he might find. On reaching the wall at the back of the sofa the Beanbag came upon a small wooden door set into the skirting board. The door was strangely engraved and had a prominent knocker right in the middle.

The Beanbag knocked and the door was opened, just a crack, by a very ancient white silicone ball. The Beanbag had never met one of these exalted spheres before but he knew that they were *very* wise and magical characters and should be treated with the utmost politeness.

"Oh it's you" snapped the Silicone Ball, which was rather odd because they had never met before. "I really should get that knocker removed." He looked the Beanbag up and down and harrumphed as if he didn't like what he saw very much.

"Excuse me sir, —" said the Beanbag politely, but the Silicone Ball interrupted.

"I suppose you have some great ambition that you'd like me to help you achieve? Well, I find this whole Master and Apprentice business rather tiresome so I've retired and moved here for some peace and quiet. Do you know I used to live on the top of a mountain thousands of miles from anywhere? I still got pestered, day and night, year in and year out. There was one youngster..."

The old sphere looked wistful for a moment, as if remembering past adventures, and then seemed to take

Zenith and the Art of Pattern Maintenance...

pity on his young guest.

"What *do* you want anyway?."

"I want to be a juggling club, sir," said the Beanbag.

The Silicone Ball raised its eyebrows, "—and why?"

"Because there must be more to life than being dropped and that's all a beanbag like me is really for."

"I'd agree with that," said the Silicone Ball, "but there is an Art to being dropped which I could teach you a lot about if you had a mind."

"Thank you very much sir, but I really would rather learn how to be a club. I have a fascination for the way that they spin in the air. It's my greatest wish to be able to do that."

The Silicone Ball looked quite hurt by this and announced, "I can't help you. Spinning through the air like a juggling club is completely against your nature —you might just as well learn to swim!" The door slammed shut and the Beanbag was left alone once more.

"And what would be wrong with that?" thought the Beanbag, "Why does everybody seem so determined to discourage me from trying anything new?"

And so it was that the Beanbag travelled on, searching for an answer and finding none until, after many adventures, he found himself at the shore of a lake and

remembering the words of the Silicone Ball, he decided to put them to the test.

He dropped in with a splash and found that he floated really rather well, even if the cold water did feel very ticklish inside. Against his nature indeed! The old Silicone Ball had been quite wrong, it was perfectly possible for him to swim as was plainly obvious from the way he bobbed so easily in the waves. He was quite enjoying himself, even if the water was beginning to make him feel a little heavy and sluggish. What tremendous fun! Mind you, he did seem to be sinking a little deeper and really was starting to feel quite bloated, and sick. In fact, he felt very sick indeed. He had never felt so awful in his life.

The Beanbag, realising that he had made a dreadful mistake, floundered towards the edge of the lake. But by the time he got there it was too late. The seeds inside him had been taking on water from the moment he had entered the water and they were now swelling uncontrollably. The stitches of his seams stretched horribly and as he tumbled out onto the shore his sides split wide open with a ghastly rip, spilling his contents onto the shore. The Beanbag was no more.

It wasn't *quite* the end though, for in time the seeds that had been his stuffing sprouted and took root. Some years ater a bushy grove had sprung up in the place where the beanbag had met his end. He must have contained quite a mixture of seeds because in the middle of the grove there grew a fine tall tree of exceptionally straight grain.

The tree was eventually cut down and sold for timber which was bought by a maker of circus props who used it to make a set of juggling clubs. These were bought by an ambitious young juggler called Zenith who practised his Five Club Cascade with them for many long hours without much success.

Zenith always complained that his clubs seemed to be intended more for dropping than staying in the air

Nobody knows whether the Silicone Ball had expected things to turn out this way but they are rumoured to be *very* wise and magical characters.

*   *   *

Zenith woke again in disbelief, unable to make up his mind about which of the two dreams was the more absurd.

"If it goes on like this," thought Zenith, adjusting his pillow, "I'll take to staying up all night instead!"

Instead he promptly fell asleep again.

*   *   *

Night. A vast flat empty place stretching evenly to a dark horizon in all directions. Overhead a billion stars pricked the deep black sky. Zenith stood completely alone. There was not a sound, not a breath of wind, and not a single sign of life for as far as he could see.

Feeling that this was not the place to be, he walked for a little while and then stopped and stood somewhere else. Nothing had changed. The ground was so featureless that it seemed to be exactly the same place as before.

"Perhaps this desert goes on forever," thought Zenith, feeling a little alarmed at being so utterly alone.

His eyes turned upwards and he gazed at the countless stars that shone in the moonless and cloudless sky. The apparently endless desert had made him feel small but the sense of scale that came from staring into the unimaginably huge vastness of space was beyond any sort of comprehension at all. How could he hope to understand the relationship between Zenith the person and the Universe as a whole?

"Half!" came a strangely familiar voice from behind.

"The Universe as a Half is what you are relating to," came the voice again. Zenith turned to see who had spoken.

It was, of course, the old Master.

"Half, because you seem to ignore the ground on which you stand, despite its incredible usefulness to a juggler like you as a means of preventing your missed catches from plummeting below foot level.

"And a further half because if you removed the ground altogether you would find yourself in such an absence of gravity that you would have more different kinds of *up* than you would know what to do with, and double the amount of sky to stare into which is roughly the right amount when you are considering the proportion of Zenith the person weighed against the Universe as a Whole, rather than the rather shoddy approximation you were considering a moment ago."

The mathematics seemed wrong to Zenith, who wondered if three halves making a whole didn't make a half equal to a third of whatever you were thinking of before.

"It's not important anyway," said the Master, "It doesn't really matter how much of everything there is out there."

The Master waved casually in the general direction of everything and magical sparks floated from his fingertips. "The real problem is the problem of your relationship to it. Understand that and it all becomes easy! Hold this!"

Zenith looked up and saw the shape of five clubs made of stars turning in a perfect cascade above him. His hands took control of the pattern and it rolled on through the air

without missing a beat. Zenith was amazed. This was his ambition, *This* was what it felt like to juggle five clubs. He tried to remember whether this was a dream or not but he wasn't quite sure.

"Surely I can't really do this?"

"It's not a complicated thing," said the Master. "Five levers to operate, one at a time, interchangeable parts cheap to run and completely indestructible."

"How can it be indestructible, I mean, what if I drop?"

"Of course it's indestructible, it's only an idea —an invention of the mind. Besides, this is a dream, dropping doesn't come into it, that's something you do when you're awake."

Zenith tried to dream a drop. It was just as impossible as *not* dropping when *not* dreaming.

"Think of the pattern as a sculpture," said the Master. "A very special work of art that is constantly collapsing and falling apart right in front of you. The juggler's job is to repair it, constantly."

Zenith hadn't thought of it this way before, it seemed a pretty strange analogy. Surely the collapsingness of the cascade was part of its very nature, balanced by the building-upness of the throws?

"That's right!" Said the Master, seeming to read his mind. "See what a clever thing the Five Club Cascade is!

t's even built the fact that it's always falling apart into its design. Such a Work of Art!"

"Hang on," thought Zenith. The Master was making it sound as though the Five Club Cascade was its own creator. Surely that couldn't be right. Surely it was something that jugglers do, something that *they* create.

"You are so near to Perfect Understanding, Zenith, and yet still so far! Let me tell you how it is; a Five Club Cascade and a Five Club Juggler are just two things that are possible in this amazing Universe and you cannot have one without all three."

The Master paused for a moment to let the remark sink in. Zenith tried to follow the reasoning as his hands continued to juggle the cascade.

"—They are all part of the same thing you see. Just as the Five Club Juggler needs to maintain a Five Club Cascade in order to *be* a Five Club Juggler so the Five Club Cascade, which is only an Idea, needs to maintain its Five Club Jugglers in order to *be* a Five Club Cascade."

Zenith considered this carefully, fully aware that the whole conversation was being dreamt in the very head that was trying to follow its own argument. The resulting mental activity resembled a failed attempt to tie a sheep shank knot by the 'parlour method'. The Five Club Cascade rolled on through his hands.

The Master continued.

"The Five Club Cascade is a very difficult trick. It exists only because it is an Idea of such appeal that it can entice people like yourself into the long, lonely hours, days, weeks, months and years of practice required to attain it."

"The skill that this juggling pattern displays in acquiring jugglers to juggle it is just as extraordinary as the skill of the jugglers themselves, and it is even more extraordinary when you consider that the Five Club Cascade is not a conscious thing with a mind of its own, but simply an Idea that survives on its own merits. That the Five Club Cascade is virtually useless as a practical object except as a device for entertainment may in some perverse way contribute to its appeal. You see, useless things may have no definite positive qualities, but neither do they do anybody any harm. They may actually do some good by being a distraction from dreadful things like sitting around getting bored, striving for wealth, or starting wars.

"I'm telling you all this, Zenith, because I also am just an idea in your head and I've noticed that your pursuit of the Five Club Cascade has not so far been an enjoyable one. You have seen the pattern simply as a problem to be overcome, a battle to be fought and to hell with the cost. You have failed to see that you are not really the driving force in this battle. The Five Club Cascade has chosen you as one of its jugglers and it will survive whether you master it or not. It is, like you, just a part of the Universe and when you drop it, it is not destroyed but continues for as long as it suits the Universe to contain it."

There was a sound of magic happening and Zenith turned his eyes away from the pattern to see what had happened.

The Master had completely vanished but what was more extraordinary was that so had the ground he was standing on and the entire desert along with it. He was surrounded by stars in every possible direction. In his distraction he had released the Five Club Cascade and it fell away, not down because it wasn't quite clear where down was any more but out, through the stars, spinning in perfect time with itself —off into the vast space of the Universe as a Whole through which it would travel, perhaps forever, picking up a few lucky jugglers along the way.

*   *   *

Zenith woke up shortly before lunch. He had overslept.

"Interesting dreams are like that", he thought. "They must be designed to stop you from waking up. It really *was* an interesting dream too, all that crazy stuff about—

"All about what?"

He had forgotten already.

The End

Notes

Notes

Notes

Notes

Computers and the Internet

When I started work on this book, way back in 1993, the Internet was small and largely unknown to anyone living in the world outside of geekdom.

Meanwhile, personal computers were only just starting to gain general acceptance as devices that we could live with on a day to day basis. Most people simply didn't see the need for the things.

Well, that's all changed now, and there are few homes in the "Western World" that are without a personal computer and an Internet connection. These machines have, after a fairly shaky start, shown themselves to be capable of applying themselves usefully to most areas of life - including juggling.

Nobody who reads this book could possibly fail to notice my interest in the mathematical nature of juggling and juggling **Notation**.

These notations and analytical techniques have provided a solid theoretical framework that has allowed computer programmers to produce juggling simulators that you can download and run on your own computer.

Some professional acts, like the brilliant Gandini Juggling Project, now use computers to design beautiful and subtle juggling routines.

Computers are also great communication tools, and you can use your machine to link up with jugglers all over the planet.

The central location for jugglers and juggling on the World Wide Web is the **Juggling Information Service** which is located at:

http://www.juggling.org

You'll also find juggling simulators there for download.

Check it out!

Other Books from Butterfingers

Butterfingers supply a wide, nay complete, range of juggling equipment and they also publish a number of other books on juggling and related subjects.

Charlie Dancey's Encyclopædia of Ball Juggling

Everything you'll ever need to know about Ball Juggling.
224 pages
ISBN 1 898591 13 X

How to Ride Your Unicycle

By Charlie Dancey.
A beginner's guide to the most ridiculous form of transport ever invented.
30 pages
ISBN 1 898591 18 0

Coming soon...

Watch out for a great new book on **Hat Juggling** by Haggis McLeod, with illustrations by Charlie Dancey.

Butterfingers are also about to go to press with a book on **Poi Swinging**.

Both of these books are scheduled for publication in spring 2002.

Fliktriks

Fliktriks are a series of twelve animated cartoon flick books. Each contains two tricks —flick one way for one, then turn over and flick the other way. Serious juggling by silly jugglers!

- 3 Ball Cascade & Columns
- 3 Club Cascade & Chops
- Georgian Shuffle & Biting the Apple
- 4 Ball Circles & 4 Ball Columns
- The Headroll & Flips
- Boston Mess & The Armroll
- Mill's Mess & Mill's Mess Duet
- Burke's Barrage & Matt's Mess
- Rubenstein's Revenge & Luke's Shuffle
- The Box & Grace
- The Escalator & Reverse Chops
- 4 Ball Mill's Mess & 5 Ball Cascade

The Complete Juggler

By Dave Finnigan
588 pages
ISBN 0 9513240 2 0

Scarf Juggling Step by Step

16 pages
ISBN 0 9513240 3 9

Ball Juggling Step by Step

24 pages
ISBN 0 9513240 6 3

Club Juggling Step by Step

24 pages
ISBN 0 9513240 9 8

Diabolo Step by Step

24 pages
ISBN 0 9513240 4 7

Devilstick Step by Step

24 pages
ISBN 0 9513240 7 1

About the Author

CHARLIE DANCEY learned to juggle at about three o'clock in the afternoon in 1977. It has recently emerged, to everybody's complete amazement, that a very large number of people became jugglers at *exactly* this instant, quite independently all over the world. At least one of these people has tried to claim that they acquired the art a few moments *before* the others. Careful research reveals that this is not true. The false claims are simply attempts at fraudulent one-upmanship.

He has worked for many years with Haggis McLeod (who *didn't* learn to juggle at 3pm in 1977). Together they are the well-known comic juggling duo *Haggis & Charlie*. This act has been billed as being '...not so much a dazzling display of devastating dexterity —more a complete clash of personalities'.

He first set out to write a book about juggling in 1980 but found that he was encountering new tricks far faster than he could write them down, let alone actually *learn* them. It wasn't until 1994 that he had managed to catch up sufficiently to complete his first book, THE ENCYCLOPÆDIA OF BALL JUGGLING.

THE COMPENDIUM OF CLUB JUGGLING has followed naturally from his first work. Dancey realised that he could save himself a lot of time if he took the original manuscript for the ENCYCLOPÆDIA and simply changed every occurrence of the word 'ball' for the word 'club' and then made a few minor alterations to the pictures. This strategy has reduced the time it has taken to get this book ready for press from fourteen years to fourteen *months*. The result is in your hands.

Photo by Pete "Doc" Leates.

A recently discovered picture of Dancey, taken in 1975 —exactly two years before he became a juggler.

He has made an extensive study of the problem of defying gravity (of which his books form a major part) and has eventually come to the conclusion that the best solution of all is to marry an International Jet Air Hostess.

His other interests include computers, tents, signwriting, knots, mathematics, cartoons, old trucks, motorcycles, animation, inventions, sundials, gold prospecting, cyber cafés, graphic design, and the seventeen different classes of wallpaper. He has an increasing obsession with gaffer tape which may one day be the subject of another book.

He used to be a Scorpio but now he's not so sure. One thing he *was* always sure about was the so-called 'mystery' of crop circles, having always maintained that, like fire juggling, this is something that *people* do at night (except that they do it when nobody is looking).

Charlie has enjoyed writing his juggling books and is both amazed and grateful that so many people have taken the time to read them so thoroughly.